Digital Culture & Society

Vol. 6, Issue 1/2020

Cindy Kohtala, Yana Boeva, Peter Troxler (eds.)
Alternative Histories in DIY Cultures and Maker Utopias

The journal is edited by
Annika Richterich, Karin Wenz, Pablo Abend,
Mathias Fuchs, Ramón Reichert

Editorial Board
Maria Bakardjieva, Brian Beaton, David Berry, Jean Burgess, Mark Coté, Colin Cremin, Sean Cubitt, Mark Deuze, José van Dijck, Delia Dumitrica, Astrid Ensslin, Sonia Fizek, Federica Frabetti, Richard A. Grusin, Orit Halpern, Irina Kaldrack, Wendy Hui Kyong Chun, Denisa Kera, Lev Manovich, Janet H. Murray, Jussi Parikka, Lisa Parks, Christiane Paul, Dominic Pettman, Rita Raley, Richard Rogers, Julian Rohrhuber, Marie-Laure Ryan, Mirko Tobias Schäfer, Jens Schröter, Trebor Scholz, Tamar Sharon, Roberto Simanowski, Nathaniel Tkacz, Nanna Verhoeff, Geoffrey Winthrop-Young, Sally Wyatt

[transcript]

Bibliographic information published by the Deutsche Nationalbibliothek
The Deutsche Nationalbibliothek lists this publication in the Deutsche Nationalbibliografie; detailed bibliographic data are available on the Internet at http://dnb.d-nb.de

© 2020 transcript Verlag, Bielefeld

All rights reserved. No part of this book may be reprinted or reproduced or utilized in any form or by any electronic, mechanical, or other means, now known or hereafter invented, including photocopying and recording, or in any information storage or retrieval system, without permission in writing from the publisher.

Cover layout: Kordula Röckenhaus, Bielefeld
Typeset: Michael Rauscher, Bielefeld

ISSN 2364-2114
eISSN 2364-2122
Print-ISBN 978-3-8376-4955-0
PDF-ISBN 978-3-8394-4955-4

Content

Introduction
Alternative Histories in DIY Cultures and Maker Utopias
Cindy Kohtala, Yana Boeva and Peter Troxler   5

I Field Research and Case Studies

Craft and Artisan Initiatives of the Salvadoran Civil War (1980–1992)
Emilio Velis, Kate Samson, Isaac Robles and Daniel Rodríguez   37

Histories of Technology Culture Manifestos
Their Function in Shaping Technology Cultures and Practices
Ellen K. Foster   57

From Hacking to Making
The Commodification of Spanish DIY Spaces Since the 1990s
David Cuartielles Ruiz and César García Sáez   85

II Entering the Field

Tracing the History of DIY and Maker Culture in Germany's Open Workshops
Regina Sipos and Kerstin Franzl   109

"What You Can Invent over the Weekend" and the Recurring History of Corporate DIY
Samantha Shorey   121

III In Conversation with …

Makers and Design in South Africa
Technology and Craft Cultures and their Antecedents
Felix Holm and Suné Stassen in Conversation with Cindy Kohtala and Yana Boeva   135

The Exhibition of People's Technology, 1972
Peter Harper in Conversation with Simon Sadler   153

IV Moments in Alternative (Hi)stories

The Craft of Small Wind Turbine Making
The Windmills of Scoraig and the Alternative
Technology Movement in the UK
Kostas Latoufis and Aristotle Tympas   187

Made in the Russian North
Narratives of Inventiveness from the Geographic Periphery
Svetlana Usenyuk-Kravchuk   193

Czech DIY
A Historically Contingent Landscape
Petr Gibas and Blanka Nyklová   197

Halasuru Traverses
Alternative Local Histories
Anupama Gowda   199

The Trade Educators' Syndicate
Making 10 Retirement Lathes in the Twilight
of Australian Manufacturing
Jesse Adams Stein   203

Politics of Patents
Researching, Making and Wearing Alternative Histories
of Clothing Inventions
Kat Jungnickel   207

Biographical Notes   211

Introduction
Alternative Histories in DIY Cultures and Maker Utopias

Cindy Kohtala, Yana Boeva and Peter Troxler

Digital maker culture is increasingly studied for its impact on production and consumption patterns, technological innovation, educational potential and citizen engagement in design and technology. As making practices proliferate globally and begin to institutionalise, research on these practices is also maturing beyond mere conceptual speculation and propositional dogma. Nevertheless, particular terminologies tend to dominate beyond their Anglo-Saxon contexts (even the term "maker" itself), and technocultural histories of digital making are often rendered as over-simplified technomyths and hagiographies of selected gurus. Such story-making reinforces a specific represented history in the maker imaginary: typically, a white, male, well-educated (often engineering or computer science), middle-class, Western-situated narrative.

This special issue presents a targeted examination of DIY maker culture that profoundly acknowledges and investigates some of its diverse historical precedents, which play an important role in present practices and strategic visions even if unseen. Maker culture tends to refer to current communities, activities and projects in shared community workshops (fab labs and makerspaces), and/or electronics tinkering projects documented in online repositories and glossy magazines, but these endeavours are informed by more diverse practices than are always recognised (Richterich/Wenz 2017b). Activities considered "low-tech", the non-digital in DIY (Do-It-Yourself) cultures, are often pushed aside in the rush to promote the most photogenic high-tech tools, such as 3D printers, laser cutters and computer numeric-controlled (CNC) routers. Meanwhile, individual inventors are lauded as solitary heroes belying the collective efforts underpinning "DIT" (Do-It-Together) and "DIWO" (Do-It-With-Others). DIY stemming from former visions of self-sufficiency, handiwork and technical skill in the home has been reframed as an all-encompassing, all-embracing, universal, modernised and global "maker culture".

Much is being written about maker culture as a phenomenon, its meanings and possible future pathways, but discussion on its technocultural antecedents has been highly limited. Often referenced are the Homebrew Computer Club and its related garage tinkering cultures. Relevant counterculture movements that have fed its development are not always brought into the conversation, from hacking and community technology to DIY craft and building, media art and activist publishing and much more (e.g. Atkinson 2006; Medina/Marques/Holmes 2014; Krewani 2017). Moreover, the commonly espoused maker narrative frames Silicon

Valley as a geographical and metaphorical locale, as the culture centre of DIY maker values, which radiate across the globe through commercial Maker Faires and the growing network of Fab Labs and makerspaces. Maker practices in other contexts – other continents than Europe and wealthy Anglo-Saxon nations, as well as the forgotten, neglected cities inside them – manifest differently, build on other local industrial and technological histories, and use other terminologies for their endeavours (Lindtner 2015; Usenyuk/Hyysalo/Whalen 2016; Braybrooke/Jordan 2017).

Such fragmenting of historical representations, even deliberate suppression, is cause for worry in these turbulent times, when makers' promises of empowerment, agency, inclusion, democratisation and openness of apparently everything too easily serve to render nothing as open or empowering (Powell 2012; Pomerantz/Peek 2016). The promises of making to ease the socio-economic ills of unfettered capitalism, not to mention environmental destruction, appear fragile and vulnerable to enclosure, commodification and colonisation (Fonseca 2015; Irani 2015; Lindtner/Lin 2017). Current dominant narratives, apparently stemming from the grassroots, are bloated with techno-optimism and techno-solutionism. They serve to shape a hegemonic sociotechnical imaginary (Jasanoff/Kim 2015; Stein 2017; Turner 2018) in ways that cause concern for researchers as to what is rendered invisible and voiceless: we need to re-examine and re-focus on who and what is left out. If DIY making is to be truly democratic and democratising, inclusive and equitable, accessible, empowering and capacity building, there is a role for research to unmask these alternative histories. We thus build on this journal's previous special issue on "Making and Hacking" (Richterich/Wenz 2017a) to place emphasis on legacies and foundations: thinking in terms of history places the emergent and fast-changing phenomena of DIY making practices into a broader and richer frame.

Our call for papers for this Special Issue "Alternative Histories in DIY Cultures and Maker Utopias" aimed to elicit contributions from cultural-historical perspectives, technology and design histories and historiographies, alternative histories related to postcolonial resistance, and studies that highlight how historical elements and historicising play a role in mythmaking and the creation of social imaginaries. In the following sections, we will review several key themes with regard to DIY, tinkering and inventing, community technology, user innovation, shared workshops and their histories and historiographies, as well as the benefits of learning through history and historicising. We then summarise the contributions that appear in this special issue before concluding briefly with some considerations as to why historical knowledge matters.

Historicising as a Tool

Over several decades, researchers in Science & Technology Studies (STS) and closely related approaches in feminist studies, indigenous and postcolonial studies, design, human-computer interaction (HCI) and so on have sought to overcome the broader image of science and technology practised exclusively by "white elite groups" (e.g. Kline/Pinch 1996; Oudshoorn/Pinch 2003; Mavhunga 2017). Recent contributions have emphasised the hegemony of Western technology design and engineering cultures as not only driving the perception of who gets to define the "future", but also who from the past is to be revered. Anthropologist Arturo Escobar (2018) asks us to reconfigure these dominant, colonialising models of technology design by examining practices and movements among the indigenous and Afro-descended people in Latin America. Ron Eglash and Ellen Foster (2017) emphasise how fixer practices and *se débrouiller* (making do) in African maker cultures are as much about spiritual lineages, a collective ethos, creative play and subversive intelligence, as they are about economic necessity. Cindy Lin Kaiying, Silvia Lindtner and Stefanie Wuschitz (2019) demonstrate how Indonesian biohacker collectives provide an alternative narrative of DIY making and hacking, by positioning their practices in relation to distinctly Indonesian political, cultural and material antecedents. Daniela Rosner's volume (2018) challenges the dominant history of computing innovation as well as design practice as being void of traditional craftwork legacies. These examples and others make visible multifarious design and technology practices and repressed or forgotten histories.

DIY making and hacking has also often purposefully presented alternatives to the mainstream, which means individuals and groups are presenting counter-objects and "counter-contexts" where design, technology and engineering are wrested from hegemonies and given new meaning (Pfaffenberger 1992; Kohtala/Hyysalo/Whalen 2020). People's reasons for engaging in such making are political, whether that means explicitly rebelling against "the system" (Cuartielles/García 2020, in this issue; Foster 2020, in this issue); being compelled to invent to meet needs (Jungnickel 2020, in this issue; Latoufis/Tympas 2020, in this issue); taking on hobbies within a capitalist work ethic (Shorey 2020, in this issue; Stein 2020, in this issue); making do with what is to hand (Gibas/Nyklová 2020, in this issue; Usenyuk-Kravchuk 2020, in this issue; Sipos/Franzl 2020, in this issue); or finding solace and solidarity in handwork in conditions of adversity (Gowda 2020, in this issue; Velis et al. 2020, in this issue).

For historians of design, acknowledging politics and meanings entails examining not only consumption and production, but also mediation – the relations between designer, consumer, use and meaning-making (Lees-Maffei 2009), which, in DIY making "prosumption", shift fluidly. Moreover, scholars of STS and material culture have long argued that users are also innovators and have been more deeply involved in technology production, and for much longer, than many have been willing to give them credit for (Hyysalo/Jensen/Oudshoorn 2016). A history of innovation and technology bound only to what is considered "high-tech", is unmoored from what people themselves do, design, innovate and make – which includes also sewing and clothes, growing food, making furniture and even making and fixing cars.

As historians of consumer technology Ruth Schwarz Cowan (1987) and Joy Parr (1999) point out, we can benefit from shifting our focus from studying celebrated inventors and corporations to the practices of everyday life. Following their recommendation, several historians of technology and culture have explored the multiple paths and DIY practices of different user groups covering the development of transportation, household and computation technologies over the 20th century. These studies have captured the early automobile use and DIY tinkering by car owners (Franz 2005) and vehicle convergence to meet local energy supply needs and other farming necessities in the rural United States (Kline/Pinch 1996), through amateur ham radio hobby cultures in North America, Europe and Japan and their intricate relationship to professional identity-shaping (Takahashi 2000; Haring 2007), to more general treatments of maintenance work of electronics and electronic-based technology (Orr 1996).

DIY Material Practice Before Stabilisation: On Car Owners and Hams

For historian Kathleen Franz, car tinkering empowered users, particularly women, to minimise the imbalance between their desires and one standardised technology – the early Ford Model T. Drawing upon various examples in the contemporary popular literature, advice journals and travel logs, Franz reveals that women in this period were encouraged and very determined to tinker with their cars. Whether car owners had some previous mechanical know-how or not, they "were eager to tinker with the new machine" (Franz 2005: 1), and the combination of hands-on work on the vehicles, advice literature and exchange with others taught them to maintain and modify those. Women learned that in repair shops, through experimentation or by recalling their observations of technicians' work (ibid). Even the *Ladies Home Journal* published illustrated instructions on car maintenance. Such approaches to repair and maintenance vividly bring to mind how contemporary DIY making functions at times – by being messy, exploratory and to some degree sustainable (see Holm/Stassen/Kohtala/Boeva 2020, in this issue). Yet, the connection to these historical precedents within DIY maker cultures remains unaccounted. These ingenious DIY practices mostly disappeared in Western countries with their growing automotive industries, especially once vehicles were stabilised in terms of their design (ibid). Franz's study presents a limited perspective considering gender, race, class and geography, but her dedication to female car owners and their practices provides a glimpse of liberation and system opposition similarly experienced by women through DIY and craft practices in Kat Jungnickel's study of Victorian female cyclists (2018; 2020, in this issue).

Whereas necessity, sustainability, resourcefulness and also counteraction were associated with these previous examples, it was mostly hobbyism and pleasure that initially determined the tinkering with electronics. With the growing economic importance of electronic technology in the post-war period, it also gained significance for technical work. Both Haring and Takahashi describe tinkering with ham radios as essential for the professional activity of technicians and in repair work. The difference between their studies, however, is that most Western tinkerers were doing it from a hobbyist perspective, while Japanese tinkerers were motivated by the economic conditions of occupation-era Japan. Western hams often turned to their amateur personas at work to sustain professional success (Haring 2007). Professional education and the industry during this period disconnected tinkering, DIY and material practice from (engineering) design, as Haring indicates, the "advocacy of tinkering as opposed to research and design allied the amateur and professional electronics communities with separate traditions of practice" (ibid: 90). These activities took place in individuals' private time and space and often remained uncelebrated outside that. Maker culture, the fab lab structure and contemporary STEM education, on the contrary, have been lauding DIY, tinkering and the entire ecosystem around it for increasing creativity and the potential of innovation. Moreover, this maker ecosystem has enforced a global, entrepreneurial Silicon Valley culture of worship (Irani 2019). The prevalence of entrepreneurial narratives around DIY making, however, fails to represent the wider cultural history related with hands-on practices, whether that includes electronics, computational technologies or remains non-digital.

DIY Making as "Critical Fabulations": On Gender, Race and Tech

The development of computer science as a discipline, computer engineering and its affiliated industry often portray their history by neglecting hands-on material user practices and the people involved in them, as many computer historians and HCI scholars have pointed out. There are multiple reasons for this. First and more comfortably aligning with computer/tech cultures, hands-on experimentation is difficult to structure and break down into discrete (binary) entities. Second, the restructuring and renaming of computer-related jobs in wartime and in the post-war period aimed at securing gender boundaries and ended up devaluing women's contribution to this field (Light 1999; Abbate 2012; Hicks 2017). The exclusion from historical memory, writes Jennifer Light (1999), further relates to implicit assumptions that the low status of women's occupations in computing are not deemed innovative. Many feminist scholars studying DIY, making and craft have noted a similar trend in Maker Media's disposal of Craft magazine and its relocation within a few pages of *Make:*, suggesting that "feminised" craft is less worthy of attention.

Early programming, before being labelled as "software engineering", resembled telephone switchboard operations which made it "more handicraft than science [and technology], more feminine than masculine" (Ensmenger 2010: 15). Programming then began deploying textile-based manufacturing practices such as in the core memory for NASA's Apollo 8 mission by line workers (Rosner et al. 2018) or the Fairchild semiconductor by Navajo women (Nakamura 2014), both executed by women mastering the craft of weaving. While line workers were hired for their particular textile craft skills required in the production of electronics, Navajo women's mastery of weaving served to support a racialised labour rhetoric based "heavily on existing ideas of Indians as creative cultural handworkers" (ibid: 921). For many indigenous women, textile crafts are deeply entangled with cultural values, traditions as well as forms of subsistence (see Velis et al. 2020, in this issue). Their appropriation within tech culture narratives rarely serves to present an alternative, more nuanced but also problematic history of material and DIY-based shaping design and technology. Instead, as Nakamura argues, "[i]t posits that indigenous design informed electronic circuit design – a kind of colonialism in reverse – despite the lack of involvement of indigenous people in the company's research and development arm" (2014: 932). In other words, it becomes a whitewashing of historical accounting.

Lately, research in the history of computing informed by approaches and epistemologies in the study of women, gender and sexuality, of race, ethnicity and postcoloniality as well as disability studies, has expanded the common trajectories of the white male or Western institutions and corporations as those who have shaped user practices and technological development. These projects combine digital DIY making with research methods to write alternatives, not just as a gesture of inclusiveness but as conceivably primary histories of technology and tech cultures. Some of them look at how historical tools, crafts and practices inform interaction design (Fernaeus/Jonsson/Tholander 2012); others take more exploratory and playful approaches to question the dominant paradigms of what counts as scientific and technical practice (Posch/Kurbak 2016; Boeva et al. 2017; Rosner/Bjørn 2019).

DIY Making's Visible Histories and Hagiographies

DIY maker culture's represented history within makers' own narratives has been limited to garage innovators such as the Homebrew Computer Club and oriented mainly to engineering and computer science technical cultures. In pursuing an imaginary that brings new forms and aesthetics to humanise – or even replace – mass production and consumption, makers' writings often also reference the Arts and Crafts movement of William Morris, lending their cause a tie to craftsmanship and artisan production. Such techno-utopianism tends to overlook the luxury of time and resources these objects and activities entail, and how the principles behind the Arts and Crafts movement later became forgotten as its products became commodified for wealthy, elite consumers (Sivek 2011; Cramer 2019). Moreover, offering a consumerist view of DIY making and hacking as the most valued – trajectories that end in best-selling products and multinational corporations – belies the very real traditions of many hacklabs and makerspaces in, for example, squatter, anarchist and social justice communities (Oldenziel/Hård 2013; Costanza-Chock 2020).

Several historians have noted how alternatives get "written out" of history until they are later rediscovered and become utopian – or re-utopianised. DIY maker culture has built upon garage tinkering, but also upon traditions of community organising and alternative value creation, whose terminologies, ideologies and operating principles are easily "written out" (cf. Cuartielles/García 2020, in this issue). In the case of cooperatives, for instance, as neoclassical economics became the canon, discussion on cooperatives was dropped from economics textbooks; this in turn meant cooperatives were overlooked for their potential to address social problems (Kalmi 2007). Similar issues arise with documenting informal economies and gift economies in many regions, where DIY making clearly resides, not least with regard to repair, maintenance and material flow networks (Ahmed/Mim/Jackson 2015; Eglash/Foster 2017). In the same way, small craft production was written out of the history of mass production – often in itself presented as a linear trajectory – as if it never co-existed alongside globalising centralised production (Carson 2010). For historians such as Charles Sabel and Jonathan Zeitlin (1985), small firms and maker-craft production did not denote a traditional or subordinate form of economic activity. Their visionary figures, such as French philosopher Pierre-Joseph Proudhon, often inspired or even mobilised further cooperative production projects, using ideas and a political vocabulary unknown to the "well-schooled theoreticians of mass production" who thus rendered these alternative idioms obsolete through neglect or outright scorn (ibid: 142–143). Rediscovering technocultural phenomena may allow us to imagine new visions, recreate utopias and remake narratives of how to act in the world and how to be embedded in webs of life, in times of complexity and health, environmental and economic crises. This is particularly pressing now when it is unimaginable to see outside of capitalism and *homo oeconomicus*, and beyond ready-made solutions (Daily 2017).

Tool Domestication and Beyond: DIY and DIT

Numerous authors have summarised the histories of DIY as related to home maintenance and handicrafts, while others have included later music and self-publishing subcultures related to punk's explicit use of DIY terminology and a particular aesthetic. Florian Cramer (2019) assigns the roots of DIY culture to the romantic reaction to alienating industrial or institutional production – such as the Arts and Crafts movement, at least in Western cultures – which implies that Do-It-Yourself as a term lacks sense for eras or regions that are pre-industrial or less industrialised. DIY is thus both conservative and anti-conservative, depending on what is rejected or preserved (Cramer 2019). Paul Atkinson points to the "sometimes contradictory elements of need versus desire and creativity versus assemblage" when one attempts to categorise DIY activities (2006: 2). Linking DIY histories to "democracy" and people's agency in different eras, Atkinson suggests categories of "pro-active DIY", activities that are self-directed; "reactive DIY" which entails mediation through kits; "essential DIY", that is, home maintenance performed through economic necessity, and "lifestyle DIY", where the motivation for home renovation lies more in conspicuous consumption (ibid: 3). Historian of technology Rachel Maines (2009) introduced the duo of utilitarian and hedonised DIY, the former referring to activities done out of necessity and the latter out of pleasure, to illustrate how under particular circumstances in Western countries utilitarian DIY became hedonised DIY. One and the same DIY activity, for example, needlework, could simultaneously be rendered utilitarian and hedonised depending on when it is performed and by whom.

In a similar quest to avoid technological determinism and chronological linearity when examining people's DIY practices over time, Knott (2013) proposes a taxonomy of prosumption that is not principally embedded in Western capitalism, as Toffler had conceptualised it (having coined the term prosumption in *The Third Wave*, 1980). Knott's categories for prosumers are those who "follow", that is, "the prosumer who follows the rules" when provided with kits, toolkits and instructions, such as paint-by-number kits; those who "reject" those provisions of capitalism and "pursue self-sufficiency", symbolised by the launch and subsequent influence of the *Whole Earth Catalog* (further discussed below); and those who "adapt" through hacking and ad hoc bricolage, such as "IKEA hacking" (2013: 45). For Ruth Oldenziel and Mikael Hård (2013), active users have been investing time, skills and resources as "consumers", forming user movements, "tinkerers" who appropriate technology and modify machines, and "rebels" who protest technology introduction such as surveillance software and hardware. Such DIY making and hacking includes computer tinkering, wind turbine and cargo-bike building, and children's engineering toy kits, which have shaped European infrastructures and technologies (Oldenziel/Hård 2013).

Domestic and Public DIY

Within the broader set of historical examples, some of the cultural antecedents of DIY making are squarely placed in the domestic sphere. The activities related to early car owners, farmers and amateur radio hobbyists often took place within the household confines, but they rarely addressed the needs of the home as a place and building and its individual caretakers. The aftermath of the Wars, especially in the United Kingdom, economic recessions but also the proliferation of hardware stores, manuals and instructions media, turned the house and home into a DIY site (see Gelber 1997; Hackney 2013). In activities like home renovations and repairs, homeowners engaged in utilitarian DIY activities out of financial necessity, household duty and an absence of qualified craftspeople; on other occasions, hedonised DIY provided an opportunity for artistic self-expression and pastime (see Edwards 2006). Similar to feminised care-work, repair and maintenance, however, utilitarian DIY gets limited attention from a historical and contemporary perspective. The home with its actors and activities is often treated as a marginalised space, placed out of the focus of collectively relevant attention and productive influence, but mostly as the site of gendered work and homemaking crafts that has little value to contribute (ibid). Besides, the ongoing hedonisation of

DIY practices and technologies connected to increase of wealth and resources in predominantly Western countries enables individual expression and exploration celebrated for its creative and libertarian attributes (see Gelber 1997; Powell 2012). These diverse studies suggest that a closer analysis of the histories of domestic and everyday DIY as a marginalised practice obscures present-day visions of DIY making as the locus of creative tech innovation.

Utilitarian DIY making in an improvement sense has recently taken a more political stance as cities and their residents feel pressure through ongoing gentrification, the ramifications of de-industrialisation and the absence of municipal support. In several cases, this has led to civic engagement through DIY actions such as urban gardening, neighbourhood exchange of goods and services as well as other forms of meaningful transformation of public space. Such examples have their own antecedents dating further back than most contemporary DIY-related activities, but tend to be overlooked once tech-based maker and hacker cultures are presented as the answer to communal issues.[1] Other renditions of these histories such as the DIY revitalisation practices for "gray spaces", that is, public spaces forgotten or abandoned by municipalities, carried out by local Detroiters from diverse cultural and ethnic backgrounds get little credit and public attention, as the study by geographer Kimberley Kinder (2016) illustrates. DIY revitalisation practices of public space and community, based on self-provisioning, however, lead to growth of local subcultures around common goals and methods (ibid).

Utilitarian DIY also characterised much DIY activity in regions such as the Soviet Bloc, where the scarcity and low quality of goods met authoritarian regimes' quashing of consumerism. A culture of craft, repair and bricolage developed, enacted in private homes, summer homes and gardens, and shared public spaces, and propagated through television programmes and DIY magazines (Gerasimova/Chuikina 2009; Oldenziel/Hård 2013; Gibas/Nyklová 2020, in this issue; Usenyuk-Kravchuk 2020, in this issue; Sipos/Franzl 2020, in this issue). At the same time, Soviet teens performed their own rebellion during the Cold War by appropriating blue jeans – a symbol of American capitalism – and making, customising and personalising them (Oldenziel/Hård 2013).

Punk Rebellion

DIY's lineage can further be traced in the punk subculture of the 1970s/1980s fostering the production of self-made media known as zines. Zines made with

---

1   One fitting example is the 2016 exhibition "Fix the City" curated by London's Machines Room makerspace as part of the London Design Festival. Though many of the projects created by the designers and makerspace members showed good intentions, only few embraced actual local craft and DIY traditions such as those required for houseboat living and maintenance and combined them with the means of digital fabrication (Foster/Boeva 2019).

cut-n-paste techniques, photocopying and collages, as well as hand and typewritten text not only created a particularly appealing subversive aesthetic that countered the commercial style of popular culture, but aligned (youth) interests and practices with direct action politics, feminism, anti-colonialism and more recently digital production (see McKay 1991; Triggs 2006; Foster 2020, in this issue). While the cultural histories of zine making and DIY print media with their idiosyncratic aesthetics often get credited in maker and hacker histories to emphasise their envisioned countercultural background, they have limitations in explaining the rather standardised design of mainstream online DIY instructions and media such as Instructables or GitHub. Instead, their current form puts these squarely in the style and logics of technical writing and tech culture (Cole/Perner-Wilson 2019), thus neglecting the diversity of DIY practices and their needs for representation.

Interestingly, the word "punk" stems from the late 1800s and meant "inferior" or "bad", and it was slang for a "worthless person" or young hoodlum in the early 1900s (Online Etymology Dictionary n. d.). The punk aesthetic and ethos from the hardcore music scene of the 1970s, with its imagery of hoodlums and rebellion against commercialism, has later informed the more political and protest-oriented subcultures in "craftivism" (Greer 2008). Craftivism entails handicraft performed individually or in groups, such as knitting circles, but directed to political activism, environmental advocacy, artistic protest and/or radical feminism (Minahan/Cox 2007). Particularly when connected to digital technologies, craftivism seeks to resist narratives of traditional gender roles and how they are associated with utilitarian craft, as well as the exclusion of women from innovation and technology imaginaries. Early craftivist communities were forerunners exploring novel networked possibilities to use "Web 2.0" as well as digital fabrication in creating new material cultures and alternative maker practices. As with the other DIY practices we have reviewed here, relationships of punk and protest-oriented DIY with mainstream mass production and consumption structures are never straightforward – subject as they are to sanctioned marginalising and invisibilising, or appropriation and commodification (Hebdige 1979). Today, despite the many espoused benefits, DIY maker practices and spaces have potential to contribute to neighbourhood gentrification and involuntarily to the more neoliberal sides of a "participation society" (Kelty 2017; Cardullo/Kitchin/Di Feliciantonio 2018; Cramer 2019); its punk, rebellious roots in protest and stimulating new politics are too easily ignored.

Collective Tools and DIWO

DIY making and hacking encompass individually oriented, often domestic or private, DIY, as well as socially oriented DIT – in public, private or third spaces, or in virtual spaces via online sharing. In 2006, the art collective Furtherfield coined DIWO, Do-It-With-Others, to denote art projects that were collaborative and distributed (Garrett 2006) – arguably more explorative, expressive and open-ended than projects such as free/libre open-source software, which are typically associated with maker culture by business analysts. Handicrafts have always had their knitting circles and common workshops, while communities have long established alternative spaces for new materialist and peer-learning pedagogies or workshops for self-sufficiency and autonomy. Where motivations multiply, so does the variety of DIWO spaces, as Regina Sipos and Kerstin Franzl illustrate in their examination of Germany's Open Workshops (Sipos/Franzl 2020, in this issue).

While there is not space in this Introduction to elaborate on the histories of hacklabs and hackerspaces, they have clearly contributed to global maker culture evolution and diversity, particularly with regard to bringing media activism literacies, as well as surveillance and privacy issues into the realm of concerns and practices. Hacker cultures and their histories in Europe and the United States have been covered by Maxigas (2012), Jordan (2016), Autistici/Inventati (2017) and others, while Sasha Costanza-Chock (2020) summarise further examples of hacklabs in the Global South. Some technology collectives emerged from clearly anti-authoritarian social movements such as squatting; others were inspired by and worked in "participatory culture" (Jenkins 2006): alternative media and telecommunications, net art, fanzines, etc. Still others (and obviously these groups overlap) gelled around computer geek culture, such as the demoscene, which gave birth to several hacklabs especially in Europe, such as Bitraf in Oslo (Silvast/Reunanen 2014; Autistici/Inventati 2017).

Scholars have also noted that paying attention to histories of making activities and shared artisan workshops contribute more to our understanding of localised and low-tech innovation patterns that do not conform to the Silicon Valley corporate model. Shadreck Chirikure (2017), for instance, questions why scientific research and technological innovation are regarded as more legitimate when done in giant, high-tech laboratories funded by global capitalist regimes, as "mass production" for mass markets. (See Figure 1 for an example of a grassroots technology park in India.) Chirikure (2017) compares the Western notion of progress to the knowledge production accomplished through craft and making in fields and houses for small, local communities in the precolonial history of African technology – and their spiritual and cultural significance beyond their innovative capacities. For Chirikure, places for pottery and metallurgy were "sites of work and knowledge production", which were "often embedded in, and were eschewed for being in, the living space and the natural world" (2017: 73). Chirikure asks directly, should Western concepts always have African equivalents? (2017: 73). What is a fabrication laboratory for, and for whom?

Tool Citizenship: When "Sustainability" Arrived

One of the most popular references in DIY historiographies is Stewart Brand's *Whole Earth Catalog*, first issued in 1968, which took DIY out of the home and into the sheds, shacks, barns, fields and even domes of a counterculture, energy-conscious, self-sufficient utopia. The Catalog featured merchandise and plans for self-reliance, from building to agriculture – small-scale tools for an individualist, autonomous citizenship – targeted to the back-to-the-land commune movement of California in the late 1960s and early 1970s (Turner 2006; Sadler 2012; Turner 2018). Brand envisioned the Catalog also as a research tool, networking people and their stuff in a way that clearly brings to mind today's maker repositories: "nifty projects everywhere, earnest folk climbing around on new dome designs, solar generators" (cited in Turner 2006: 79). The network would be designed as a learning system steeped in the cybernetics movement that Brand both moved in and was instrumental in kindling, while the Catalog also inspired environmentalists worldwide (Boyle/Harper 1976; Turner 2006; Sadler 2012). (And domes persist in maker culture; see Figure 2.)

Emerging Cyberculture

The milieu in California's Bay Area in the 1960s, its movements and counterculture, evolved into the globally influential, individualist and libertarian capitalism we see today. Fred Turner, Simon Sadler, Richard Barbrook and Andy Cameron, among others, observe how a heady mix of McLuhan-inspired community media activism, hippie ecotopia and free market ideologues formed a "bizarre hybrid" only made possible "through a nearly universal belief in technological determinism" (Barbrook/Cameron 1996: 50; also Turner 2006; 2018; Sadler 2012). Pragmatic tool-making, prototyping and networked information sharing birthed mythical artefacts of California innovation and making such as the "virtual community" and WELL (Whole Earth 'Lectronic Link), and garage tinkering such as the Homebrew Computer Club (Wozniak 1984; Rheingold 1993; McGetrick 2017). Decades later, Chris Anderson, one of the editors of Wired magazine, published the capitalist maker bible *Makers* (Anderson 2012) and O'Reilly Media began publishing *Make:* magazine in 2005 – critiqued by some for representing and reproducing maker culture as hyperconsumerist technomyth (Sivek 2011; Shorey 2020, in this issue).

The *Whole Earth Catalog* connected to and had an influence on movements beyond California emphasising ecology, environmentalism and community technology. The (Anglo-Saxon) 1970s saw the rise of the appropriate technology and alternative technology movements, both of which sought to "devise technologies which offer genuine alternatives to the large-scale, complex, centralized, high-energy life forms which dominate the modern age" (Winner 1979: 80). The Appropriate Technology movement was conceptualised and popularised through E. F.

Schumacher's influential book *Small is Beautiful* (1973) – and is a framing that many makers and maker-researchers adopt today for their work, particularly in emerging economies reflecting its early focus on development (e.g. Pearce 2012; Guzmán/Reynolds-Cuellar 2018). Alternative Technology groupings conducted hands-on experiments with and provided information on renewable energy, eco-building, organic food production, water and sanitation, and cooperative ways to develop and use useful technologies by people and for people (Smith 2005; Harper/Sadler 2020, in this issue).

"Science and technology for the people" movements also unfolded in, for example, France, Latin America and India (Quet 2013; Smith et al. 2017). In India, People's Science Movements set the stage for the later incarnations of fab labs and hackerspaces to develop alternative technologies (Smith et al. 2017). Vigyan Ashram, for example, has been involved in education as well as the development of rural technologies since the early 1980s and established a Fab Lab in 2002 (Kulkarni 2016). (See Figure 1.)

Figure 1: Technology Demonstration Park, Vigyan Ashram, Pabal, India, 2017. Photographs: Cindy Kohtala.

Figure 2: Dome demonstrator (left), Vigyan Ashram, Pabal, India, 2017. Hacker dome (right), Koppelting maker festival, Amersfoort, the Netherlands, 2016. Photographs: Cindy Kohtala.

Anti-capitalism and Anti-design

DIY counterculture in the 1960s and 1970s presented pragmatic-utopian visions of shared machine shops, community technology workshops and "laboratory situations" that drew their inspiration from Ivan Illich, the Situationists and anarchist writers such as Murray Bookchin, Pyotr Kropotkin and Pierre-Joseph Proudhon (Boyle/Harper 1976; Hess 1979; Borgonuovo/Franceschini 2018) – distinguishable from current maker hagiographies that espouse the sole-genius-inventor narrative. Especially beloved are anarchist illustrator Clifford Harper's utopian "visions" in the Alternative Technology publication *Radical Technology* (Boyle/Harper 1976), of shared workshops for handicraft and small-technology production, community workshops for larger projects, and others (Figure 3).

Some visions were actualised, such as the Centre for Alternative Technology (CAT) in Wales, now an educational centre on sustainability, and the Australian CERES Community Environment Park established in 1982, which was promoted as a "vision for Brunswick (called 'The People's Republic of Brunswick' in the press) as a decentralised/distributed DIY neighbourhood" featuring "local community sharing systems that included tool libraries, community gardens; fruit trees in streets, worm production, plant nurseries; and much more".[2] CERES had an impact on later formal design education in Australia. The early counterculture visions particularly heralded later initiatives that were informed by and more explicitly aligned with anarchism, feminism and ecosocialism as a reaction to neoliberal austerity politics, such as New Municipalism (Roth/Russell 2018; Thompson 2020). These translocal movements also call attention to compelling new practices for developing the digital tools for solidarity organising and participatory democracy, which become entangled with the material tools for making, living and working together in cities.

DIY countercultures also entailed the "adhocism" of self-built architecture, Drop City domes and projects built from waste materials (Jencks/Silver 2013 [1972]; see also Balkin/Harbison 1990). The radical technology groupings' focus on ecological solutions was labelled as anti-design and practitioners as "design outlaws" (Zelov/Cousineau 1997). North Italy too saw alternative Radical Architecture and Radical Design movements such as Global Tools that rebelled against the capitalist orientation of industrial design by promoting embodied peer learning about craft and materials, survival, the human body and philosophy in designated "laboratories" (Borgonuovo/Franceschini 2018). The collective sought to redress design's indifference to the political economy of the day, rife with the threat of nuclear war, racism, pollution and consumerism, by adopting an "anti-design", "anti-school" approach to design and pedagogy that – while avant-garde, provocative and speculative – contributed to later Environmental Design curricula in Italy

---

2 Chris Ryan, founder of CERES and professor of sustainable design, personal correspondence with Cindy Kohtala, 27 April 2020.

(Formia 2017). These rebellious acts from the periphery have thus had lasting impact on the field of sustainable design and how formal design education has incorporated elements of 1960s/1970s counterculture making.

Figure 3: Vision 5/Community Workshop illustration by Clifford Harper, pages 200–201 of Radical Technology *(Boyle/Harper 1976).*

Anti-militarism and Protest

Another characteristic marking DIY countercultures was protest: many groups were active in demonstrations denouncing the Vietnam War, for instance. Peter Harper from CAT collaborated with a Stockholm activist group called PowWow to organise the Exhibition of People's Technology in Stockholm, to take place during the 1972 United Nations Conference on the Human Environment (UNCHE) (see Simon Sadler's interview with Harper, Harper/Sadler 2020, in this issue). PowWow also organised protests against the Vietnam War during the spring and summer months of 1972 and aimed to challenge the governments attending UNCHE in what they saw as centralised environmental decision-making far from citizens and highly impactful techno-solutionism, what we would call ecomodernism today (Björk n.d.; Scott 2016). In fact, Stewart Brand shows up even here, bringing the activist group Hog Farm with him to stage an initiative called Life Forum – a performative act that many members of PowWow resented as American interference and an attempt by Brand to detract attention from the Vietnam protests (Björk n.d.; Scott 2016).

In 2015, two European initiatives (OuiShare and Open State) collaborated on a circularity- and open-source-oriented maker camp called POC21 (Proof of Concept), in anticipation of the UN Conference of the Parties assembly COP21 in France the same year. Inventors prototyped their solutions using a temporary fab lab, while eating, sleeping and working together in a commune-like environment (Conrad 2016). The materiality of the camp, commune and demonstrations of inventions respond to the aesthetics of the 1970s counterculture at the same time as bringing in Silicon Valley rhetorics and practices such as mentoring and pitching (Berglund/Kohtala 2020). Like PowWow and the Exhibition of People's Technology, POC21 aimed to draw attention to grassroots solutions by connecting to high-level summitry (Smith et al. 2017). Unlike PowWow, however, POC21 did not seek to protest elite environmental decision-making nor question the processes of how the UN defines sustainability for the people of the world. Indeed, in many maker subcultures, explicit protest and political critique are relatively rare. Beliefs that "science is neutral" and "technology is neutral" are remarkably tenacious, and pragmatic prototyping is clearly emphasised even in initiatives explicitly oriented to environmentalism and/or social good.

That said, critiques do arise regarding maker culture's apparent determination to remain depoliticised. Aligning with military partners and the petrochemical industry has been contested in maker and fab lab subcultures, even when the funding is earmarked for "good" educational initiatives (Altman 2012; Troxler 2014). The legacy of radical technology's alternative milieu – particularly its readiness for protest and critique – is thus most visible in today's most overtly political spaces, such as DIYbio and biohack labs; alternative spaces such as feminist hacklabs and Green Fab Labs; and Critical Making projects, some of which address privacy, anti-surveillance and sousveillance (Ratto 2011; Hertz 2012; Toupin 2014; Delgado/Callén 2016). Boston's South End Technology Center, for example, was initially established in the milieu of the civil rights struggle, as a technology training site for black Boston youth. Founder Mel King moved from protest and activism to political strategy, aligning with MIT, a predominantly white, elite institution, to connect a Fab Lab with the existing SETC, thus also enabling MIT to enact objectives aiming at diversity and inclusion (McIlwain 2020).

DIY Geographies: On Peripheries and Centres

One of our desired results has been to include geographical and spatial contexts of DIY maker practices beyond the well-represented ones in the Global North. However, the attempt to represent a "global" or in other terms world history of making within the limited scope of this special issue as well as from our own positionality (in northern/western Europe) further problematises this endeavour. As the growing scholarship on making, hacking, DIY, craft and its associated topics reveals, the prevalence of English as a lingua franca for exchange and in publications reduces the opportunities to include voices and stories that remain unheard. This can already fail because of something deemed negligible such as understanding a call for papers or the absence of an accurate translation of concepts like *jugaad* in Hindi, *urawaza* in Japanese, *gambiarra* in Brazilian Portuguese and many more denoting something similar to DIY. In other words, the dominance of western DIY making and its histories begins with the language behind it. Other issues with expanding the geographic representation relate to the research methods required to uncover untold histories – DIY practices are not overtly represented in archives and scholars rely on oral histories, cues by research informants and interviewees, or even the actual reconstruction of artefacts (see Jungnickel 2020, this issue; Boeva et al. 2017).

Even so, a few ethnographic studies on contemporary maker culture have provided insights into other local industrial and technological histories as well as their manifestations that allow us to challenge the dominance of the Western and predominantly colonial perspective. The enduring link between education and DIY maker culture, often praised for its direct descent from Dewey, Piaget or Montessori's philosophy, is at the centre of several studies. Anita Say Chan's study (2014) of Peru's nationwide adoption of the One Laptop Per Child (OLPC), another MIT spin-off, in the early 2000s questions the long-lasting binary of centre and periphery. In capturing different events and strategies around OLPC's distribution in the country, she discovers how local indigenous educators and students from the Puno altiplano develop their own training programmes reflecting the culture of local Aymara and Quechua people, all leading up to the creation of Peru's first rural hack lab collective (ibid). Similar to Chan's work, Morgan Ames (2019) points out that not all DIY, constructivist educational models underlying projects like the OLPC translate well within the combination of Western "techno-utopian" schemes and metropolitan governmental enterprises of the Global South through her study of the OLPC programme in Paraguay.

Another strand on DIY making in less visible regions considers the connections to industry, manufacturing and innovation. Denisa Kera's comparative study (2012) of hackerspaces in Indonesia, Singapore and Japan demonstrates how such spaces mediate between high-tech/industrial and vernacular knowledge and traditions as much as between technology development and community building. Singapore's earliest hackerspace, for instance, is situated in a neighbourhood full of paradoxes – seafaring, colonial pasts, diverse religions reside next to IT innovation companies, commerce and entertainment areas – and it takes credit for that (ibid). Chinese DIY maker cultures and the growing DIY manufacturing businesses in Shenzhen are the focus of Silvia Lindtner's multi-year ethnography (2015; 2020). Studying how contemporary practices draw upon the culture of local Chinese manufacturing traditions, her work exemplifies how informal manufacturing systems, also known as *shanzhai*, that follow a DIY ethos were established in this region. Counted as prime examples of Chinese grassroots creativity and today the centre of governmental support, these places and activities have a marginal or shadow existence in comparison to the Western (especially American) maker tech economy which paradoxically relies on the industrial infrastructures of production in Southeast Asia (Tanenbaum et al. 2013). The ignorance of local craft and make-do traditions as much as their co-optation into Western design, innovation and entrepreneurship paradigms builds the core of Lilly Irani's argument in her decade of fieldwork in a Delhi design studio (2019). She vividly illustrates how the process of casting designers, developers and non-governmental organisation workers as drivers of innovation in India conceals the contribution of local craftspeople, regular workers and activists to the country's development, which even gets framed as obstructive (ibid).

The review presented here is by no means expansive; it only captures the scholarly worlds closer to ours. Moreover, it is also afflicted by the same language issues described above. To expand the geographies of alternative DIY maker practices and their histories would likely require confronting research methods and practices (What counts as a history? When does it begin?), the research privileges of academia (Who gets to tell stories? And about whom?) and the deeply embedded colonial and marginalising structures of the technological and scientific worlds (Why is DIY making as the "economy of one" more valuable for society than making out of necessity and to fight poverty?).

In This Issue

Three full papers in the section *Field Research and Case Studies* present novel perspectives on alternative DIY maker histories. In "Craft and Artisan Initiatives of the Salvadoran Civil War (1980–1992)", Emilio Velis, Kate Samson, Isaac Robles and Daniel Rodríguez place Latin American craft strongly within a maker culture that elsewhere often devalues handicraft in favour of technology-oriented innovation practices and rhetoric. As digital makers do today, the artisans in the authors' study taught and practised craft making in workshops as an outlet for personal expression and even therapy, a way to develop technical skills for personal and collective empowerment, and as an opportunity for creative learning. The authors give voice to people not often heard in today's technology-addled maker circles – refugees, women, veterans and disabled people, all of them bonded as participants of artisan collectives during the strife of the Salvadoran Civil War in the 1980s.

In "Histories of Technology Culture Manifestos: Their Function in Shaping Technology Cultures and Practices", Ellen K. Foster examines the rhetoric, contexts, aesthetics and materialities of well-propagated feminist, maker and hacker, repair, and cyberfeminist and feminist hacker manifestos developed in different periods and geographies. Analysing these as historical artefacts, Foster makes a case for manifestos as tools for identity shaping as well as for laying the knowledge foundations of individual groups. Yet as the better-known examples of the maker, hacker and tech-related communities demonstrate, the values behind them often result in the maintenance of a status quo instead of its uprooting. Instead, Foster proposes to expand the perspective towards radical feminist manifestos and their configurations which critically question power relations and account for diverse backgrounds around class, gender, race and geography.

The third full paper explores the recent history of Spanish DIY spaces. In "From Hacking to Making – The Commodification of Spanish DIY Spaces Since the 1990s", David Cuartielles Ruiz and César García Sáez survey the broader context of the country's different techno-social movements and spaces and the possible reasons why many of them underwent a double transformation through the commercialisation of DIY culture and a loss of its values associated with it. Capturing data from a broad range of sources including an online survey, social media and community channels, the authors present a compelling "Spanish DIY culture timeline" that includes the entry and exit points of some of these spaces, relevant media publications, public events, as well as policies and governmental reforms imposing changes on Spain's DIY spaces.

Two exploratory papers in the *Entering the Field* section open our perspectives on the diversity of DIY activities, communities and spaces. In "Tracing the History of DIY and Maker Culture in Germany's Open Workshops", Regina Sipos and Kerstin Franzl take the proliferation of contemporary makerspaces in Germany to trace their beginnings in the two formerly separated 20th-century countries. Combining oral histories and document analysis, their initial study illustrates how the different sociocultural and economic infrastructures of both countries constructed distinct DIY cultures – one being more countercultural and leisurely oriented, the other pursuing the education of future generations of young workers. Despite such differences, their commonality was an underlying idea of community-making.

The combination of hobbies/leisure time and workforce education through DIY is explored from a different perspective in "'What You Can Invent over the Weekend' and the Recurring History of Corporate DIY" by Samantha Shorey. The paper presents a comparative study of two sets of DIY texts – a collection of printed DIY booklets from the 1950s and 1960 provided by General Motors (GM) to their production employees, and the first issues of *Make:* magazine from the early 2000s. In studying the topics, projects, tools, materials and their intended audience turned makers in both printed sources, Shorey questions the argumentation for DIY as a practice and place for self-improvement and innovation, further noting that the techno-utopian celebration of making, craft and DIY within contemporary tech-cultures as unmapped sites of (workers') creativity deviates from GM's intentions for their workers' education and leisure time.

In the section *In Conversation With...*, we present two compelling interviews with practitioners and founding figures of alternative DIY movements. The first interview "Makers and Design in South Africa: Technology and Craft Cultures and their Antecedents" with Felix Holm, co-founder of the Maker Station in Cape Town, and Suné Stassen, founding director of Open Design Afrika, was conducted over video conference with two of the guest editors days before the global pandemic shut down nearly everything. Here, Holm and Stassen reflect on how their engagement in making, design and creative practices has supported establishing infrastructures that reflect South Africa's diverse DIY traditions and empower local communities in a meaningful way. In "The Exhibition of People's Technology, 1972", Peter Harper, co-editor of the famous *Radical Technology* source, recapitulates in his conversation with design historian Simon Sadler the contents and topics of the 1972 Stockholm exhibition dedicated to it and its broader implications. Supplemented with a plethora of visual materials presenting some of the "alternative technologies" and instructions on how to rebuild them, the conversation reconnects contemporary tech DIY making with many of its initial promises around sustainability, democracy and diversity.

To illustrate an even richer landscape of DIY making's alternative histories, in the section *Moments in Alternative (Hi)stories*, we invited researchers and practitioners to contribute short vignettes that combine historical, ethnographic and practice-based research. Following from the Alternative Technology movement, Kostas Latoufis and Aristotle Tympas describe small wind turbine making and design in an isolated Scottish island community that has grown to a global group of supporters. In a similar way, extreme weather conditions and extremely remote locations engender ingenuity through DIY, as Svetlana Usenyuk-Kravchuk illustrates the wonderful bricolaged solutions for mobility crafted by inventors in the Russian Arctic. Socialism and the transition to a democracy created another locally contextual form of DIY in what is now the Czech Republic, merging necessity with leisure, as Petr Gibas and Blanka Nyklová's contribution reveals. Anupama Gowda looks at history from a different angle, that of using her fab lab to allow local children to explore the histories of their own urban neighbourhood of Halasuru in Bangalore, India. The experiences of educators are also at the heart of Jesse Adams Stein's vignette on the collective action of highly skilled engineering patternmakers teaching at a trade school in Melbourne during a stern period of de-industrialisation. The ultimate example, written by Kat Jungnickel, explores how historical clothing patents, in particular from the Victorian era, help uncover the unlauded inventiveness of women and marginalised people, created in a manner and with the motivation similar to other DIY cultures, but also how the actual DIY act of re-making these textile "technologies" creates seminal knowledge about the individuals and societal norms missing in the paper records.

Conclusions

The examination of DIY cultures and maker utopias confirms their importance paradoxically through their very marginality. By framing and reframing, appropriating and reappropriating, DIY making and hacking – understood through a wider set of people and practices – allows individuals and social groupings to reassert control, choose how to spend their time in leisure or productivity, learn and bond, and have multiple orientations to "innovation". While the terminology of DIY is pegged to industrialisation and rendered irrelevant or colonising in less industrialised contexts, there is room for epistemological consideration as to how "maker culture" can be re-expanded to allow low-tech, handicraft and bricolage to inform. Historical examinations also serve to complicate problematic technology determinist views of innovation.

By remaining stalwart at the grassroots and the peripheries, alternative DIY maker cultures have created technocultural conditions by which technologies could be prototyped and eventually adopted more widely. The Alternative Technology movement, for instance, played a role in the mainstreaming of wind turbines in Denmark (Boyle/Harper 1976; Smith 2005). The antecedents to current maker culture are important with regard to how they contribute to making "enduring technologies" (such as bicycles or windmills), maintaining and resurrecting interest in repair and small-scale environmental technologies (Oldenziel/Trischler 2015: 5; see Latoufis/Tympas 2020, in this issue; Harper/Sadler 2020, in this issue). As such technologies become embedded in people's everyday lives, even at the fringes, they act as "pockets of persistence" which are rooted in routines, materiality and cultural reframings (Shove 2012: 372, cited in Oldenziel/Trischler 2015: 6). From the perspective of the history of technologies, then, it is less helpful to see innovations as having linear histories, moving in a trajectory towards stabilisation, than it is to observe how technologies and movements wane and revive in cycles and their relations to other technologies and practices (Shove 2012; Oldenziel/Trischler 2015). This appears particularly important with regard to how the contemporary maker culture takes up or disregards low-carbon technologies and to which technology narratives groups align.

Today's DIY maker communities and their spaces may take inspiration and even strategic guidance from the global commodified "maker movement", but they are geographically situated and actual practices and tactics are informed, explicitly or implicitly, by groups and norms that precede the makerspace and its community (Dunbar-Hester 2014; Costanza-Chock 2020). If articulated, currently invisible histories can tell us much about how such practices could be made more relevant, better answer local needs and gain staying power in their own localities (Soppelsa 2011). Historical knowledge can feed back into actual practice, strengthen the potential for positive socio-environmental impact, inform policy and more generally foster plurality of voice and agency.

Acknowledgements

We are grateful to the reviewers for their valuable contributions to this Special Issue. The work has been supported in part by the Nessling Foundation (Grant 201900394).

References

Abbate, J. (2012): Recoding Gender: Women's Changing Participation in Computing. Cambridge, MA: The MIT Press.

Ahmed, S. I./Mim, N. J./Jackson, S. J. (2015): "Residual Mobilities: Infrastructural Displacement and Post-colonial Computing in Bangladesh." Proceedings of the 33rd Annual ACM Conference on Human Factors in Computing Systems. New York, NY: ACM, pp. 437–446.

Altman, M. (2012): "Do Funding Sources Matter? Why I Chose to Stop Helping at Maker Faire After They Received Military Funding (For a Good Cause)." In: G. Hertz (ed.), Critical Making: Make. Hollywood, CA: Telharmonium Press. Retrieved from http://conceptlab.com/criticalmaking/PDFs/CriticalMaking2012Hertz-Make-pp01to10-Altman-DoFundingSourcesMatter.pdf.

Ames, M. G. (2019): The Charisma Machine: The Life, Death, and Legacy of One Laptop Per Child. Cambridge, MA: The MIT Press.

Anderson, C. (2012): Makers: The New Industrial Revolution. New York, NY: Random House Business Books.

Atkinson, P. (2006): "Do It Yourself: Democracy and Design." Journal of Design History 19(1), pp. 1–10.

Autistici/Inventati. (2017): +Kaos: Ten Years of Hacking and Media Activism (English edition). Amsterdam: Institute of Network Cultures.

Balkin, A./Harbison, J. (1990): Lackluster Bad-Ass Homes. Lackluster No. 2 [zine].

Barbrook, R./Cameron, A. (1996): "The Californian Ideology." Science as Culture 6(1), 44–72.

Berglund, E./Kohtala, C. (2020): "Collaborative Confusion among DIY Makers: Ethnography and Expertise in Creating Knowledge for Environmental Sustainability." Science & Technology Studies 33(2), pp. 102–119.

Björk, T. (n.d.): Challenging Western Environmentalism at the United Nations Conference on Human Environment in Stockholm 1972. Association Aktivism. Retrieved from http://www.aktivism.info/rapporter/ChallengingUN72.pdf.

Boeva, Y./Elliott, D./Jones-Imhotep, E./Muhammedi, S./Turkel, W. J. (2017): "Doing History by Reverse Engineering Electronic Devices." In: J. Sayers (ed.), Making Things and Drawing Boundaries: Experiments in the Digital Humanities. Minneapolis, MN: University of Minnesota Press, pp. 163–176.

Borgonuovo, V./Franceschini, S. (eds.). (2018): Global Tools 1973–1975: When Education Coincides with Life. Rome: Nero.

Boyle, G./Harper, P. (eds.). (1976): Radical Technology. London: Wildwood House.

Braybrooke, K./Jordan, T. (2017): "Genealogy, Culture and Technomyth: Decolonizing Western Information Technologies, from Open Source to the Maker Movement." Digital Culture & Society 3(1), pp. 25–45.

Cardullo, P./Kitchin, R./Di Feliciantonio, C. (2018): "Living Labs and Vacancy in the Neoliberal City." Cities 73, pp. 44–50.

Carson, K. A. (2010): The Homebrew Industrial Revolution: A Low-Overhead Manifesto. Charleston, SC: Booksurge.

Chan, A. S. (2014): "Beyond Technological Fundamentalism: Peruvian Hack Labs & 'Inter-technological' Education". Journal of Peer Production 5. Retrieved from http://peerproduction.net/issues/issue-5-shared-machine-shops/peer-reviewed-articles/beyond-technological-fundamentalism-peruvian-hack-labs-and-inter-technological-education/.

Chirikure, S. (2017): "The Metalworker, the Potter, and the Pre-European African 'Laboratory'." In: C. C. Mavhunga (ed.), What Do Science, Technology, and Innovation Mean from Africa? Cambridge, MA: The MIT Press, pp. 63–77.

Cole, D./Perner-Wilson, H. (2019): "Getting Lost and Unlearning Certainty: Material Encounters in an Electronic Craft Practice." In: L. Bogers/L. Chiapiani (eds.), The Critical Makers Reader: (Un)learning Technology. Amsterdam: Institute of Network Cultures, pp. 107–126.

Conrad, A. (ed.) (2016): We are All Crew: The POC21 Innovation Camp Report. Open State and OuiShare. Retrieved from http://www.poc21.cc/THE_POC21_REPORT.pdf.

Costanza-Chock, S. (2020): Design Justice: Community-Led Practices to Build the Worlds We Need. Cambridge, MA: The MIT Press.

Cowan, R. S. (1987): "The Consumption Junction: A Proposal for Research Strategies in the Sociology of Technology." In: W. E. Bijker/T. P. Hughes/T. Pinch (eds.), The Social Construction of Technological Systems: New Directions in the Sociology and History of Technology. Cambridge, MA: The MIT Press.

Cramer, F. (2019): "Does DIY Mean Anything? – A DIY Attempt (= Essay)." Anrikningsverket Journal 1, pp. 54–72.

Daily, L. (2017): "'Change Your Underwear, Change the World': Entrepreneurial Activism and the Fate of Utopias in an Era of Ethical Capital." In: A. Day (ed.), DIY Utopia: Cultural Imagination and the Remaking of the Possible. Lanham, MD: Lexington Books, pp. 227–252.

Delgado, A./Callén, B. (2016): "Do-it-Yourself Biology and Electronic Waste Hacking: A Politics of Demonstration in Precarious Times." Public Understanding of Science 26(2), pp. 179–194.

Dunbar-Hester, C. (2014): "Radical Inclusion? Locating Accountability in Technical DIY." In: M. Ratto/M. Boler (eds.), DIY Citizenship: Critical Making and Social Media. Cambridge, MA: The MIT Press, pp. 75–88.

Edwards, C. (2006): "'Home is Where the Art is': Women, Handicrafts and Home Improvements 1750–1900." Journal of Design History 19(1), pp. 11–21.

Eglash, R./Foster, E. K. (2017): "On the Politics of Generative Justice: African Traditions and Maker Communities." In: C. C. Mavhunga (ed.), What Do Science, Technology, and Innovation Mean from Africa? Cambridge, MA: The MIT Press, pp. 117–135.

Ensmenger, N. L. (2010): The Computer Boys Take Over: Computers, Programmers, and the Politics of Technical Expertise. Cambridge, MA: The MIT Press.

Escobar, A. (2018): Designs for the Pluriverse: Radical Interdependence, Autonomy, and the Making of Worlds. Durham, NC: Duke University Press.

Fernaeus, Y./Jonsson, M./Tholander, J. (2012): "Revisiting the Jacquard Loom: Threads of History and Current Patterns in HCI." CHI '12: Proceedings of the SIGCHI Conference on Human Factors in Computing Systems. San Diego, CA; New York, NY: ACM, pp. 1593–1602.

Fonseca, F. (2015): Repair Culture. Retrieved from http://efeefe.no-ip.org/livro/repair-culture.

Formia, E. (2017): "Mediating an Ecological Awareness in Italy: Shared Visions of Sustainability Between the Environmental Movement and Radical Design Cultures (1970–1976)." Journal of Design History 30(2), pp. 192–211.

Foster, E. K./Boeva, Y. (2019): "Making Sense of Place: Research Reflections from Two Multi-sited Ethnographies." Making Futures: Crafting a Sustainable Modernity – Towards a Maker Aesthetics of Production and Consumption Vol. 5. Retrieved from https://drive.google.com/open?id=1hb-vXJTJRd3lVKklxLYYT4IgYGj2r3me.

Franz, K. (2005): Tinkering: Consumers Reinvent the Early Automobile. Philadelphia, PA: University of Pennsylvania Press.

Garrett, M. (2006): "D.I.W.O." [blog entry]. Furtherfield. Retrieved from http://www.furtherfield.org/lexicon/diwo.

Gelber, S. M. (1997): "Do-It-Yourself: Constructing, Repairing and Maintaining Domestic Masculinity." American Quarterly 49(1), pp. 66–112.

Gerasimova, E./Chuikina, S. (2009): "The Repair Society." Russian Studies in History 48(1), pp. 58–74.

Greer, B. (2008): Knitting for Good!: A Guide to Creating Personal, Social, and Political Change Stitch by Stitch. Boston, MA: Trumpeter.

Guzmán, S. B./Reynolds-Cuellar, P. (2018): "Achieving Grassroots Innovation Through Multi-lateral Collaborations: Evidence from the Field." Journal of Peer Production 12. Retrieved from http://peerproduction.net/issues/issue-12-makerspaces-and-institutions/peer-reviewed-papers/achieving-grassroots-innovation-through-multi-lateral-collaborations/.

Hackney, F. (2013): "Quiet Activism and the New Amateur: The Power of Home and Hobby Crafts." Design and Culture 5(2), pp. 169–194.

Haring, K. (2007): Ham Radio's Technical Culture. Cambridge, MA: The MIT Press.

Hebdige, D. (1979): Subculture: The Meaning of Style. London: Routledge.

Hertz, G. (2012): Critical Making: Projects. Hollywood, CA: Telharmonium Press.

Hess, K. (1979): Community Technology. New York, NY: Harper & Row.

Hicks, M. (2017): Programmed Inequality: How Britain Discarded Women Technologists and Lost Its Edge in Computing. Cambridge, MA: The MIT Press.

Hyysalo, S./Jensen, T. E./Oudshoorn, N. (eds.). (2016): The New Production of Users: Changing Innovation Collectives and Involvement Strategies. New York, NY: Routledge.

Irani, L. (2015): "Hackathons and the Making of Entrepreneurial Citizenship". Science, Technology, & Human Values 40(5), pp. 799–824.

Irani, L. (2019): Chasing Innovation: Making Entrepreneurial Citizens in Modern India. Princeton, NJ: Princeton University Press.

Jasanoff, S./Kim, S.-H. (eds.) (2015): Dreamscapes of Modernity: Sociotechnical Imaginaries and the Fabrication of Power. Chicago: The University of Chicago Press.

Jencks, C./Silver, N. (2013): Adhocism: The Case for Improvisation (Expanded and updated edition). Cambridge, MA: The MIT Press.

Jenkins, H. (2006). Convergence Culture: Where Old and New Media Collide. New York, NY: New York University Press.

Jordan, T. (2016): "A Genealogy of Hacking". Convergence 23(5), pp. 528–544.

Jungnickel, K. (2018): Bikes & Bloomers: Victorian Women Inventors & their Extraordinary Cycle Wear. London: Goldsmiths Press.

Kalmi, P. (2007): "The Disappearance of Cooperatives from Economics Textbooks." Cambridge Journal of Economics 31(4), pp. 625–647.

Kaiying, C. L./Lindtner, S./Wuschitz, S. (2019): "Hacking Difference in Indonesia: The Ambivalences of Designing for Alternative Futures." Proceedings of DIS'19 the Designing Interactive Systems Conference. New York, NY: ACM, pp. 1571–1582.

Kelty, C. M. (2017): "Too Much Democracy in All the Wrong Places: Toward a Grammar of Participation." Current Anthropology 58(S15), pp. S77–S90.

Kera, D. (2012): "Hackerspaces and DIYbio in Asia: Connecting Science and Community with Open Data, Kits and Protocols." Journal of Peer Production 2. Retrieved from http://peerproduction.net/issues/issue-2/peer-reviewed-papers/diybio-in-asia/.

Kinder, K. (2016): DIY Detroit: Making Do in a City without Services. Minneapolis, MN: University of Minnesota Press.

Kline, R./Pinch, T. (1996): "Users as Agents of Technological Change: The Social Construction of the Automobile in the Rural United States." Technology and Culture 37(4), pp. 763–795.

Knott, S. (2013): "Design in the Age of Prosumption: The Craft of Design after the Object." Design and Culture 5(1), pp. 45–67.

Kohtala, C./Hyysalo, S./Whalen, J. (2020): "A Taxonomy of Users' Active Design Engagement in the 21st Century." Design Studies 67, pp. 27–54.

Krewani, A. (2017): "Urban Hacking and Its 'Media Origins'." Digital Culture & Society 3(1), pp. 139–146.

Kulkarni, Y. (2016): "Fab Lab 0 to Fab Lab 0.4: Learnings from Running a Lab in an Indian Village." Proceedings of the Fab 12 Research Stream, FAB12: Fabricating the Future, 8–14 August, Shenzhen, China. Retrieved from https://archive.org/details/Fab12Kulkarni.

Lees-Maffei, G. (2009): "The Production-Consumption-Mediation Paradigm." Journal of Design History 22(4), pp. 351–376.

Light, J. (1999): "When Computers were Women." Technology & Culture 40(30), pp. 455–483.

Lindtner, S. (2015): "Hacking with Chinese Characteristics: The Promises of the Maker Movement against China's Manufacturing Culture." Science, Technology, & Human Values 40(5), pp. 854–879.

Lindtner, S. (2020): Prototype Nation: China and the Contested Promise of Innovation. Princeton, NJ: Princeton University Press.

Lindtner, S./Lin, C. (2017): "Making and its Promises". CoDesign 13(2), pp. 70–82.

Maines, R. (2009): Hedonizing Technologies: Paths to Pleasure in Hobbies and Leisure. Baltimore, MD: John Hopkins University Press.

Mavhunga, C. C. (2017): "Introduction: What Do Science, Technology, and Innovation Mean from Africa?" In: C. C. Mavhunga (ed.), What Do Science, Technology, and Innovation Mean from Africa? Cambridge, MA: The MIT Press, pp. 1–44.

Maxigas. (2012): "Hacklabs and Hackerspaces: Tracing Two Genealogies." Journal of Peer Production 2. Retrieved from http://peerproduction.net/issues/issue-2/peer-reviewed-papers/hacklabs-and-hackerspaces/.

McGetrick, B. (2017): "More is Better: Making Makers in California." In: J. McGuirk/B. McGetrick (eds.), California: Designing Freedom. London: Phaidon Press, the Design Museum, pp. 116–153.

McIlwain, C. D. (2020): Black Software: The Internet and Racial Justice, from the AfroNet to Black Lives Matter. New York, NY: Oxford University Press.

McKay, G. (ed.) (1991): DIY Culture: Party & Protest in Nineties Britain. London: Verso Books.

Medina, E./Marques, I. C./Holmes, C. (eds.). (2014): Beyond Imported Magic: Essays on Science, Technology, and Society in Latin America. Cambridge, MA: The MIT Press.

Minahan, S./Cox, J. W. (2007): "Stitch'nBitch: Cyberfeminism, a Third Place and the New Materiality." Journal of Material Culture 12(1), pp. 5–21.

Nakamura, L. (2014): "Indigenous Circuits: Navajo Women and the Racialization of Early Electronic Manufacture." American Quarterly 66(4), pp. 919–941.

Oldenziel, R./Hård, M. (2013): Consumers, Tinkerers, Rebels: The People Who Shaped Europe. London: Palgrave Macmillan.

Oldenziel, R./Trischler, H. (2015): "How Old Technologies Became Sustainable: An Introduction." In: R. Oldenziel/H. Trischler (eds.), Cycling and Recycling: Histories of Sustainable Practices. New York, NY: Berghahn, pp. 1–12.

Online Etymology Dictionary (n. d.): "punk" [entry]. Retrieved from https://www.etymonline.com/word/punk.

Orr, J. (1996): Talking about Machines. Ithaca, NY: Cornell University Press.

Oudshoorn, N./Pinch, T. (2003): How Users Matter: The Co-construction of Users and Technologies. Cambridge, M: The MIT Press.

Parr, J. (1999): Domestic Goods: The Material, the Moral, and the Economics in the Postwar Years. Toronto: University of Toronto Press.

Pearce, J. M. (2012): "The case for Open Source Appropriate Technology." Environment, Development and Sustainability 14(3), pp. 425–431.
Pfaffenberger, B. (1992): "Technological Dramas." Science, Technology, & Human Values 17(3), pp. 282–312.
Pomerantz, J./Peek, R. (2016): "Fifty Shades of Open". First Monday 21(5). Retrieved from https://journals.uic.edu/ojs/index.php/fm/article/view/6360/5460.
Posch, I./Kurbak, E. (2016): "Crafted Logic Towards Hand-Crafting a Computer." Proceedings of the 2016 CHI Conference Extended Abstracts on Human Factors in Computing Systems (CHI EA '16). New York, NY: ACM, pp. 3881–3884.
Powell, A. B. (2012): "Democratizing Production Through Open Source Knowledge: From Open Software to Open Hardware." Media, Culture & Society 34(6), pp. 691–708.
Quet, M. (2013): "Science to the People! (and Experimental Politics): Searching for the Roots of Participatory Discourse in Science and Technology in the 1970s in France." Public Understanding of Science 23(6), pp. 628–645.
Ratto, M. (2011): "Critical Making: Conceptual and Material Studies in Technology and Social Life." The Information Society 27(4), pp. 252–260.
Rheingold, H. (1993): The Virtual Community: Homesteading on the Electronic Frontier. Cambridge, MA: The MIT Press.
Richterich, A./Wenz, K. (eds.) (2017a): Making and Hacking [Special Issue]. Digital Culture & Society 3(1).
Richterich, A./Wenz, K. (2017b): "Introduction: Making and Hacking." Digital Culture & Society 3(1), pp. 5–21.
Rosner, D. K. (2018): Critical Fabulations: Reworking the Methods and Margins of Design. Cambridge, MA: The MIT Press.
Rosner, D. K./Bjørn, P. (2019): "Fabulating Historical Data by Hand: AtariWomen and Historical Re-Telling." Conference paper presented at the Annual Meeting of the Society for the History of Technology (24–27 October 2019). Milan, Italy.
Rosner, D. K./Shorey, S./Craft, B. R./Remick, H. (2018): "Making Core Memory: Design Inquiry into Gendered Legacies of Engineering and Craftwork" (Paper 531). Proceedings of the 2018 CHI Conference on Human Factors in Computing Systems. New York, NY: ACM.
Roth, L./Russell, B. (2018): "Translocal Solidarity and the New Municipalism." ROAR 8, 26 September, p. 7.
Sabel, C./Zeitlin, J. (1985): "Historical Alternatives to Mass Production: Politics, Markets and Technology in Nineteenth-Century Industrialization." Past & Present 108, pp. 133–176.
Sadler, S. (2012): "The Dome and the Shack: The Dialectics of Hippie Enlightenment." In: I. Boal/J. Stone/M. Watts/C. Winslow (eds.), West of Eden: Communes and Utopia in Northern California. Oakland, CA: PM Press, pp. 72–80.
Schumacher, E. F. (1973): Small is Beautiful: A Study of Economics as if People Mattered. London: Blond & Briggs.

Scott, F. D. (2016): Outlaw Territories: Environments of Insecurity/Architectures of Counterinsurgency. Cambridge, MA: The MIT Press.

Shove, E. (2012): "The Shadowy Side of Innovation: Unmaking and Sustainability." Technology Analysis & Strategic Management 24(4), pp. 363–375.

Silvast, A./Reunanen, M. (2014): "Multiple Users, Diverse Users: Appropriation of Personal Computers by Demoscene Hackers." In: G. Alberts/R. Oldenziel (eds.), Hacking Europe: From Computer Cultures to Demoscenes. London: Springer, pp. 151–163.

Sivek, S. C. (2011): "'We Need a Showing of All Hands': Technological Utopianism in MAKE Magazine." Journal of Communication Inquiry 35(3), pp. 187–209.

Smith, A. (2005): "Environmental Movements and Innovation: From Alternative Technology to Hollow Technology." Human Ecology Review 12(2), pp. 106–119.

Smith, A./Fressoli, M./Abrol, D./Arond, E./Ely, A. (2017): Grassroots Innovation Movements. Abingdon, UK: Routledge.

Soppelsa, P. (2011): "Intersections: Technology, Mobility, and Geography". Technology and Culture 52(4), pp. 673–677.

Stein, J. A. (2017): "The Political Imaginaries of 3D Printing: Prompting Mainstream Awareness of Design and Making". Design and Culture 9(1), pp. 3–27.

Takahashi, Y. (2000): "A Network of Tinkerers: The Advent of the Radio and Television Receiver Industry in Japan." Technology and Culture 41(3), pp. 460–484.

Tanenbaum, J. G./Williams, A. M./Desjardins, A./Tanenbaum, K. (2013): "Democratizing Technology: Pleasure, Utility and Expressiveness in DIY and Maker Practice." Proceedings of the SIGCHI Conference on Human Factors in Computing Systems. New York, NY: ACM, pp. 2603–2612.

Thompson, M. (2020) "What's so new about New Municipalism?" Progress in Human Geography, in press, 1–26.

Toffler, A. (1980): The Third Wave. New York, NY: Morrow.

Toupin, S. (2014): "Feminist Hackerspaces: The Synthesis of Feminist and Hacker Cultures." Journal of Peer Production 5. Retrieved from http://peerproduction.net/issues/issue-5-shared-machine-shops/peer-reviewed-articles/feminist-hackerspaces-the-synthesis-of-feminist-and-hacker-cultures/.

Triggs, T. (2006): "Scissors and Glue: Punk Fanzines and the Creation of a DIY Aesthetic." Journal of Design History 19(1), pp. 69–83.

Troxler, P. (2014): "Fab Labs Forked: A Grassroots Insurgency Inside the Next Industrial Revolution." Journal of Peer Production 5. Retrieved from http://peerproduction.net/issues/issue-5-shared-machine-shops/editorial-section/fab-labs-forked-a-grassroots-insurgency-inside-the-next-industrial-revolution/.

Turner, F. (2006): From Counterculture to Cyberculture: Stewart Brand, the Whole Earth Network, and the Rise of Digital Utopianism. Chicago, IL: University of Chicago Press.

Turner, F. (2018): "Millenarian Tinkering: The Puritan Roots of the Maker Movement." Technology and Culture 59, pp. S160–S182.

Usenyuk, S./Hyysalo, S./Whalen, J. (2016): "Proximal Design: Users as Designers of Mobility in the Russian North." Technology and Culture 57(4), pp. 866–908.

Winner, L. (1979): "The Political Philosophy of Alternative Technology: Historical Roots and Present Prospects." Technology in Society 1(1), 75–86.

Wozniak, S. (1984): "Homebrew and How the Apple Came to be." In: S. Ditlea (ed.), Digital Deli: The Comprehensive, User-Lovable Menu of Computer Lore, Culture, Lifestyles, and Fancy. New York, NY: Workman Pub.

Zelov, C./Cousineau, P. (eds.). (1997): Design Outlaws on the Ecological Frontier. Easton, PA: Knossus.

Field Research and Case Studies

Craft and Artisan Initiatives of the Salvadoran Civil War (1980-1992)

Emilio Velis, Kate Samson, Isaac Robles and Daniel Rodríguez

Abstract

This article describes the testimonies of two arts and crafts collectives during the Salvadoran Civil War in the 1980s. These collectives, open to victims and refugees of the war, emerged as creative spaces during a time of significant social unrest. As participants learned to make and produce arts and crafts, these activities encouraged individual expression and allowed them to heal traumatic experiences. By describing the aspects that motivated and discouraged the involvement of participants over time, we show how the individual and collective aspects of making *are important for the sustained participation of the people who engage in maker culture. We draw comparisons between the struggles of these historical movements and of current embodiments of the maker culture, in order to draw conclusions regarding how making can be a personal catalyst in the face of social hardship, the importance of economic sustainability in maker initiatives and how unjust gender dynamics take place in these spaces. The ability to compare and learn from these historical initiatives serves to unpack maker culture as a social asset that can be described beyond the mere use of digital tools and to repurpose it as a more inclusive concept that takes into account narratives from a broader range of expressions of* making.

Keywords: maker culture, Salvadoran Civil War, El Salvador, arts and crafts, makerspaces

Introduction

The term *making* describes the way in which humans interact with the physical world to express their creativity, but in recent years, the surge of technological and digital tools has changed how some communities use this term. On the one hand, since *making* can describe most human activities, all humans can be considered makers (Dougherty 2012). On the other hand, a more recent depiction of *making* implies the use of digital tools to recreate and make artefacts (Foster 2017: 6; Papavlasopoulou/Giannakos/Jaccheri 2017) and to share them over the Internet (Mikhak et al 2002; Walter-Herrmann 2013).

It is critical to note that before the dawn of the technological age, people were making. Across cultures, local artisans have engaged with materials and with each other to solve practical problems; in their collective spaces, a Do-It-Yourself culture was accepted as a given. It has only been more recently that a predominant white and male narrative has redefined the value given to creative manual labour through concepts such as *maker culture*, which are mostly used in the Global North to describe communities of avid learners, creators and technologists.

With the spread of concepts such as fab labs and makerspaces, two main challenges exist to the mainstream definition of these concepts. The first one is the need of a more inclusive maker culture with opportunities for a more diverse group of makers. Artisans from traditional arts and crafts often take part in events such as Maker Faires, for example, but they soon find themselves at the low end of power inequalities compared to users of more modern technologies. The community has made a distinction between *crafters* and *makers*, where the former activities are regarded as "feminine" and "frivolous" (Britton 2015). Makers, in contrast, are usually less culturally diverse and mostly male, with activities and creations more valued by the movement.

The second one is a challenge to the Western paradigm that celebrates individuals for their creations, based on the myth of artists and inventors as "unique, different or better than others" (Sawyer 2006: 140), whereas a collectivist paradigm is more common in non-Western cultures, limiting individualism and personal autonomy to embrace social interdependence (Markus/Kitayama 1991: 36). Furthermore, a Hegelian view of personhood as inseparable from the artist's creation has widened the gap between individual and collective creations and led to shaping our current intellectual property laws, on which inalienable moral rights are automatically granted to authors (Knowles 1983; Priya 2008). As a result, creations with a name attached to it are more worthy of protection and thus more valuable, while the protection of collective and anonymous works is sometimes complicated and cumbersome (Dutfield 2017).

With this in mind, it is clear why non-Western craft movements are outside of the definition of maker culture due to their lack of digital technology, use of traditional techniques and their relation to collective ethno-cultural expressions. They do not fit into an academic definition of art and are often relegated to be lower-quality expressions of creativity (González 2018: 32). For this reason, we pose that handicrafts throughout Latin America – which are perceived as an integral part of contemporary maker culture – are also sources of personal creativity and self-actualisation, and that this is the reason why they are still present in rural communities, suburban areas and informal settlements, as a living, evolving movement and even a relevant medium for therapy and self-expression.

This article will describe the recollections of people who took part in two Salvadoran crafts collectives from the 1980s. In the first section, we will describe the interviews with two refugees who took part in embroidery workshops in Colomoncagua and Mesa Grande, as well as a member of the ceramics cooperative ACOGIPRI. The war context section describes the role of crafts in the Salvadoran Civil War through a narrative that focuses on the historical context and the motivations of our informants.

In the subsequent section, we will explore the struggles and demotivators of participants in the movement, which we have grouped as follows: (1) making as a psychological escape, (2) economic sustainability and (3) gender inclusion. Our discussion then connects the struggles and demotivators with the current state of the *maker movement* and ways in which these are addressed. Finally, in the conclusion, we will reflect on the importance of including non-Western narratives into the current definition of *making* and maker culture.

Interviews and Informants

Central American wars were fought mostly in cities and rainforests but had their beginnings among the intellectual circles that developed its underlying ideological front. In El Salvador, this process was started by groups of organised students and artists around ideological causes; one important example of this is the Committed Generation literary movement. Support for insurgency gained force within these groups and permeated even to rural areas through the support of radicalised members of the Catholic Church and the University of El Salvador (Chávez 2017: 79), whose work in rural communities focused on cooperativism, literacy and the Catholic faith. This process unified the movement and led to the formation of common groups that engaged in the war as ideologues, community organisers or fighters.

The contribution of peasant leaders to the Civil War has been widely documented through the testimonies of fighters and peasants who supported the movement. However, the intellectual value of peasant intellectualism and its role in the war "has been greatly underestimated in the academic literature" (ibid: 73), and we argue that even the narrative of peasant participation is biased towards the stories of more educated outsiders who taught skills to naïve and uneducated artisans, instead of it being an appropriation of these skills into an already existing and rich worldview. In order to address the intellectual contribution of rural communities in the Civil War, this article will explore *making* as a reflection of personhood and collectivity as well as the shared values and social practices of civilians in two of many creative collectives that were organised across El Salvador during its Civil War (1980–1992).

We interviewed members from two collectives of arts and crafts made up of people who were directly affected by the Civil War to learn about their motivations to invest time in making artistic and utilitarian products, and how this mirrors characteristics of a modern maker culture. By exploring the intellectual role of *making*, we are broadening the scope of the social narrative in this social period and of maker culture as a richer historical movement. The first account explores the experiences of two Salvadoran women who lived several years in the refugee camps of Colomoncagua, Honduras. A group of refugees – mostly women – fled their hometowns in Morazán around 1980 due to fear of retaliation from the military after a series of massacres in the region. At the camp, refugees organised workshops that produced for internal consumption and, to some degree, for external use: refugees also began to make products to support the guerrillas. Photographer Steve Cagan describes them: "[...] men, women and children (when they were not in school) worked together. They produced furniture, clothing, shoes, hats, hammocks, metal utensils (such as bowls, pitchers, buckets) and other items. The refugees were learning genuine skills, both occupational and social" (2016: 56). Interviews were conducted with Marisela and Marta, two women originally from Jocoaitique and Osicala, who became refugees at a young age and participated in the embroidery workshops with other women from the camp.

The second account is of Élida, a leader of ACOGIPRI, a cooperative formed in 1979 – which is still active – that offered learning opportunities for individuals with disabilities. As the civil war progressed, the workshops quickly became a space to help them to develop craftsmanship skills and to reintroduce them to a productive life. The cooperative received support from international cooperation funding, which allowed them to transition into producing ceramics. Individuals with disabilities honed their techniques over time and the cooperative was able to stabilise operationally under a formal business model. At one point during the war, the cooperative saw an influx of former guerrillas and military members who became injured during the war. Given their discipline, as well as training in combat and defence, they helped make the workshops safe spaces for others while they learned to cope with their new life realities.

Motivations for Making: The War Context

The political conflict surrounding the Salvadoran Civil War started in the 1970s and brought a military-led Salvadoran government against a coalition of insurgent leftist guerrilla groups (later merged into the FMLN, Farabundo Martí Liberation Front) in the mid-1980s. El Salvador was dragged into an environment of social distress with harsh actions against impoverished communities and thousands of cases of forced disappearances, homicides and massacres. At the end of the twelve-year conflict, the death toll rose to over 75,000 out of a population of 5 million. The largest percentage of these deaths were caused by government-backed forces against civilians (La Comisión de la Verdad para El Salvador 1993; Chávez 2015).

Since the 1950s, arts and the intellectual collectives of musicians, poets and graphic design artists became a starting point for the formation of the New Left in El Salvador. Social activism and avant-garde aesthetics became part of the movement (Chávez 2017). During the Civil War, these artistic expressions were used for the creation of a revolutionary identity, with folk music and poetry expressions being encouraged by the guerrillas in areas under their control or as part of their communications strategy (Consalvi 2010). As people in rural areas came in contact with the movement, handicrafts and other expressions of *making* were influenced by these intellectuals, who used creative activities as an avenue for recruitment.

We argue, however, based on our first-hand testimonies as well as secondary sources, that despite this narrative by which peasants were taught how to *make* by intellectuals, many of these initiatives grew from the bottom up and out of concern with survival and autonomy. For example, for Salvadoran refugees living in Honduras in camps – such as the one described in one of our testimonies – the act of making would become an avenue for "personal liberation" (Todd 2010: 162). In order to depend as little as possible on international cooperation, refugees started repurposing oil cans to make their own utensils and set up workshops to teach both men and women different activities such as cooking, metalwork, embroidery and growing vegetables. Regardless of how they began, these initiatives were appropriated and led by the refugees.

The two main motivations of these groups were (1) an adherence to a collective narrative that values community and a cultural tradition rather than the glorification of a specific individual or creative genius in the movement and (2) an individual motivation to cope with their situation by acquiring autonomy and learning new skills. These commonalities so far serve to connect these local initiatives to the philosophy of maker culture, most specifically by how people engaged in creative learning and applying technical skills to transform their physical environment, by developing agency and desire for self-actualisation and through the development of a collective narrative that served to forge a movement ascribed to a place and time.

The aspiration to become part of a community, based upon experimentations with machines to create new things, is the ethos of the mainstream view of maker culture expressions such as fab labs (Hielscher 2017). The reports by the informants, however, tell how the traumatic loss and social distress caused by the war was a strong motivator to form these craft workshops in two different, war-related, contexts. In both cases, members were driven by either an immediate need to survive, to cope with the violence of their environment or to heal from the post-traumatic state of loss of the war. This led them to establish and sustain communities around *making*. The creative opportunities of their chosen craft thus served a therapeutic role for their members.

Struggles and Demotivators

The manner in which these groups displayed their motivations, as we will show, will allow us to set a starting point for comparisons and the establishment of common ground for groups that engage in *making*: people who come together to learn, create and share have more things in common beyond the technologies or techniques used in their craft: people in these groups used machines and techniques as means to satisfy personal and collective needs. For this reason, it is worthwhile noting some of the social difficulties that modern makers have in common with other historical movements focused on *making*.

These specific craft movements were born as a response to the context of the Salvadoran Civil War within a set of specific cultural, political and economic conditions. Examples of social tension related to privilege and inequality, however, can help us compare them to modern embodiments of maker movements that aim to create open and inclusive dynamics. We will explore (1) how their activities served as psychological escape, (2) how individual expression is undermined by the need to earn a living and (3) the conflict of inclusion and gender. These tend to be less addressed through a critical lens because they are more subtle or overlooked due to an illusion of openness and meritocracy on which there lies a structure of privileges around gender, class and race (Toupin 2014).

Many of the current digital technologies that are central to maker culture are rooted in practices that are not socio-economically equitable across cultures. For this reason, it is not uncommon for emergent narratives to only highlight historical representations of makers from wealthy nations in which the population is predominantly European and Anglo-Saxon, has access to technology and creates out of a desire for leisure or an entrepreneurial activity that differs from a regular job (Tanenbaum et al. 2013). Other expressions such as arts and crafts may be accepted only if they fit into this dominant narrative. Examples of this include the use of intellectual property for traditional products in order to infuse market potential into them (Chan 2008), or the top-down imposition of digital technology to how artisans work, in an effort to modernise traditional knowledge. Instead of this view, we illuminate the importance of including a diversity of cultural narratives into what we consider to be maker culture. Regardless of their use of technology, makers from different backgrounds share common social dynamics and motivations, and therefore, this must be taken into account when defining what maker culture is.

Craft initiatives told by our informants do not fit into a narrative of collectiveness much different from how a modern maker collective would. The narrative often used to depict them, however, carries a connotation that deprives them of autonomy and individuality. A good example of this is the art of Fernando Llort, an acclaimed Salvadoran artist. Llort is regarded as the founder of the *La Semilla de Dios* cooperative in 1972. Llort lived for a period in La Palma, a city north of San Salvador, where he taught arts and helped educate and organise artisans into a cooperative. During this period, he developed a *naif* art style alongside the members of the cooperative. His biography, however, gives sole credit to Llort in the development of the art style, through a romantic narrative around his individual inspiration: "Walking through the streets of La Palma, Fernando found a kid rubbing a little seed against the ground [...] he [took the seed and] painted it with very small and colourful drawings" (Llort 2019). The artist and the cooperative in which he participated shared similar, unique styles until the death of Llort in 2018. Their work, despite being similar in style, is regarded as art in the case of Llort, as opposed to the crafts made by the cooperative (Figure 1). This example shows how an outside influence can seek to redefine or impose a cultural ideology based on the need to give recognition to an individual artist or *originator* (Ballengee-Morris 2002: 239).

The *La Semilla de Dios* cooperative sought to distance themselves from a narrative that robbed them from a sense of autonomy. They stated on their now defunct website that "our style has changed and evolved" (La Semilla de Dios 2009), possibly due to the collective motivation that drives their work. It is important to note that these tensions between modes of authority are also present in certain instances of modern maker culture (Powell 2016). These interpersonal struggles between individuals and collective narratives existed in collectives throughout the duration of the war but have been obscured by the privileged narrative of the groups which were considered as more intellectual. While it is notable that in both cases there were external influences that helped these movements to initiate and develop (e. g., the presence of instructors as leaders in the execution of workshops), the culture *within* the cooperatives enabled artisans to appropriate the styles and techniques as they learned them, and most importantly, to explore new avenues of personal expression and personal healing through them. We explore these narratives in the following sections.

Figure 1: Decorative stamps at ACOGIPRI with textures and animal motifs using the style of La Palma. Photograph: Emilio Velis.

Making as Psychological Escape

It is important to notice from the interviews how participants of both collectives were in similar positions of having to cope with the trauma of loss and violence during the Salvadoran Civil War. For instance, people with physical disabilities found in *making* the means for self-expression and an avenue for healing, catalysed by a newfound sense of agency and freedom. Élida described the motivations of participants during the formation the cooperative as follows:

For a group with disabilities, this was a way to spend time outside. We provided transportation back and forth from their homes. For someone with a disability, living in a place where they couldn't even use their wheelchair properly outside their home, [coming to the workshops] meant [...] a way out, it meant to be free. It allowed them to feel as themselves again. (Personal communication, 10 September 2019)

Figure 2: Depiction of a guinda, *an escape from Salvadoran military raids to villages. [Embroidery]. "Colección Bordadoras de memoria [Embroiderers of Memories Collection]", Museo de la Palabra y la Imagen, San Salvador, El Salvador.*

Similarly, women at the refugee camps discovered that they could use their newly acquired embroidery skills to express and represent their lives at the camps. Embroidery became a medium to communicate their life stories and aspirations. This form of expression was impressive because it was unexpected: nobody asked the women to depict their life stories, but it happened because the women shared a desire to communicate their triumphs and tribulations throughout their journeys as refugees (Figure 2). Texts and images of these embroidered pieces depict, for example, stories of families drowning while crossing the river and being massacred by armed forces. They also depict life at the refugee camp and collective aspirations of the collective. According to Marisela,

[Women] began making [embroidered] representations, after finishing other decorative pieces in the same workshops. They portrayed teachers and their blackboards and students at the school; [...] agricultural motifs [...], women making tortillas, the workers at the hammock workshop [...], people cooking [...] our "corn fertility festivals" [...] women used photographs of these events as a basis to make the designs. This initiative came from the refugees themselves, because we needed to portray our reality. (Personal communication, 26 September 2019)

The ritualised routine imposed by regular group activities at the camp, such as cooking and making things at the workshops, allowed for the creation of a sense of community and purpose. This process can be seen in the deliberate choice the collective made to support the guerrillas, by giving them part of their production, such as shoes, clothing, socks or belts. According to Marisela, these activities, while aiding the cause for the guerrillas, created a consistent new routine that gave them a sense of purpose and maintained a community cohesion despite being in a different, and sometimes hostile, environment.

The end of the war brought a breaking point for both groups and their lifestyles. For example, members of the cooperative who had seen their activities as an avenue to express themselves at a challenging moment in life shifted their motivations towards a need for economic stability. In the case of the refugees' return from the Colomoncagua camps back to their hometowns, it was enough to dissolve the sense of collectiveness, and with it, participants moved on to different lifestyles. According to Marta, who after the war left for the city and later returned to the Segundo Montes Community, former refugees no longer maintain the collective values that were shared at the camp:

None of the sense of collectivity is left. Many people migrated to the United States and others returned to their hometowns; some others moved to the capital. Everything has changed completely. I believe that many came to question themselves as much as I did, wondering what to do next, where to go and live. I think that we all felt the same. We left looking for opportunities; otherwise, we wouldn't have amounted to anything. (Personal communication, 22 July 2018)

In the years after the war, some groups of people have tried to restart the workshops, but production has been negligible. After 20 years, the *Bordadoras de memoria* collective started to revisit their work with survivors through commemorative workshops. This group maintains a monthly workshop, supported by the Museum of the Word and Image, in which older women teach children and young women about the history of maker culture during the Salvadoran Civil War. They encourage participants to illustrate their current historical narratives in the embroidered pieces they create during the sessions.

Similar relationships between arts and crafts and social crises can be found in how these activities become commonplace during not only wartime but also in times of distress, economic depression or grievance (Stannard/Sanders 2014: 100). Women who participate in embroidery activities are found to share a deep connection to others in a space of intimacy and support, while their material products are part of the process of transforming their reality (Pérez-Bustos/Piraquive 2018).

The Conflict of Sustainability

While arts and crafts could be seen as pathways for identity and freedom, the process of finding and securing resources for its continuity quickly became a source of personal tension. It was clear from the interviews how *making* became a way for self-actualisation, but collective decisions and governance of the groups would often require uniformity as a way to ensure well-being for the majority. Élida described how the original members of the cooperative dealt with the lack of resources to begin operations:

We had two teachers: one taught us how to draw and another taught us sewing. At the time, we had the teachers but not the machines (laughs), but we started writing letters and asking for donations. [The five original members] put together some money and bought used machines in order to teach.

ACOPRIGI originally consisted of two groups: individuals born with disabilities – the original group for which the cooperative was intended – and individuals who had been injured or lost a limb during the armed conflict. As the war waged on, the second group multiplied. Élida mentioned that for this group, money was initially not important, and they were willing to give away their work for free.

Most gave us [their work] for free because they were *athletes* [...] For the war-disabled, at that time they believed that drawing and painting was the only thing they could do, either because they had lived in combat for so long or because they had become disabled. Those who were born with a disability would only spend their time at home. So when they came and saw [our work], everyone was excited and wanted to take a brush. They immediately wanted to learn to paint.

She believed that for people with recent war traumas, as well as for those who simply had developed a new expressive skill, financial success was not the initial motivation to participate in these workshops. Instead, as Élida posits, engaging in crafts through the workshops allowed individuals to create art for the sake of learning as well as for personal enjoyment (Figure 3):

[...] for example, the boys who were with us at that time [...] imagine the armed conflict. They would start creating: "What are we going to make now? What are we going to paint on these cups?" Someone would say: "Let's draw a Snoopy or a Mafalda [an Argentinian comic book character]."

The need to ensure sustainability, especially financially, became an increasingly bigger issue. This left smaller opportunities for these activities to be personal and leisurely. Élida explained how this transition was guided by the mentors of the cooperative, who urged them to focus on developing a more successful business model. This slowly brought artisans to pursue new objectives for their work:

They would begin to draw [cartoon characters], but [Álvaro Cuestas, a mentor from the University of El Salvador] told them: "Do you expect that people will like these, or are you just drawing them for yourselves?" At the beginning, a few product ideas came from the artisans, but the truth is that we had the need to pay our rent, electricity, water [...] and a part of these costs were no longer being covered by the project because this money went to pay for our teacher, purchasing the materials to work, and a transportation service for all the participants.

Élida believed that nowadays people with disabilities see economic mobility as a bigger motivator, because current opportunities for inclusion are opening doors to jobs at call centres and supermarkets, which pay better wages than the arts and crafts.

Figure 3: Ceramic artisan working at ACOGIPRI. Photograph: Emilio Velis.

A different reality existed for refugees at the camps. Money was non-existent and to some degree forbidden, since they were not able to leave the premises of the camp while they remained in Honduras as refugees. For this reason, they traded everything that they made. Marisela remarks,

No one received money [at the camp]. Work was performed without expecting money [...] as a matter of fact, it was forbidden. When Hondurans of the area wanted to trade, they passed us guavas and lemons, and asked us to give them rice or something else. This was forbidden, however, because if you went through the fence of the camp no one would guarantee your safety, as you were supposed to stay inside.

The community developed a collective culture around *making* due to their need to survive, so they accepted the lack of economic incentives. The ideals did not remain, however, after the end of the war. Upon their return from the camps at the end of the civil war, many refugees expressed their intentions of returning to the Segundo Montes Community and vowed to continue their production practices, with little success.

An important aspect of this part of the story is the vital support to the development of these collective workshops from international aid during the war. They supplied the raw materials and training for the members of the workshops. Most economic support to this region halted at the end of the war, and without an internal understanding of how to administer these initiatives, they quickly died out.

Social Inclusion and Feminism

Throughout the interviews, participants made remarks regarding a strong participatory component common to both cases. The formation of individual and collective narratives and the social cohesion through collective decisions around money were elements that served to create a sense of intimacy, understanding and participation. From the testimonies, these arts and crafts initiatives helped to create a sense of belonging and equality (Figure 4). When questioned about the challenges of engaging with members of both sides of the conflict, Élida mentioned that former fighters found in the cooperative a safe space from the climate they had come from into the new reality of their disability:

In the end, there were no remarks [among participants] such as "you are on this side or the other [of the war]". We didn't have any of that.

Figure 4: "Mujer con bordado [Woman with embroidery]". Photograph: Museo de la Imagen y la Palabra, MUPI, San Salvador, El Salvador.

Despite the effort towards gender inclusion in this space, there was a separation of activities among its members. As Élida remarks, "Most [male participants] were from San Salvador. Many had seen military service, but those were part of the drawing and painting workshops. Sewing was done by young women who wanted to learn something new". The sewing and drawing workshop at the cooperative – that would later focus on ceramics – became for many of the veterans a temporary refuge from their new personal reality of having a disability. This sense of social cohesion and engagement was short-lived, however, since it faded away as they gained acceptance.

The change from creative workshops into a more serious for-profit endeavour ended up favouring activities performed by men. This eroded the interest from other participants. As the war was ending, and with the creation of more opportunities for people with disabilities, many members left the cooperative. Élida believed that this seems to have affected women more than men, making the case for an imbalance in power against women:

They became bored because at the beginning we were just a centre for learning, but at one point we had to sell everything we made. It wasn't going to be easy. Many people left; about fifteen of us remained. We closed the sewing workshop and left only the ones for drawing and painting. More men than women continued working with us.

Women took more managerial roles than men at the cooperative (at least six women to one man directed the cooperative from 1981 to 1995), while most of the workers remained men. To some degree, women became less interested in the workshops when the focus shifted from drawing and sewing to ceramics.

For both cases, it could be said that women took part in initiatives according to traditional gender roles. However, in the case of the refugee women, there was a bigger change in the views of these roles in the time of the war, especially due to the fact that these camps were mostly populated by women, children and the elderly, while the men participated in the guerrilla. Women had to leave their husbands and children in order to protect the area. According to Marisela, "All the women had to separate from their husbands because they stayed [in Perquín, Morazán]. Imagine, some couples had just gotten married, but when the war started, they had to separate". Women took a very active role in supporting the camp with activities of securing the space as well as logistics. This is similar to the most common roles of women in the guerrilla. Their tasks usually consisted of food preparation and transportation, as well as the logistics for medicines and clothes; men in these spaces constituted "an image of protection more than of real support" (Aguiñada Deras 2001). Over time, some women took over important roles of leadership, but at a high cost.

Many other stereotypes did remain in place. One of them is the idea that some activities were exclusive to women, something that women seemed to enforce as a way to maintain cohesion. Of the workshops in Colomoncagua and Mesa Grande, sewing and embroidery were only done by women and girls of different ages. As a result, this space opened up the possibility for women to create embroidery with artistic motifs in a safe space to express themselves, something that led to creating the embroidered depictions of life at the camp and of their tragic testimonies, while men worked on the making of uniforms and shoes for soldiers. Workshops served a purpose as a safe space for women at the camps. They looked out for each other, physically and emotionally. Eventually, women took leadership roles in the spaces for crafts at the camps, which ultimately transformed the roles of women. This wove, in the social fabric of the camp, a sense of equal importance and division of work among genders.

Discussion

By starting with an inclusive view of who are considered *makers*, we propose that individuals and groups involved in *making* develop narratives that correspond to a broader definition of maker culture, regardless of whether the technologies being used in these cases are digital or not. For the cases studied in our testimonies, we believe that the individual and collective motivations of makers were important to their success, and therefore, there are lessons to enrich the current embodiments of maker culture.

Maker culture is a powerful vehicle for therapy and violence prevention. From the interviews, it is clear that both collective initiatives started out of a practical need to survive over a short period, especially in the most acute moments of social need. As individuals engaged in *making*, however, their motivations developed towards the realm of personal expression, such as the desire to feel independently and uniquely as themselves (Sawyer 2006: 141). These expressions also supported their personal healing, as in some cases, crafts served as a material medium for storytelling.

A recent study makes a similar point about the pictorial expressions of the *Piraq Causa (Who Caused It?)* collection. This modern interpretation of a traditional art style called *Sarhua Boards* was created by artists from the farming community of Sarhua in the Department of Ayacucho, in Peru. These pieces depict the "Times of Danger", a period of war between government and the insurgent and violent Maoist forces of the Shining Path Party in the region during the 1980s who had taken control over Sarhua. The paintings depict how, with support from the Peruvian government, a highly organised community regained their freedom and defeated the local leader of the Shining Path:

The Piraq Causa [...] allowed them to render testimony but also served as a vent to express their "anger toward the injustices committed against innocent farmers" [...]. As an action, venting has a cathartic quality since it is about relieving the stress and anxiety resultant of suppressing painful memories and feelings. In this way, testimonial art involves the function of rendering testimony as well as the elaboration of the trauma. (González 2015: 113)

Nowadays, the therapeutic benefit of maker programmes and collectives is called on by international development initiatives throughout a diversity of communities and social settings. For example, maker-centred workshops are used as tools for youth violence prevention in programmes directed towards marginalised minorities in the United States (Barton/Tan/Greenberg 2016). Also, international cooperation agencies have observed the social, interpersonal and psychological benefits of implementing makerspaces and fab labs in conflict zones around the world (Blanchard 2014; Njambi-Szlapka 2019).

As a takeaway from these experiences, it is critical for new initiatives to consider the most foundational and immediate needs of participants such as funding sources of food, childcare and transportation, so that individuals are able to overcome pre-existing entry barriers as they engage in a safe space and become motivated to discover new means of expression through *making*. Makerspaces established in conflict zones and low-income communities worldwide must consider a holistic view of the needs and priorities of the intended participants in order to ensure that community members can engage without restrictions. Finally, these programmes must also guide participants towards self-actualisation, especially in activities that are solely focused in survival. For fab labs and makerspaces, this could mean showcasing and studying the techniques and products made by artisans, while challenging the notion that adding digital technologies will automatically infuse value into them.

A good organisational structure and administrative skills may ensure sustainability. From the testimonies in interviews, we learned how the fragility of these movements is caused by lack of resources, financially and beyond. For this reason, good administration is key to ensure the continuity of maker spaces and programmes, a challenge that fab labs and makerspaces struggle with (Waldman-Brown et al. 2016). We believe, for this reason, that the formation of a strong organisational structures among members of collectives, as evidenced in the ACOGIPRI cooperative, was key to the survival of grassroots maker initiatives during the Salvadoran Civil War.

As ACOGIPRI grew, members continued to perceive their work as valuable and their retribution as fair, which led to a continued investment in the collective. A good organisational structure at the cooperative led to more learning opportunities for participants and the development of a business model, which allowed the cooperative to last longer. Investing in administrative training and fundraising may allow for better chances of sustainability, despite being seen as a financial burden for maker collectives, especially in places where resources are scarcer.

Nowadays, funding challenges continue to function as entry barriers for artists or makers who may not be able to afford rent in a studio space, and an exclusion criterion for artists who may create niche designs, ultimately narrowing the scope of who has the opportunity to participate in maker culture exclusively for personal expression.

Gender inclusion must be a permanent change, not a cultural experiment. Maker culture places a higher value on refined expertise through the use of digital fabrication machines in makerspaces (e.g., 3D printers, laser cutters and other Computer Numerical Control machines), which are undoubtedly male-dominated. In these spaces, the concept of technology is overwhelmingly seen as merely digital, rendering non-digital technologies invisible or subordinate (Fox/Ulgado/Rosner 2015; Lorenzi/Sanches 2019).

An example of this is the lack of representation of crafts in publications by Make Media: "There is a vibrant indie craft movement running parallel, and often overlapping, with the Maker movement [...] the craft component is rarely – if ever – discussed in the discourse. Technical making is perceived as requiring more skill and holds higher status compared to low-tech activities, like crafting, even when crafters use technical components in their work" (Britton 2015). This description is strikingly similar to how handicraft skills, such as embroidering with needles and textile construction with sewing machines, were described in informant testimonies as much more frequently practised by women than men and considered less important. This gendered divergence of practices and interests is one of the reasons that ACOPRIGI ended up with only male artisans despite having many female members in the past. This process of domination of a certain activity by men has been documented in other handicrafts cultures over time (Vainio-Korhonen 2000) and continues to be a problem to be solved in current embodiments of maker culture (Toupin 2014).

Finally, it is important to note that despite being seen as less important, many of these handicraft traditions were oral traditions – they were passed from one generation to the next through elders who taught younger women (Todd 2010: 168). At the refugee camps, women started learning basic embroidery skills and used these techniques to develop textile expressions of their personal histories. Methods were not written in manuals and handbooks, and thus, the techniques themselves were intrinsically social. Perhaps it is for this reason that a devaluation of soft fabrication emerged initially in the historical narrative. These gendered differences can be seen throughout historical contexts, though contemporary social changes have allowed more women to come forward with anecdotal evidence of their gendered experiences in making. For makers in our current contexts, the documentation of so-called *soft* material activities such as sewing and knitting, as well as immaterial ones such as design, facilitation and storytelling are key to ensuring that skills and cultural assets are reproduced and passed down as effectively as the use of machinery or coding.

Conclusion

By analysing social commonalities among maker initiatives across demographic and geographic contexts, we can learn how makers organise together to *make* things – a view supported by an all-encompassing definition of design as a relationship between "thinking, acting, and utilising" (Sant'Anna 2013: 51). From a cultural perspective, individuals make because they are committed to individual and collective values, be it the survival of the group, a political ideal or the Free Software definition. In this sense, *making* is unequivocally a material medium for social justice, which is collective by definition.

These collective values are also present in the formation of an imaginary in our testimonies, created through a set of well-established rules, social dynamics and motivations that are shared among all individuals. These become formalised as organisations emerge to embody these values: from an initiative to teach crafts to war veterans with disabilities into organising as a cooperative; from being a group of refugees into a collective of peasants who shared a narrative of the Salvadoran Civil War that will transcend their time. The social dynamics and struggles can serve not only to implement and maintain maker culture initiatives in developing countries or impoverished contexts, but to learn about personal motivations and power inequalities in makerspaces and fab labs around the world.

Today, makers and maker communities face challenges similar to those experienced by makers in older, historical contexts, but with an unprecedented condition: a seemingly limitless collection of open source resources are available for makers worldwide, and yet the pressure to create palatable deliverables for a capitalist consumer market continues to constrain artistic expression. Quality materials are expensive, and international politics continue to drive tariff increases for imported goods. When facing these obstacles, makers today can reference historiographical accounts from the past while formulating plans for the future. In these cases, the lack of machines, financial struggles and lack of inclusion are not far from the struggles that have created tensions in previous embodiments of the maker culture in other parts of the world.

References

Aguiñada Deras, D. (2001): "Una mirada feminista sobre la participación de las mujeres en la guerra. El caso de El Salvador." Hommes armés, femmes aguerries : Rapports de genre en situations de conflit armé. Genève: Graduate Institute Publications. Retrieved from https://books.openedition.org/iheid/6146.
Ballengee-Morris, C. (2002): "Cultures for Sale: Perspectives on Colonialism and Self-Determination and the Relationship to Authenticity and Tourism." Studies in Art Education 43(3), pp. 232–245.
Barton, A. C./Tan, E./Greenberg, D. (2016): "The Makerspace Movement: Sites of Possibilities for Equitable Opportunities to Engage Underrepresented Youth in STEM." Teachers College Record 119(6), pp. 11–44.
Blanchard, M. (2014): "Maker Movement and Hope in a Developing Country Context: A Community Empowered Through Hope and Creativity." Strategic

Foresight & Innovation Master Research Project. OCAD. Retrieved from http://openresearch.ocadu.ca/id/eprint/107/2/SFI%20MRP%20MBlanchard%20September%202014.pdf.

Britton, L. (18 March 2015): "Power, Access, Status: The Discourse of Race, Gender, and Class in the Maker Movement." In: The Technology & Social Change Group (TASCHA). Retrieved from https://tascha.uw.edu/2015/03/power-access-status-the-discourse-of-race-gender-and-class-in-the-maker-movement/.

Cagan, S. (2016): "Salvadoran Refugees in the Camp at Colomoncagua, Honduras, 1980–1991." In: ReVista: Harvard Review of Latin America. Retrieved from https://revista.drclas.harvard.edu/book/salvadoran-refugees-camp-colomoncagua-honduras-1980-1991.

Chan, A. S. (2008): The Promiscuity of Freedom: Development and Governance in the Age of Neoliberal Networks (Doctoral dissertation, Massachusetts Institute of Technology).

Chávez, J. M. (2015): "How Did the Civil War in El Salvador End?". The American Historical Review, 120(5), pp. 1784–1797.

Chávez, J. M. (2017): Poets and Prophets of the Resistance: Intellectuals and the Origins of El Salvador's Civil War. New York, NY: Oxford University Press.

Consalvi, C. H. (2010): Broadcasting the Civil War in El Salvador: A Memoir of Guerrilla Radio. Austin, TX: University of Texas Press.

Dougherty, D. (2012): "The Maker Movement." Innovations: Technology, Governance, Globalization 7(3), pp. 11–14. Retrieved from https://www.mitpressjournals.org/doi/pdf/10.1162/INOV_a_00135.

Dutfield, G. (2017): "TK Unlimited: The Emerging but Incoherent International Law of Traditional Knowledge Protection." The Journal of World Intellectual Property 20(5–6), pp. 144–159.

Foster, E. K. (2017): Making Cultures: Politics of Inclusion, Accessibility, and Empowerment at the Margins of the Maker Movement (PhD dissertation, Rensselaer Polytechnic Institute).

Fox, S./Ulgado, R. R./Rosner, D. (2015): "Hacking Culture, Not Devices: Access and Recognition in Feminist Hackerspaces." In Proceedings of the 18th ACM conference on Computer Supported Cooperative Work & Social Computing. New York, NY: ACM, pp. 56–68.

González, O. (2015): "Testimonio y secretos de un pasado traumático: los tiempos del peligro en el arte visual de Sarhua." Anthropologica, 33(34), pp. 89–118.

González, W. (2018): El impacto de la tecnología en la artesanía peruana. CIDAP. Retrieved from http://documentacion.cidap.gob.ec:8080/handle/cidap/1805.

Hielscher, S. (2017): "Experimenting with Novel Socio-technical Configurations." Digital Culture & Society, 3(1) pp. 47–72.

Knowles, D. (1983): "Hegel on Property and Personality." The Philosophical Quarterly 33(130), pp. 45–62.

La Comisión de la Verdad para El Salvador (1993): "De la locura a la esperanza: la guerra de 12 años en El Salvador." New York, NY: United Nations. Retrieved from https://www.marxists.org/espanol/tematica/elsalvador/organizaciones/naciones-unidas/cv-es/informe_cv_es.pdf.

La Semilla de Dios. (27 March 2009). "La Semilla de Dios – Quiénes Somos." Retrieved from Internet Archive website https://web.archive.org/web/20090327050441/http://www.cooperativasemilladedios.com/historiaartesania.htm.

Llort, F. (1 October 2019). "Fernando Llort – The Artist." Retrieved from https://www.fernando-llort.com/biography.

Lorenzi, E./Sanches, M. (2019): "Diseño y contexto: pensando en abierto desde la moda." dObra [s]: revista da Associação Brasileira de Estudos de Pesquisas em Moda 12(26), pp. 245–262.

Markus, H. R./Kitayama, S. (1991): "Cultural Variation in the Self-concept." In: J. Strauss/G. Goethals (eds.), The Self: Interdisciplinary Approaches. New York, NY: Springer, pp. 18–48.

Mikhak, B./Lyon, C./Gorton, T./Gershenfeld, N./McEnnis, C./Taylor, J. (2002): "Fab Lab: An Alternate Model of ICT for Development". Paper presented at the 2nd International Conference on Open Collaborative Design for Sustainable Innovation. Retrieved from http://cba.mit.edu/docs/papers/02.00.mikhak.pdf.

Njambi-Szlapka, S. (2019): Youth and Technology: A Desk Review of the Makerspace Phenomenon and Its Potential to Enhance Youth Employment and Empowerment. Retrieved from http://theresiliencecollective.org/docs/ODIdeskreviewonyouthtechnologyempowermentfinalreport.pdf.

Papavlasopoulou, S./Giannakos, M./Jaccheri, L. (2017): "Empirical Studies on the Maker Movement, a Promising Approach to Learning: A literature review." Entertainment Computing 18, pp. 57–78.

Pérez-Bustos, T./Piraquive, A. C. (2018): "Bordando una etnografía: sobre cómo el bordar colectivo afecta la intimidad etnográfica." Debate Feminista 56, pp. 1–25.

Powell, A. (2016): "Hacking in the Public Interest: Authority, Legitimacy, Means, and Ends." New Media & Society 18(4), pp. 600–616.

Priya, K. (2008): "Intellectual Property and Hegelian Justification." NUJS Law Review 1(2), pp. 359–365.

Sant'Anna, H. C. (2013): Design sem Designer. Brasil: Edição do autor.

Sawyer, R. K. (2006): Explaining Creativity: The Science of Human Innovation. Oxford: Oxford University Press.

Stannard, C. R./Sanders, E. A. (2014): "Motivations for Participation in Knitting Among Young Women." Clothing and Textiles Research Journal 33(2), pp. 99–114.

Tanenbaum, J. G./Williams, A. M./Desjardins, A./Tanenbaum, K. (2013): "Democratizing Technology: Pleasure, Utility and Expressiveness in DIY and Maker Practice." Proceedings of the SIGCHI Conference on Human Factors in Computing Systems. New York, NY: ACM, pp. 2603–2612.

Todd, M. (2010): Beyond Displacement: Campesinos, Refugees, and Collective Action in the Salvadoran Civil War. Madison, WI: University of Wisconsin Press.

Toupin, S. (2014): "Feminist Hackerspaces: The Synthesis of Feminist and Hacker Cultures." Journal of Peer Production 5. Retrieved from http://peerproduction.net/issues/issue-5-shared-machine-shops/peer-reviewed-articles/feminist-hackerspaces-the-synthesis-of-feminist-and-hacker-cultures/.

Vainio-Korhonen, K. (2000): Handicrafts as Professions and Sources of Income in Late Eighteenth and Early Nineteenth Century Turku (Åbo): A Gender Viewpoint to Economic History." Scandinavian Economic History Review 48(1), pp. 40–63.

Waldman-Brown, A./Hurtado, M./Thongsouksanoumane, P./Balta, C./Gandhi, A./Leonard, J./Agustini, G./Vargas, M./Anderson, R. (2016): "Failure Modes of Academic Makerspaces". Proceedings of the 1st International Symposium on Academic Makerspaces. Cambridge, MA: Massachusetts Institute of Technology, pp. 192–194.

Walter-Herrmann, J. (2013): "FabLabs – A Global Social Movement?" In: J. Walter-Herrmann/C. Büching (eds.), FabLab: Of Machines, Makers and Inventors. Bielefeld: transcript, pp. 33–45.

Histories of Technology Culture Manifestos
Their Function in Shaping Technology Cultures and Practices

Ellen K. Foster

Abstract

Taking impetus from a collaborative conversation about writing a feminist repair manifesto, this article is focused on examining radical feminist manifestos, new technology manifestos, and their intersecting themes and influence upon cyberfeminist manifestos. Its theoretical underpinnings include histories of repair and maintenance and the manifesto as technological form. As a practice, repair and theorisations of repair regarding technology take into account invisible labour and create a relationship of care not only within communities, but in relation to everyday technologies. Since this work to write a feminist fixers' manifesto was inspired by the iFixit Repair Manifesto, the NYC Fixers Collective manifesto, as well as manifestos from radical feminist technology movements, it seemed appropriate to consider and critically engage the function of manifestos in these various maker and digital technology communities, as well as the history of radical feminist manifestos in response to cultural oppression. By looking more deeply at specific historical instances and their function, I aim to uncover the importance of such artefacts to give voice to alternative narratives and practices, to subvert systemic oppressions while at other times reproducing them in their form. I argue that there is power in iterating and proliferating manifestos with a critical stance and work to establish the knowledge-producing and world-making potentials of manifesto writing.

Keywords: feminist, manifesto, repair, hacker, maker

Introduction

During the autumn of 2018, a colleague inquired if I had ever come across a feminist repair manifesto. Like her, I had never come across such a document, even during my six years of research into maker, hacker and fixer cultures for my dissertation. There were numerous fixer, maker and hacker manifestos associated with new technologically based movements, but what would it look like to collectively shape an explicitly *feminist* repair manifesto? This became a continuing conversation and led to a collective rewriting session at a workshop in Montreal in spring of 2019. Coincidentally, I began to formulate a historical task of looking through not only maker, fixer and tech-oriented manifestos, but also manifestos put forth by radical feminist collectives and movements. I felt it important to consider the historical underpinnings and foundations upon which we might want to think critically about our own manifestation project.

I was interested to find what is the function of the manifesto as historical artefact for alternative stories and what is the function of the manifesto as a technology to establish certain practices, values and commitments? In this article, I argue that the manifesto, particularly the technology culture manifesto, is a tool for establishing new epistemological ground towards world-making, specifically a way for collective public thought to take shape as part of the knowledge-producing process of social movements to shift societal values.[1] Each one tells a story through their content, but also via their materiality – the form they take and the modes in which they were printed, made and shared. They also have a winding narrative of prior movement building, political strategising or previous manifestos of influence.

While many of the technology culture manifestos I analyse push for new modalities of knowledge and identity, I also argue that they have the possibility of reproducing deeply embedded oppressive systems. The contentious issue within current maker and hacker cultures is that dominant narratives have established a universalising quality around their democratisation of technology. This reproduces a surface-level attempt at diversification and inclusion grounded in keeping the status quo – and it shows in the wording, aesthetics and values put forth in their manifestos. Attention to various histories and their effects on current technology movements is prescient to arguments for diversity in Science, Technology, Engineering, Mathematics (STEM), as well as critical studies of science and technological practice.

The first part of this work looks specifically at the manifesto form and its function as a historical artefact. I then detail historical and Science and Technology Studies (STS) theorisations of repair and fixing, as related specifically to narratives of technology use, expertise and knowledge-sharing. These sections inform the subsequent description and analysis of primary source material, manifestos which have been primarily accessed digitally via the Digital Manifesto

---

1   My work is informed by Eyerman and Jamison's (1991) "cognitive praxis" model of social movements, which conceptualises social movements as practices by which individuals create new kinds of knowledge and identities, both for themselves and for the cultures as well as societies in which they exist. However, divergent from Eyerman and Jamison, my take on this model is that the purview of written and spoken forms created to transmit meaning and knowledge is not just the work of important figureheads within the movement, but a collective effort.

Archive, and a collection of radical feminist manifesto essays gathered by the Diásporas Críticas (a Barcelona-based arts research collective founded in 2014).[2] I look at the materiality, values and knowledge-shaping potentials that come up in radical feminist manifestos, technology movement manifestos and finally at their intersection via specifically feminist tech movements such as cyberfeminism. Cyberfeminists acknowledge a hybrid reality of nature-culture and technology in which a return to the "natural" would never be possible, and they cultivate imaginaries that engage the liberatory potentials of digital and computing technologies for reframing identity formations.[3]

I aim to uncover the importance of manifestos to give voice to alternative narratives and practices. In particular, I unpack how radical feminist manifestos diverge, diffract and iterate in a way that seeks to intervene upon the reproduction of technological oppressions and establish new epistemological modes that value diverse positionalities in relation to technology and cultures. I argue for the liberatory and epistemological purchase gained through the specifically radical feminist manifesto and its intention at reworlding. This form of reworlding can be tied up with the act and form of repair – more so in the act of unravelling and mending preceding creeds, manifestos and technology cultures. This directly correlates to a feminist repair manifesto, which seeks not to destroy Do-It-Yourself (DIY) fixer and repair culture, but instead create an alternative space in conversation with it.

The Manifesto Form as Technology and Genre

The manifesto might be broadly construed as a written text or performance that uses political, discursive and cultural interventions with the intention to rally like-minded peoples towards collective action. At times playful, at times serious, their written form often includes bold claims that can portray a dogmatic stance. Manifestos are a desire for change and a formulation of how practices, institutions and systems might be otherwise, something which even comes across in their materiality and forms of dissemination, from Marx onward to the Hacker Ethic.

2   https://www.digitalmanifesto.net/.
3   Cyberfeminism was established in the early 1990s – some having attributed it to Donna Haraway's *Cyborg Manifesto* (1989) which proclaims at the end, "I would rather be a cyborg than a goddess" (204). Her statement suggests that feminism should embrace hybrid realities of nature-culture and technology, rejecting essentialist ecofeminist narratives that a return to pure "nature" without technological intervention was even possible. Cyberfeminists also take issue with male-dominated cultures of digital technology, seeking to create alternative space, practices and methods for reconstituting what such technologies might entail and the worlds they might foster. For further exploration of cyberfeminist histories and practices beyond this article, see Evans (2016) and Dunbar-Hester (2020).

In this section, which informs my subsequent analysis, I consider other scholarly engagements of the manifesto form, seeking to establish it as a technology and epistemological artefact along with its role as a narrative document.

Scholars looking at manifestos of modernism in art (Puchner 2006), writing (Winkiel 2008) and architecture (Buckley 2014) demonstrate how their creators used manifestos to embody a particular ideology of making as well as to critique the techniques and technologies upon which their professions and artistic practices were predicated, often via unique technologies of publication. In his examination of the manifesto and its relation to the avant-garde of the 20th century, Martin Puchner establishes that while the form existed previously, Marx and communist-socialist networks to which he belonged developed our current understanding of the manifesto genre. According to Puchner, Marx establishes that it is "[the manifestos'] form, not their particular complaints and demands, that articulates most succinctly the desires and hopes, maneuvers and strategies of modernity" (Puchner 2006: 2). Thus, due to Marx, "[m]anifestos do not articulate a political unconsciousness that needs to be excavated through careful analysis [...]; rather, they seek to bring this unconscious into the open" (ibid: 2). I take his argument that the different material forms, aesthetics and modes of dissemination of manifestos have political, cultural and social implications and are predicated on context, resulting in a co-construction of the artefact.[4] Radical print cultures that foster the manifesto form have been reconfigured according to accessible technologies – they are co-constructed not only by human collective action, but by the technologies and discourse in which they are situated.

Jacqueline Rhode's work focuses on how manifestos from the feminist liberation movements of the 1960s and 1970s use discourse to articulate identity work, often in the form of collaborative, "temporary" texts. Rhodes argues that the very "rhetoric of radical feminism was a rhetoric of manifestos", focused on political interruptions geared towards refiguring politics of the family, sexuality and gender (Rhodes 2005: 1) – a relevant argument when considering the writings of feminist hacker groups. Highlighting the importance of historicising the lineage of manifestos, Janet Lyon argues the act of writing them is to take part "in a history of struggle against dominant forces" (1999: 4). Mary Ann Caws (2001) observes that they arise in moments of crisis, which is prescient for more critically engaged

---

4 For example, in 1848, Marx and Engels' communist manifesto was published by the Communist League and eventually printed by various communist and socialist groups in other countries (Puchner 2006). Meanwhile, the Lesbian Avengers (who will be discussed in the radical feminist section) handed out manifestos and calls to action at rallies and protests to further solidify the intention behind their playful disruptions. The Lesbian Avengers were founded in New York City in the early 1990s and led direct actions about lesbian visibility as well as their own survival. Their intention grew out of feeling their own issues were not being addressed while they put energy into activist issues such as abortion and AIDS.

digital technology manifestos that point to the slow, ongoing crisis of oppressive systemic structures in technology tied to global north capitalism, environmental racism, toxic masculinity and so forth.

In her work about feminist manifestos, Felicity Colman unpacks how they leverage hope and articulations of frustration, while also engaging epistemology. Colman explains how for feminist groups, "[t]he manifesto form offers an accessible epistemology – or anti-epistemology – for an event marked as a temporally determined gender activity" (2010: 376). The tension of hope-frustration she identified surfaces in many cyberfeminist texts, as they employ utopian/dystopian tropes. Working to gather feminist manifestos in a global context, Anyley Marin Cisneros and Rebecca Close tie the form to the colonial industrialisation of writing – pamphlets are able to be cheaply iterated and made more accessible. In digital form they are further proliferated widely via email, message boards and personal posting. This is important for their own work, since "[a]cknowledging the coloniality of the manifesto pushes us to consider how spatial realities and the materiality of the voice are fields of *technological intervention*" (Cisneros/Close 2018: 91, emphasis in original). They consider the flow of materials and knowledge, via translation and language as well as means of access. This has particular implication for radical cyberfeminist manifestos that play with language and critique colonialist, global north narratives of knowledge hierarchy and definitions of technology. In the next section, I provide theoretical underpinnings from histories of repair and feminist technoscience that further unpack these issues of hierarchy and politics in technology cultures.

Theorisations and Historical Contexts of Fixing, Repair and Care in Technology Cultures

Narratives of repair in technology cultures have often been relegated to a lower status than those of innovation, typically due to capitalist ideals of productivity and growth – a valuation which has certainly affected the maker movement and DIY cultures. The cultivation of repair-focused values in technology cultures is intended to break down dominant hierarchies, making their appearances in the manifesto form epistemologically predicated. Engaging repair-focused lines of inquiry in the history of technology and within STS is helpful to better understand certain strains of critique in feminist repair initiatives.

For the purposes of this article, I define "repair" as re-making to a functional state (understanding that "functional" is contextually, personally and culturally contingent) that which was once considered broken or causing harm. While often imagined as fixing electronics such as computers and cell phones, repair can also encompass the mending of clothing, umbrellas, chairs, inaccessible design or oppressive systems. As a practice, it takes into account invisible labour, creates a relationship of care not only within communities but in relation to everyday technologies, and gives weight to discontinuity and behind-the-scenes actualities of what might otherwise be seen as seamlessly lived modern realities.

Repair has been theorised as a way of considering technological world assemblages, such as Steven Jackson's "Broken World Thinking" (2014).[5] In querying whether it is possible to establish a "standpoint epistemology of repair" Jackson asks: "Can breakdown, maintenance, and repair confer special epistemic advantage in our thinking about technology? Can the fixer know and see different things – indeed, different worlds – than the better-known figures of 'designer' or 'user'?" (ibid: 229). Thus, the valuation of repair establishes a different viewpoint for analysing digital technology cultures and their embedded power dynamics.

Narratives of maintenance in the history of technology, as highlighted by The Maintainers network co-founded by Lee Vinsel and Andrew Russell, also inform formulations of feminist repair.[6] Ruth Schwartz Cowan's (2018) research on technology involved in maintaining the home and gender biases related to forms of labour is particularly relevant. Cowan argues that technologies for home maintenance in the early 20th century did not simply lessen work, but instead shifted it from physical to organisational and administrative, in some ways creating more demands and tasks to fit into newly found "free time". Such labour was historically undervalued due to its position as unwaged and being labelled culturally as feminine.[7] Mierle Ukeles's (1969) art on maintenance engaged not only gender, but also race and socio-economic class via social art practice in collaboration with waste management employees in the United States. Through her writing of a "Maintenance Art Manifesto" (1969), she examined the valuation put upon production-centric work versus that upon maintenance work and the disillusion of this binary system. Both Cowan and Ukeles work to reveal often invisible labour practices that are becoming more recognised today via current research into fixing, repair and maintenance (Rosner 2014; Rosner/Turner 2015; Graziano/Trogal 2017; Russell/Vinsel 2018; Houston 2019).

Feminist STS work in the politics of care in technoscience and "matters of care" (de la Bellacasa 2011) relate to these histories of repair and maintenance and are values that cyberfeminist practitioners also explore (Foster 2019; Dunbar-Hester 2020). Feminist STS scholars theorise the agency of objects in a way that

---

5 This work comes out of Lara Houston, Daniela K. Rosner and Steven Jackson's ongoing "Reclaiming Repair" project. See http://faculty.washington.edu/dkrosner/repair/index.html.
6 http://themaintainers.org/.
7 Cowan's work has since been critiqued for its lack of considering dynamics of socio-economic class and race, but it still makes a strong case on the devaluation of particular forms of labour that have been historically gendered feminine – primarily maintenance, care and repair work. Further arguments could be made that when such labour is labelled masculine (such as electronics or car repair and maintenance), the valuation is flipped and it is considered of import.

decentres human agency, acknowledging the importance of materiality (Barad 2007). Their critiques also focus on the analytical purchase gained in paying attention to the politics involved in care practices (Martin/Myers/Viseu 2015; Murphy 2015). They thus give room for refusal of repair and acknowledge care practices as possible ways for enacting violence or reproducing problematic power dynamics. These feminist critiques reflect the importance of historicising technology cultures as well as the radical feminist desire to iterate diverse manifestos from different standpoints and positionalities.

Both histories of maintenance in technology and feminist critiques of care in technology cultures create a ground upon which to consider the various narratives and values in the subsequent sections. Tania Pérez-Bustos's work on creation through destruction via analysis of the *calado* weavers in Colombia is especially relevant. She identifies a kind of stitching together apart that takes place through unravelling of cloth, wherein an object is given new meaning and intention. Pérez-Bustos describes how:

Fabrics weaken in [the] process of unraveling. Then, *calado* stitches mend the partially destroyed cloth, weaving new threads within the holes of the generated grid, and so creating a new pattern in the structure. In König's words (2013: 578) this process modifies the original identity of the fabric, reworking it in a way that changes its meaning. (2017: e)

The works of radical cyberfeminist groups use similar methods in their modes of manifesto development predicated on their technological practices and values. They eat away at dominant cultural framings of technology cultures, teasing apart and then stitching back together the fabric of that which they are both within and without. The intended result is for alternative spaces, practices, framings, and epistemic cultures in which they can subsist, possibly eventually shifting dominant cultural mind-sets.

Radical Feminist Manifestos: Establishing Alternative Worlds and Epistemological Valuations

In this section, I focus on the radical feminist manifesto. Historically, such manifestos have been formulated in response to sociocultural oppression, to solidify collective intentions, and as tactical intervention of the status quo. I direct my focus this way as cyberfeminist and feminist hacker groups seek to cultivate liberation through technological interventions and reworlding. As opposed to creating space for women in the current state of things, which they view as hostile and broken, radical tech feminists seek to formulate new modes of being, creating technological knowledge and engaging digital technologies.

One radical manifesto that grapples with lived experience aligned with identity is the Combahee River Collective Statement of 1978, which established the importance of black feminism having its own set of values different from mainstream as well as radical separatist lesbian feminism of the time. Meanwhile, the Redstockings Collective Manifesto written on 7 July 1969 calls upon women to collectively work together to see their struggles not as individual, but as the result of greater structural inequities built into social systems such as patriarchy, racism, capitalism and colonialism. They argue that male domination is the root of the others, something with which not all feminist movements necessarily agreed.

In the playfully rebellious Lesbian Avengers pamphlet (1993, see Figure 1), the collective rings out a call to arms for Lesbians to get up and get out into the street. They do not focus on the need for legislative changes alone, but also for radical cultural shifts. They encourage the use of what they call "creative activism" as tactics for establishing community and bringing attention to matters of concern for them. The rhetoric of the pamphlet instils urgency with the use of exclamations and directive commands. These pamphlets were often handed out during actions or marches – not only telling the receiver to do something but demonstrating what that might be in the very moment. They were proliferated through Xerox copier technology, which was readily available to university students, teachers, and white-collar workers at that time, who were eager to seize the means of production to shift oppressive cultures they faced both within and outside of the institutions to which they were connected.[8]

Figure 1: Excerpt from transcription of a Lesbian Avengers Pamphlet (Lesbian Avengers 1993).

```
              CALLING ALL LESBIANS
               WAKE UP! WAKE UP!

IT'S TIME TO GE OUT OF THE BEDS, OUT OF THE BARS AND INTO THE
STREETS
TIME TO SEIZE THE POWER OF DYKE LOVE, DYKE VISION, DYKE
ANGER, DYKE INTELLIGIENCE, DYKE STRATEGY.
TIME TO ORGANIZE AND IGNITE
Time to get together and fight
We're invisible and it's not safe. Not at home, on the job, in the streets or in
the courts
Where are our lesbian leaders
We need you
We're not waiting for the rapture. We are the apocalypse
We'll be your dream and their nightmare.
```

What the Avengers called "creative activism" is often a centrepiece of radical feminist manifestos and political interventions. In the mid-1980s and early 1990s, several arts- and music-focused feminist manifestos came to the fore. In 1985, the guerrilla girls critiqued gender disparity in the arts world. Their "report card"

---

8   The original pamphlet (Lesbian Avengers 1993) with its full text and graphic design is viewable on the Lesbian Avengers archive website: http://www.lesbianavengers.com. This excerpt was retrieved from the feminist manifesto dropbox repository.

(Figure 2) may not be considered a manifesto but is along the lines of intervention that has come to be expected from the genre. They enact an institutional critique of the arts world, and thus their use of a format from another institution that suffers from systemic oppression, that of American education, concedes that there are structural issues at hand. The visual cues of elementary-school type report cards add another layer of critique, poking fun at the art institutions' high-class elitism by revealing school-boy tendencies of immaturity and politically, gendered and racially charged dealings. Both the lesbian avengers and guerrilla girls bring a satirical side to feminist critique, something that is also present in various cyberfeminist manifestos which bring levity to deeply rooted patriarchal systems within technology cultures.

Figure 2: Guerrilla Girls' Report Card (Guerrilla Girls 1986). Courtesy www.guerrillagirls.com.

GUERRILLA GIRLS' 1986 REPORT CARD

GALLERY	NO. OF WOMEN 1985-6	NO. OF WOMEN 1986-7	REMARKS
Blum Helman	1	1	no improvement
Mary Boone	0	0	Boy crazy
Grace Borgenicht	0	0	Lacks initiative
Diane Brown	0	2	Could do even better
Leo Castelli	4	3	not paying attention
Charles Cowles	2	2	needs work
Marisa del Rey	0	0	no progress
Allan Frumkin	1	1	Doesn't follow directions
Marian Goodman	0	1	Keep trying
Pat Hearn	0	0	Delinquent
Marlborough	2	1	Failing
Oil & Steel	0	1	Underachiever
Pace	2	2	Working below capacity
Tony Shafrazi	0	1	Still unsatisfactory
Sperone Westwater	0	0	Unforgivable
Edward Thorp	1	4	Making excellent progress
Washburn	1	1	Unacceptable

A PUBLIC SERVICE MESSAGE FROM **GUERRILLA GIRLS** CONSCIENCE OF THE ART WORLD

The riot grrrl manifesto, published in 1991 in the zine *Bikini Kill* by feminist musicians in the punk scene of the Northwest of the United States, targeted the issue of gender bias in the music industry and its subcultures, revealing misogyny within the punk and DIY scene of that time. That subcultures, even if critical of dominant cultural trends, can still often reproduce systemic oppressions is particularly relevant to cyberfeminist critiques. Riot grrrls' self-published zines also demonstrate their rejection of mass media entertainment culture of the time (such as the glossy pages of *Rolling Stone* magazine and MTV) which was heavily gender-biased. In their cultivation of alternative media, they establish how music-making and artistically creative endeavours might be otherwise. They did not want to rework their values and images to fit into the pages of *Rolling Stone*; riot grrrls wanted to create their own print culture, based in their own values and modes of expression.

In her analysis of feminist manifestos, Colman argues, first, that "the form of the manifesto is a radical signal of epistemic change; second, that for the feminist, the activation of time in the manifesto offers a break from the machinic subjectivity of patriarchal systems" (2010: 375). Unpacking the histories of feminist manifestos also demonstrates their importance in proliferating feminisms contingent on diverse contexts, standpoints, and goals. To write a specifically cyberfeminist repair manifesto certainly aims to foster epistemic shifts. It reconsiders how fixing and repair is defined, who enacts it and its purposes to intervene upon various social orders and as a radical departure from those that may have been influenced by initial maker manifestos which often fit within a capitalist logic. More generally, radical feminist manifestos aim to dismantle power relations and oppressive systems that have held back the communities which take up their demands, critiques and future visionings. The various strains of radical feminist manifestos are but one narrative that shapes feminist-focused technology manifestos. A large part of this historically contingent narrative takes origin in the proliferation of tech-based manifestos in the past decade with deeper root in various hacker manifestos.

New Technology Manifestos: The Democratisation of Technology, Personal Empowerment, Open Source and Libertarian Framings

In this section, I turn to what I am calling "new technology" manifestos, which argue for divergence of technological use from dominant systems of control, often focusing on identity politics. However, embedded within their discourse is a basis in neoliberal and technocratic framing that expects the individual to be self-empowered via particular forms of access, often overlooking systemic oppression built into technologies. The intention of this section is to acknowledge this influence and tension, even if as a foil, for cyberfeminist manifestos.

As pointed to in the previous section, the history of manifestos themselves are entangled with new technologies and distributive forms for sharing knowledge, and the more recent proliferation of tech-based manifestos follows in this entanglement. Tied up with this are the values and practices of the free and open source software movement, which pushes for the proliferation, reworking and iterating of software so as to improve the technology exponentially, democratise its development and use, and make their inner workings openly available to the public (Kelty 2008; Coleman 2012).

The appearance of manifestos in various maker, hacker and digital technology communities traces to the early days of personal computing. In his 1974 *Computer Lib/Dream Machines* text (see Figure 3), Ted Nelson argued that the

Histories of Technology Culture Manifestos   67

Figure 3: Computer Lib/Dream Machines *by Ted Nelson (1974).*

Figure 4: The "Conscience of a Hacker" text first published in the online publication "Phrack" in 1986 (The Mentor 1986).

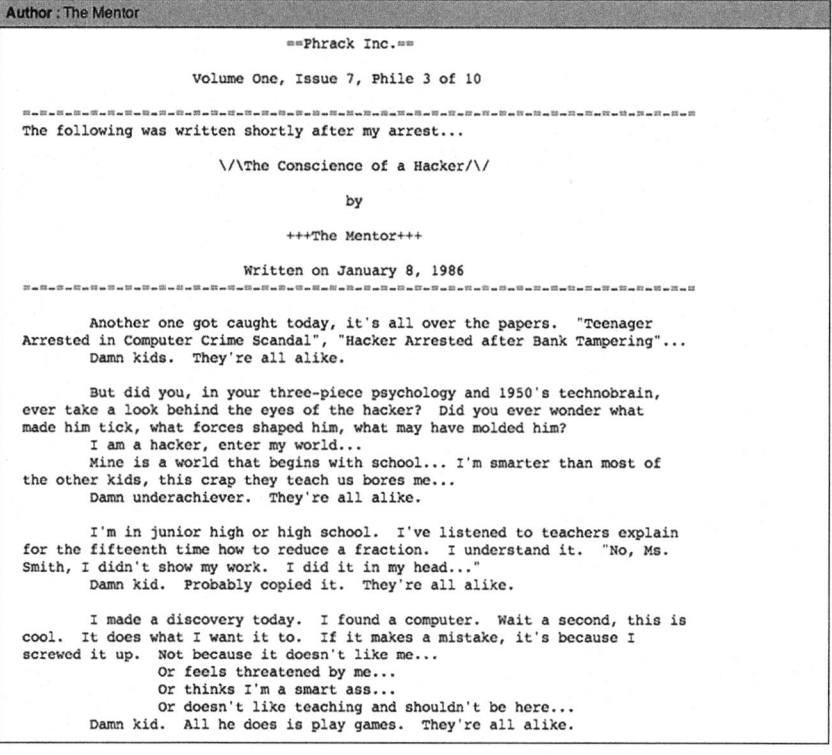

personal computer was liberatory and empowering, while corporate mainframe infrastructures and normative educational forms were oppressive and limiting. His call to organise around personal computing device infrastructures showcased libertarian or democratising themes now prevalent in various hacker, maker, and digital technology movements. These themes were further developed in "The Conscience of a Hacker" written on 8 January 1986 by The Mentor (see Figure 4). Another iteration is the Hacker Ethic. Considered an unspoken code among hackers, it was later articulated by Steven Levy (1984) in his book *Hackers* (see Figure 5).

Figure 5: Hacker Ethic Bullet points first published in Steven Levy's Hackers *(1984).*

Levy's Hacker Ethic

- Access to computers should be unlimited and total.
- All information should be free.
- Mistrust authority—promote decentralization.
- Hackers should be judged by their hacking, not bogus criteria such as degrees, age, race or position.
- You can create art and beauty on a computer.
- Computers can change your life for the better.

Both foundational texts by Nelson and the Mentor characterise the hacker as a defiant independent male fighting against top-down institutional expectations and war-based violence. Interestingly, the normative force is often gendered as woman – either in the form of the motherly corporate mainframe or as a pernickety schoolteacher "Ms. Smith" (Evans 2016). These gendered themes are not explicitly reproduced in other maker movement manifestos, but the neoliberal framing of the heroic individual resurfaces. The expectations are put on the individual critical engineer, hacker, maker or fixer to take up the manifesto's call to action for a personal narrative of change. Antithetical to this, cyberfeminist practices more often establish Do-It-Together (DIT) collective realities and point towards consciousness-raising methods for dismantling oppressive infrastructures.

Computer Lib/Dream Machines was originally self-published by Nelson (1974) and later reprinted by Microsoft Press in 1987 with a foreword by Stewart Brand, placing it squarely in the lineage of Silicon Valley new communalism and technolibertarian cyberculture (Turner 2010). The raised fist of liberation and solidarity used by Nelson becomes a recurring theme in tech-based manifestos. "Conscience of a Hacker" was shared digitally, could easily be emailed, and appeared in an issue of "Phrack", a collectively run digital newsletter by and for hackers. Using a classic computer-based font, it relies on repetition and metaphor to give it an edgy, underground-outsider energy. It presents as both written by an individual, and yet vocalised by an anonymous collective – a tension that comes up often in hacker ideologies predicated both on individualism and on collective play. Meanwhile, Levy's Hacker Ethic are embedded within a major press publication, instigating greater reach and uptake of hacker values and ethics. Here, they are cleanly listed with bullet points, often in either Helvetica or Times New Roman fonts. There are no poetics, but instead clean, concise statements and demands, a format which we see resurface in the maker movement manifestos.

The story of an initial manifesto established by the maker movement is murky, but it appears to start with the "Maker's Bill of Rights" (Torrone 2006). While the Bill of Rights (Figure 6) is largely attributed to *Make* magazine and Make Media, it was created by one of their online bloggers Mister Jalopy, with help from Phillip Torrone and Simon Hill. Torrone later reposted the Maker Bill of Rights in PDF format on the *Make* magazine website (2006).

Figure 6: "Maker Bill of Rights" published on the Make *magazine website in 2006 (Torrone 2006).*

THE MAKER'S BILL OF RIGHTS

makezine.com

- Meaningful and specific parts lists shall be included.
- Cases shall be easy to open.
- Batteries shall be replaceable.
- Special tools are allowed only for darn good reasons.
- Profiting by selling expensive special tools is wrong, and not making special tools available is even worse.
- Torx is OK; tamperproof is rarely OK.
- Components, not entire subassemblies, shall be replaceable.
- Consumables, like fuses and filters, shall be easy to access.
- Circuit boards shall be commented.
- Power from USB is good; power from proprietary power adapters is bad.
- Standard connectors shall have pinouts defined.
- If it snaps shut, it shall snap open.
- Screws better than glues.
- Docs and drivers shall have permalinks and shall reside for all perpetuity at archive.org.
- Ease of repair shall be a design ideal, not an afterthought.
- Metric or standard, not both.
- Schematics shall be included.

Make: technology on your time

The concise one-line directives seem to take inspiration from Levy's Hacker Ethic, and the use of Helvetica reads well to a minimal, tech-innovation, upper-middle class and white aesthetic.[9] Make Media ensures that they get credit, as their logo is inscribed on the bottom right and it is shared via the Make Media website as well as in their printed magazine. More in line with Levy's mass publication of Hackers, it is a fairly far digression from the "Conscience of a Hacker" code-line zine aesthetic. Such prior tech manifestos which question intentions of top-down organisations seem at odds with this one-page manifesto put forth by an organisation that profits via the proliferation of the maker movement. Even as proponents of the maker movement argue for open-source, repairable, accessible technologies and tools, some had much to gain financially by the promulgation of "Everyone a Maker" rhetoric, pushing consumers to make more through the buying of particular tools, toys, kits, devices and instructions (Sivek 2011). Thus, these maker manifestos often recapitulate capitalist narratives of innovation predicated on planned obsolescence and gadgetry.

Almost eight years later, Mark Hatch put out the "Maker Movement Manifesto" (2014) in his book about the practices of maker culture from his viewpoint as the CEO of TechShop (see Figure 7). Such tensions are illustrated by his "Tool Up" rule, which is predicated on having the right tools for the job, as well as having consistent access to them. Conveniently, TechShop provided such access to the "right" tools for a fee. This "right" tools ideology has been critiqued by those at the margins of these maker cultures, including how this framing lacks incorporation of culturally embedded or handed down traditions of making (Vossoughi/Hooper/Escudé 2016).

Like the "Maker Bill of Rights", it has a simple aesthetic. Some of the points have a dogmatic quality such as "You must learn to make". Everything is in the service of tooling up and making more, the act of which comes across as a personal and individual endeavour.[10] Like Levy's Hacker Ethic, it found wide public dissemination via a larger publisher, with further reach made during public presentations by Hatch and reproduction of the list at various makerspaces.

Both come across as politically neutral – neither confronts what making gets us, or about the political import of making to shape and shift cultures. No questions are addressed about how access might be gained for those without any prior exposure, without financial excess or those dealing with implicit barriers and biases. They purport to have a context-less, universal mentality that overlooks how Western-centric, capitalist, colonialist, white and masculinist these tech uptakes often are. This political neutrality reproduces, demarcating those who would take it up versus those who feel implicitly the maker movement is not for them. And thus, by trying to include everyone, they default to the dominant narrative of including those already

---

9   It is of interest to note that Helvetica counts as one of the best legible fonts online and is specifically designed for impact and efficiency.
10 Fred Turner has made the astute argument that such a mindset is also tied to Puritanical roots and the Protestant Ethic in American culture. See Turner (2018).

Figure 7: The Maker Movement Manifesto from Mark Hatch's book (2014). Retrieved from Digital Manifesto Archive.

Maker Movement Manifesto

MAKE
Making is fundamental to what it means to be human. We must make, create, and express ourselves to feel whole. There is something unique about making physical things. These things are like little pieces of us and seem to embody portions of our souls.

SHARE
Sharing what you have made and what you know about making with others is the method by which a maker's feeling of wholeness is achieved. You cannot make and not share.

GIVE
There are few things more selfless and satisfying than giving away something you have made. The act of making puts a small piece of you in the object. Giving that to someone else is like giving someone a small piece of yourself. Such things are often the most cherished items we possess.

LEARN
You must learn to make. You must always seek to learn more about your making. You may become a journeyman or master craftsman, but you will still learn, want to learn, and push yourself to learn new techniques, materials, and processes. Building a lifelong learning path ensures a rich and rewarding making life and, importantly, enables one to share.

TOOL UP
You must have access to the right tools for the project at hand. Invest in and develop local access to the tools you need to do the making you want to do. The tools of making have never been cheaper, easier to use, or more powerful.

PLAY
Be playful with what you are making, and you will be surprised, excited, and proud of what you discover.

PARTICIPATE
Join the Maker Movement and reach out to those around you who are discovering the joy of making. Hold seminars, parties, events, maker days, fairs, expos, classes, and dinners with and for the other makers in your community.

SUPPORT
This is a movement, and it requires emotional, intellectual, financial, political, and institutional support. The best hope for improving the world is us, and we are responsible for making a better future.

CHANGE
Embrace the change that will naturally occur as you go through your maker journey. Since making is fundamental to what it means to be human, you will become a more complete version of you as you make.

In the spirit of making, I strongly suggest that you take this manifesto, make changes to it, and make it your own. That is the point of making.

---

included in the STEM context, further solidifying a technocratic expectation that those with the "right" tools and expertise are superior. This does not only play out in discourse, but in the demographics of those who could be found in TechShops, makerspaces, FabLabs and hackerspaces across the globe, which has been aptly studied by scholars interested in the reason for feminist responses to maker and hacker culture (Toupin 2014; Rosner/Fox 2016).[11] Critiques of these issues are made explicit in critical remakes of the "Maker's Bill of Rights" specifically from the African context (Figure 8) as well as the critical making perspective (Figure 9).[12]

---

11   Similar to issues previously pointed out by myriad feminist STS scholars regarding scientific cultures (Traweek 1988; Haraway 1991).

12   Critique through reworking is a part of the ongoing development of critical making discourse and projects, a term and theoretical concept first coined by Matt Ratto in 2008 that served to later inspire projects and writing in a zine style publication in 2012 under the direction of Garnet Hertz (Ratto/Hockema 2009; Hertz 2012; Hertz 2015). In "Critical Making", a focus is put upon the process of making and the critical thinking or shifts of mind-set possible in the doing. Intentions and eventual outcomes are also geared towards politically responsive projects.

Figure 8: African-specific "Maker's Bill of Rights", stemming from the African Maker Faire (2012).

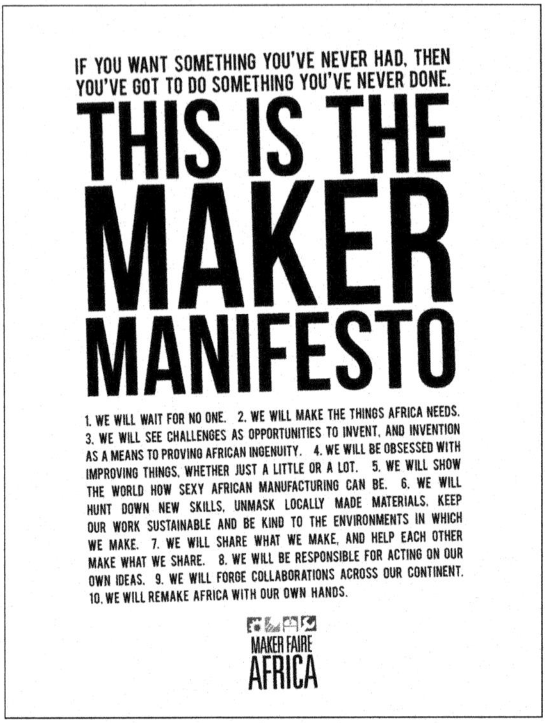

> IF YOU WANT SOMETHING YOU'VE NEVER HAD, THEN YOU'VE GOT TO DO SOMETHING YOU'VE NEVER DONE.
>
> # THIS IS THE MAKER MANIFESTO
>
> 1. WE WILL WAIT FOR NO ONE. 2. WE WILL MAKE THE THINGS AFRICA NEEDS. 3. WE WILL SEE CHALLENGES AS OPPORTUNITIES TO INVENT, AND INVENTION AS A MEANS TO PROVING AFRICAN INGENUITY. 4. WE WILL BE OBSESSED WITH IMPROVING THINGS, WHETHER JUST A LITTLE OR A LOT. 5. WE WILL SHOW THE WORLD HOW SEXY AFRICAN MANUFACTURING CAN BE. 6. WE WILL HUNT DOWN NEW SKILLS, UNMASK LOCALLY MADE MATERIALS, KEEP OUR WORK SUSTAINABLE AND BE KIND TO THE ENVIRONMENTS IN WHICH WE MAKE. 7. WE WILL SHARE WHAT WE MAKE, AND HELP EACH OTHER MAKE WHAT WE SHARE. 8. WE WILL BE RESPONSIBLE FOR ACTING ON OUR OWN IDEAS. 9. WE WILL FORGE COLLABORATIONS ACROSS OUR CONTINENT. 10. WE WILL REMAKE AFRICA WITH OUR OWN HANDS.
>
> MAKER FAIRE AFRICA

This African-specific maker manifesto advocates creating for Africa from within, working sustainably and using Africa-based materials and products. The creators have an underlying critique of the maker movement's predominant focus on production of kits, components and tools based in and for the Western context. This often creates a barrier of participation for African makers and also entails built-in assumptions about how technologies may or may not work in different contexts and cultures. The manifesto mimics the format of the "Maker's Bill of Rights" with a similar typeface, but displays the text at a tilt, suggesting a different viewpoint.

Garnet Hertz's (2018) "Maker's Bill of Rights" parodies the original 2006 version by making clear political points about gender, class and labour, resource extraction and the maker movement's branding tendency to focus on techno-solutionism. It gives room for a different kind of subjectivity in conversation with the maker movement, while also critiquing many of its implicit biases and Western-centric capitalist norms. It has been shared digitally, but also via printed stickers that Hertz would send in the mail and hand out at various conferences.

Figure 9: Hertz's remaking of "Maker's Bill of Rights" (2018).

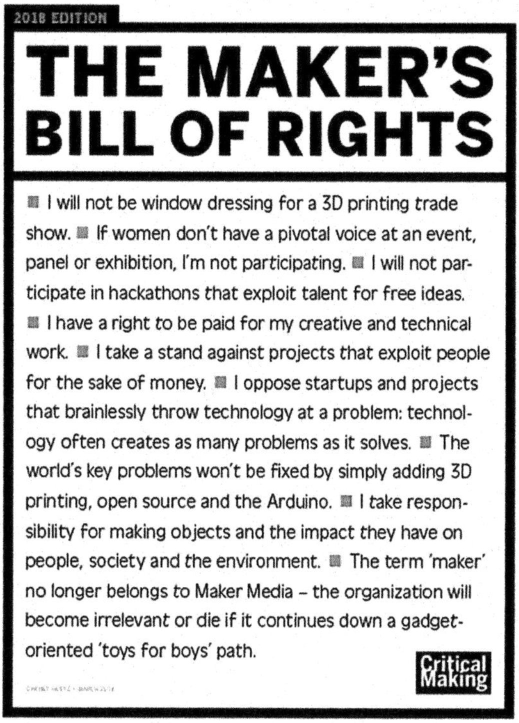

2018 EDITION

THE MAKER'S BILL OF RIGHTS

■ I will not be window dressing for a 3D printing trade show. ■ If women don't have a pivotal voice at an event, panel or exhibition, I'm not participating. ■ I will not participate in hackathons that exploit talent for free ideas. ■ I have a right to be paid for my creative and technical work. ■ I take a stand against projects that exploit people for the sake of money. ■ I oppose startups and projects that brainlessly throw technology at a problem: technology often creates as many problems as it solves. ■ The world's key problems won't be fixed by simply adding 3D printing, open source and the Arduino. ■ I take responsibility for making objects and the impact they have on people, society and the environment. ■ The term 'maker' no longer belongs to Maker Media – the organization will become irrelevant or die if it continues down a gadget-oriented 'toys for boys' path.

Critical Making

Several repair manifestos are also in conversation with and critical of the maker movement. They take repair as a personally politicised and anti-consumerist act, yet at the same time often relate fixing as a way to garner engineering skills for global market competitiveness.

The iFixit repair manifesto (Figure 10) alludes to resistance by using the wrench in a raised fist, iconography previously used by various anti-oppression movements. It also references political discourse with words such as "revolution" and "independence". While the iFixit manifesto seems to aesthetically reference the "Maker's Bill of Rights", the NYC Fixers Collective[13] has more of a scrappy and patched together aesthetic (Figure 11). It shows what it might look like to enact a world focused on repair and working with the materials at our disposal.

Like the Maker Movement Manifesto and "Maker's Bill of Rights", both repair manifestos do not confront issues of identity and the reproduction of implicit barriers within technology cultures (Eubanks 2018; Dunbar-Hester 2020). A contrast exists in the positionalities of wealthier global north or hobbyist DIY repair, done

---

13 See https://www.proteusgowanus.org/proteus-gowanus-archive/fixers-collective/index.html.

Figure 10: iFixit repair manifesto (n.d.).

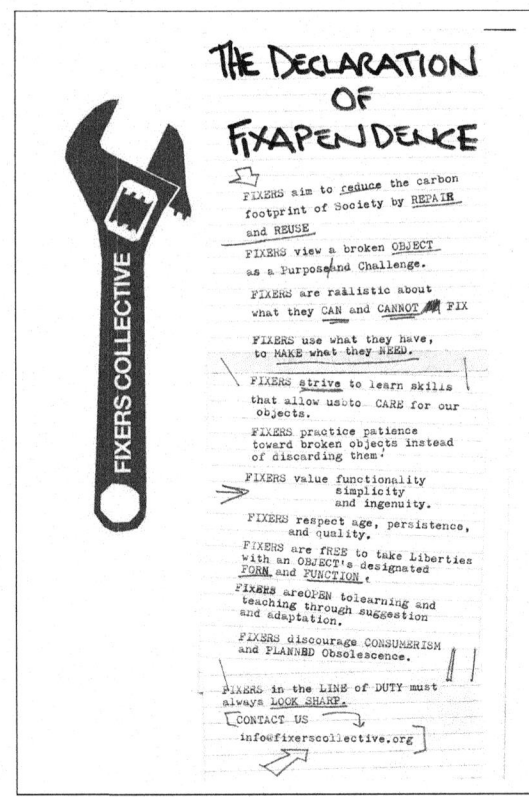

Figure 11: Fixers Collective Declaration of Fixapendence (2014). Courtesy Vincent Lai.

more so to make a statement against planned obsolescence and to garner deeper engineering skills, than for other cultures or lived experiences where repairing an object is necessary and much cheaper than buying new goods (Graziano/Trogal 2017).[14]

Feminist repair framings look to reconstitute what concerns of care towards technologies might look like. Rewriting the fixers' collective manifesto gives room for generatively playful tensions of frustration, hope and desire. Radical feminists interested in engaging DIT technology practices as a political act are invested in creating alternative spaces, discourses, and practices for engaging and unpacking these tensions. They want to consider what we gain with a decentring of innovation towards repair narratives, while also being mindful of the pitfalls of a Western-centric perspective. These valuations and critical takes on technology use and interventions are most directly tied to and found in cyberfeminist manifestos and their practices, to which I now turn.

Cyberfeminist and Feminist Hacker Manifestos: Establishing Alternative Narratives and Technology Cultures

While these movements and their associated manifestos are not sequential, I end with cyberfeminist manifestos, as I argue that they take aspects of both radical feminist and tech-based manifestos and movements. I have identified feminist hacker manifestos such as the "Cyberfeminist Manifesto for the 21st Century" put forth by The VNS Matrix in 1991 (Figure 12) and the TransHackFeminist (THF) manifesto written over a month and across global contexts by the THF network in 2014 as examples intersecting both radical feminist and technology-based movement themes. Both manifestos deal with epistemological questions as tied to technology development from a specifically feminist standpoint.

While manifestos put out by computer hackers of the 1970s and 1980s characterised oppressive infrastructures as women or motherly figures, as explicated in the previous section and detailed by Claire L. Evans (2016), VNS Matrix used their manifesto and body of work as a world-building exercise to shift this narrative. For them, the Big Daddy Mainframe is depicted as a male suit with a corporate logo instead of a head (ibid). Stepping outside of dissemination by purely digital and textual means, they also developed their manifesto as a visual format to be printed, wheat-pasted, handed out, emailed, remixed, performed and proliferated as much as possible.

---

14 Of interest here is that another theme that feminist considerations of labour and repair take into account is the value of time, and the question of who has time to make repairs or garner access to possibly expensive tools and knowledge infrastructures to foster exposure to repair.

Figure 12: VNS Matrix cyberfeminist manifesto (1991), which was widely distributed and wheat-pasted.

The fish-eye typography gives the sense of being written on a spheroid, and pink vulvar forms surround the text. Both discursively and visually, the manifesto declares that cyberspace was profoundly feminine, but not according to dominant ideas of femininity. It was a place for identity and gender play, a world unto its own where the dominant rules of engagement and gender conformity could be reconstructed for new modes of existing. Along with the analogue print version, an online version on a dedicated website ran through various phrases and imagery created by the group. They performed the piece as well with both singular dialogue and moments of speaking collectively.

Their intention was to discursively "make" and represent a new or previously unseen standpoint at the margins of technology cultures – those who both wanted to embrace the transformative and liberal possibilities of technology, while also critiquing the structures of technocratic power that both produced and were shaped by current technology cultures and the environments out of which they grew. Tied to this, feminist technology manifestos (and their associated movements such as cyberfeminism) can take on both a utopian and dystopian thematic and often play off science fiction tropes, invoking satire and irreverence to dominant framings. We see this with VNS Matrix's claims that they are "saboteurs of big daddy mainframe / the clitoris is a direct line to the matrix". In claiming a more fluid, contested engagement and definition of digital practices in terms of normalised narratives of how people identify and might act, they push against dominant framings of technology as phallocentric.

The first iteration of a THF manifesto (Figure 13) was published digitally by the Pechblenda lab, a feminist hacker lab based in the postcapitalist commune

Histories of Technology Culture Manifestos   77

Figure 13: TransHackFeminist manifesto (2014), published by the Calafou feminist hacklab Pechblenda.

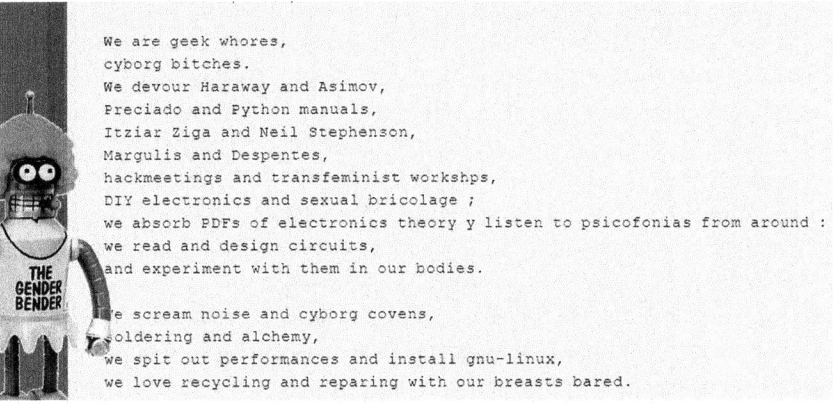
```
We are geek whores,
cyborg bitches.
We devour Haraway and Asimov,
Preciado and Python manuals,
Itziar Ziga and Neil Stephenson,
Margulis and Despentes,
hackmeetings and transfeminist workshps,
DIY electronics and sexual bricolage ;
we absorb PDFs of electronics theory y listen to psicofonias from around :
we read and design circuits,
and experiment with them in our bodies.

e scream noise and cyborg covens,
oldering and alchemy,
we spit out performances and install gnu-linux,
we love recycling and reparing with our breasts bared.
```

Figure 14: Feminist Manifest-No (Cifor et al. 2019).

The Manifest-No is a declaration of refusal and commitment. It refuses harmful data regimes and commits to new data futures.

1. **We refuse** to operate under the assumption that risk and harm associated with data practices can be bounded to mean the same thing for everyone, everywhere, at every time. **We commit** to acknowledging how historical and systemic patterns of violence and exploitation produce differential vulnerabilities for communities.

2. **We refuse** to be disciplined by data, devices, and practices that seek to shape and normalize racialized, gendered, and differently-abled bodies in ways that make us available to be tracked, monitored, and surveilled. **We commit** to taking back control over the ways we behave, live, and engage with data and its technologies.

3. **We refuse** the use of data about people in perpetuity. **We commit** to embracing agency and working with intentionality, preparing bodies or corpuses of data to be laid to rest when they are not being used in service to the people about whom they were created.

4. **We refuse** to understand data as disembodied and thereby dehumanized and departicularized. **We commit** to understanding data as always and variously attached to bodies; we vow to interrogate the biopolitical implications of data with a keen eye to gender, race, sexuality, class, disability, nationality, and other forms of embodied difference.

5. **We refuse** any code of phony "ethics" and false proclamations of transparency that are wielded as cover, as tools of power, as forms for escape that let the people who create systems off the hook from accountability or responsibility. **We commit** to a feminist data ethics that explicitly seeks equity and demands justice by helping us understand and shift how power works.

Calafou located outside of Barcelona, Spain, and the meeting place of the first THF in 2014.

It takes inspiration from the artistic and poetic forms of the VNS Matrix and reads as a collective voice. The writing is playful and infused with beliefs as well as practices that those who take part in THF enact technosocial interventions.

Available in digital form, it is flanked by imagery from the movie Metropolis, the cartoon show Futurama as well as historical figures who the THF group claim such as Ada Lovelace, Marie Curie and Alan Turing.

The Feminist Manifest-No (Figure 14) is another collaborative and anonymous document, which highlights the role of refusal in digital technology cultures in order to foster feminist data ethics (Cifor et al. 2019). Unlike many of the other new technology manifestos, it is written in the negative, stating that with which the group does not agree. It is written cleanly and clearly, with numbered refusals and commitments, and thus in form it aligns more with the Maker Bill of Rights than the THF manifesto. However, the content which unpacks the contingent politics of technology follows other cyberfeminist manifesto intent – demonstrating the heterogeneous nature of feminist technology critique. It is also written as a collective "we", demonstrating group commitment and responsibility. Conversely, many of the technology manifestos previously analysed focus on shifting individual practices as well as technologically based solutions. Responsibility is put upon the individual in a neoliberal mode. This is something from which radical feminist manifestos diverge, in that they invest in networked and community responsibility, often focusing on social infrastructures and larger cultural shifts.

Feminist technology manifestos are engaged in epistemic world-making at various scales, establishing a response-ableness in a precarious world. They establish a road map for not only shaping technologies, but also the cultures and infrastructures enacted through and surrounding them for more equitable technological engagements. Much violence has been done in the name of technoscientific work especially in the realm of engineering, and so feminist technology manifestos hope to dismantle the normative order, often in playful strains of dystopian and utopian poetics. They also often decentre efficiency, hyper-productivity, technosolutionism, and the lone inventor trope. They aspire to establish alternative spaces and cultures that can carve out new modes of becoming that acknowledge the co-constructions of identity and technology, paying close attention to embedded power relations.

Conclusion: Importance of Historical Critique for a Feminist Repair Manifesto and Accountability Towards Change in Technology Cultures

It is in this landscape that several collaborators proposed a feminist repair manifesto, with a reconstructivist (Woodhouse et al. 2002) rendering of the iFixit's Repair Manifesto, acknowledging the gendered and class-based labour practices around repair. While the group critiqued various aspects of the iFixit manifesto, such as a focus on productivity and technosolutionism, they also addressed how to shift the conversation. It felt that the group was taking on the practice of creation through destruction that Tania Pérez-Bustos (2017) studied among women weavers. However, instead of cloth, the feminist collective used an existing textual manifesto, crossing out words and phrases, while keeping and reworking certain other values and phrases, thus reimagining its intention and epistemological groundings through a feminist reframing.

This historically contingent and specifically feminist framing of DIT came out in several sessions. At play, and through conversation, the group unpacked tensions of gendered norms associated with repair and the politics of care. What resulted was a reworlding, an establishment of a framework for engaging DIY fixer practices that could be held more accountable to inherent politics predicated on context. It was also a way to garner attention and support for feminist repair practices that had been ongoing which took such issues of power more directly into account. By creating such a provocation that made direct critique of the DIY Fixer-Maker discourse currently in play (à la Hertz's critique of the Maker Bill of Rights), the group aimed to highlight issues not currently addressed, while also making space and creating ground for alternative narratives and practices.

In looking across the various manifesto groupings, they are both a product of the communities out of which they come, as well as a mode through which to further establish community identity, values, and responsibilities – in their form and aesthetics as well as content. Examples such as the African Maker Manifesto demonstrate that technology-based manifestos cannot be written for everyone, and that to do so or without consideration of diverse needs and backgrounds overlooks class, gender, geographic and race power dynamics within spheres of technology development and uptake. In the case of feminist technology-based manifestos, the manifestos acknowledge a clear connection to how technology and identity are co-constituted. Most importantly, radical feminist manifestos establish different epistemological grounds for engaging technological knowledge and outputs, bringing light to power relations and the need to shift oppressive structures in the development and sharing of knowledge. They establish how the dominant discourse made to seem universal is systemically oppressive, in visceral, emotional form. They do not stop at critique, however, but instead reformulate, and argue for new imaginaries of how the world might be otherwise. These histories and felt experiences that manifest in the genre and format of the manifesto as a mode of social critique cannot go unacknowledged, and enacting such a critique of how to move forward with technology development or use is imperative in a push for changing technology cultures towards less extractive, colonialist modes.

I have found that the manifesto's materiality, aesthetics and performative discourse reveal embedded power dynamics and diverse valuations at play in technology cultures. I have shown how both early cyberfeminist and contemporary feminist hackers and fixers build upon a legacy of radical publishing that empowers public groups to seize the means of production to share their thoughts and expertise. In using new modes of digital dissemination and collaboration, including creative reconstructions of prior manifestos, feminist technology groups institute a new meaning-making strategy which embodies the politics and values of their movement to create heterogeneous alternative technology cultures. Finally, acknowledging the manifesto as a tool for movements to enact worldmaking and establish new epistemological ground holds import for those who want to more deeply query issues of inclusion, accessibility and diversity in STEM and in the realms of science and technology development more broadly construed.

References

Barad, K. (2007): Meeting the Universe Halfway. Durham, NC: Duke University Press.
de la Bellacasa, M.P. (2011): "Matters of Care in Technoscience: Assembling Neglected Things." Social Studies of Science 41(1), pp. 85–106.
Buckley, C. (ed.) (2014): After the Manifesto: Writing, Architecture, and Media in a New Century. New York City, NY: Columbia GSAPP Books/T6 Ediciones.
Caws, M.A. (2001): "The Poetics of the Manifesto." In: M.A. Caws (ed.), Manifesto. A Century of Isms. Lincoln, NE: University of Nebraska Press, pp. xix–xxxiii.
Cifor M./Garcia, P./Cowan, T.L./Rault, J./Sutherland, T./Chan, A./Rode, J./Hoffmann, A.L./Salehi, N./Nakamura, L. (2019): "Feminist Data Manifest-No". Retrieved from: https://www.manifestno.com/.
Cisneros A.M./Close, R. (2018): "Contagion as Method." Performance Research 23(6), pp. 90–92.
Colman, F. (2010): "Notes on the Feminist Manifesto: The Strategic Use of Hope." Journal for Cultural Research 14(4), pp. 375–392.
Coleman, E.G. (2012): Coding Freedom: The Ethics and Aesthetics of Hacking. Princeton, NJ: Princeton University Press.
Cowan, R.S. (2018): "The 'Industrial Revolution' in the Home: Household Technology and Social Change in the Twentieth Century." In: A. Staub (ed.), The Routledge Companion to Modernity, Space and Gender. New York City, NY: Routledge, pp. 81–97.
Dunbar-Hester, C. (2020): Hacking Diversity: The Politics of Inclusion in Open Technology Cultures. Princeton, NJ: Princeton University Press.
Evans, C.L. (2016): "Feminist Worldbuilding in the Australian Cyberswamp." Rhizome, 27 October. Retrieved from https://rhizome.org/editorial/2016/oct/27/cyberfeminist-worldbuilding/.
Eubanks, V. (2018): Automating Inequality: How High-Tech Tools Profile, Police, and Punish the Poor. New York City, NY: St. Martin's Press.
Eyerman, R./Jamison, A. (1991): Social Movements: A Cognitive Approach. University Park, PA: Pennsylvania State University Press.
Fixers Collective. (2014): "Declaration of Fixapendence." Proteus Gowanus's Fixers Collective.
Foster, E.K. (2019). "Claims of Equity and Expertise: Feminist Interventions in the Design of DIY Communities and Cultures." Design Issues 35(4), pp. 33–41.

Graziano, V./Trogal, K. (2017): "The Politics of Collective Repair: Examining Object-Relations in a Postwork Society." Cultural Studies 31(5), pp. 634–658.

Guerrilla Girls (1986): Guerrilla Girls' 1986 Report Card (poster). Guerrilla Girls.

Haraway, D. (1989): "A Manifesto for Cyborgs: Science, Technology, and Socialist Feminism in the 1980s." Reprinted in Elizabeth Weed (Hrsg.): Coming to Terms: Feminism, Theory. Politics. New York, NY, pp. 173–204.

Haraway, D. (1991): "Situated Knowledges: The Science Question in Feminism and the Privilege of Partial Knowledge." In: J. Agnew/D. N. Livingstone/A. Rodgers (eds.), Human Geography: An Essential Anthology. Malden, MA: Blackwell, pp. 108–128.

Hatch, M. (2014): The Maker Movement Manifesto: Rules for Innovation in the New World of Crafters, Hackers, and Tinkerers. New York City, NY: McGraw Hill Professional.

Hertz, G. (ed.) (2012): Critical Making. Hollywood, CA: Telharmonium Press.

Hertz, G. (ed.) (2015): Conversations in Critical Making. Victoria, BC: CTheory Books.

Hertz, G. (March 2018): "The Makers Bill of Rights." ConceptLab. Retrieved from http://makermanifesto.com/.

Houston L. (2019): "Mobile Phone Repair Knowledge in Downtown Kampala: Local and Trans-Local Circulations." In: I. Strebel/A. Bovet/P. Sormani (eds.), Repair Work Ethnographies. Singapore: Palgrave Macmillan, pp. 129–160.

iFixit (n. d.): "iFixit Repair Manifesto." iFixit. Retrieved from https://www.ifixit.com/Manifesto.

Jackson, S. J. (2014): "Rethinking Repair." In: T. Gillespie/P. J. Boczkowski/K. A. Foot (eds.), Media Technologies: Essays on Communication, Materiality, and Society. Boston, MA: MIT Press, pp. 221–239.

Kelty, C. M. (2008): Two Bits: The Cultural Significance of Free Software. Durham, NC: Duke University Press.

Levy, S. (1984): Hackers: Heroes of the Computer Revolution (Vol. 14). Garden City, NY: Anchor Press/Doubleday.

Lesbian Avengers: (1993). The Lesbian Avengers Dyke Manifesto: "Calling All Lesbians! Wake Up!" (pamphlet). Lesbian Avengers.

Lyon, J. (1999): Manifestos: Provocations of the Modern. Ithaca, NY: Cornell University Press.

Maker Faire Africa. (20 October 2012): "Our Maker Manifesto." Maker Faire Africa. Retrieved from http://makerfaireafrica.com/2012/10/20/our-maker-manifesto/.

Martin, A./Myers, N./Viseu, A. (2015): "The Politics of Care in Technoscience." Social Studies of Science 45 (5), pp. 625–641.

Murphy, M. (2015): "Unsettling Care: Troubling Transnational Itineraries of Care in Feminist Health Practices." Social Studies of Science 45(5), pp. 717–737.

Nelson, T. H. (1974): Computer Lib: You Can and Must Understand Computers Now (first edition). N.p: Theodore H. Nelson.

Nelson, T. (1987): Computer Lib/Dream Machines (revised edition). Redmond, WA: Tempus Books of Microsoft Press.

Pérez-Bustos, T. (2017): "Thinking with Care: Unraveling and Mending in an Ethnography of Craft Embroidery and Technology." Revue d'anthropologie des connaissances 11(1) pp. a–u.

Puchner, M. (2006): Poetry of the Revolution: Marx, Manifestos, and the Avant-gardes. Princeton, NJ: Princeton University Press.

Ratto M./Hockema S. (2009): "Flwr Pwr: Tending the Walled Garden." In: A Dekker/A. Wolfsberger (eds.) Walled Garden. The Netherlands: Virtueel Platform.

Rhodes, J. (2005): Radical Feminism, Writing, and Critical Agency: From Manifesto to Modem. New York City, NY: SUNY Press.

Rosner, D. K. (2014): "Making Citizens, Reassembling Devices: On Gender and the Development of Contemporary Public Sites of Repair in Northern California." Public Culture 26(1), pp. 51–77.

Rosner, D. K./Fox, S. E. (2016): "Legacies of Craft and the Centrality of Failure in a Mother-operated Hackerspace." New Media & Society 18(4), pp. 558–580.

Rosner, D. K./Turner F. (2015): "Theaters of Alternative Industry: Hobbyist Repair Collectives and the Legacy of the 1960s American Counterculture." In: H. Plattner/C. Meinel/L. Leifer (eds), Design Thinking Research, London: Springer, pp. 59–69.

Riot Grrrl. (1991): "riot grrrl manifesto." In: Hanna, K., Bikini Kill (zine) #2. Retrieved from Digital Manifesto Archive https://www.digitalmanifesto.net/.

Russell, A. L./Vinsel, L. (2018): "After Innovation, Turn to Maintenance." Technology and Culture 59 (1), pp. 1–25.

Sivek, S. C. (2011): "'We Need a Showing of All Hands': Technological Utopianism in MAKE Magazine." Journal of Communication Inquiry 35(3), pp. 187–209.

The Mentor. (1986): "The Conscience of a Hacker." Phrack 1(7): 3 of 10. Retrieved from http://www.phrack.org/issues/7/3.html.

Torrone, P. (1 December 2006): "The Maker's Bill of Rights." Make magazine. Retrieved from https://makezine.com/2006/12/01/the-makers-bill-of-rights/.

Toupin, S. (2014): "Feminist Hackerspaces: The Synthesis of Feminist and Hacker Cultures." Journal of Peer Production 5, pp. 1–11.

Traweek, S. (1988): Beamtimes and Lifetimes: An Ethnography of the High Energy Physics Community in Japan and the US. Cambridge, MA: Harvard University Press.

TransHackFeminist (2014): TransHackFeminist manifesto. Pechblenda. Retrieved from https://pechblenda.hotglue.me/?transhackfeminism_en.

Turner, F. (2010): From Counterculture to Cyberculture: Stewart Brand, the Whole Earth Network, and the Rise of Digital Utopianism. Chicago, IL: University of Chicago Press.

Turner, F. (2018): "Millenarian Tinkering: The Puritan Roots of the Maker Movement." Technology and Culture 59(4), Supplement, pp. s160–s182.

Ukeles, M. L. (1969): "Maintenance Art Manifesto." In: K. Stiles (ed.), Theories and Documents of Contemporary Art: A Source Book of Artist's Writings. Berkeley, CA: University of California Press, pp. 622–625.

VNS Matrix. (1991): "Cyberfeminist Manifesto for the 21st Century." VNS Matrix. Retrieved from https://vnsmatrix.net/projects/the-cyberfeminist-manifesto-for-the-21st-century.

Vossoughi, S./Hooper, P. K./Escudé, M. (2016): "Making Through the Lens of Culture And Power: Toward Transformative Visions for Educational Equity." Harvard Educational Review 86(2), pp. 206–232.

Winkiel, L. (2008): Modernism, Race and Manifestos. Cambridge, MA: Cambridge University Press.

Woodhouse, E./Hess, D./Breyman, S./Martin, B. (2002): "Science Studies and Activism: Possibilities and Problems for Reconstructivist Agendas." Social Studies of Science 32(2), pp. 297–319.

From Hacking to Making
The Commodification of Spanish DIY Spaces Since the 1990s

David Cuartielles Ruiz and César García Sáez

Abstract

This article explores the history of contemporary Spanish Do-It-Yourself (DIY) spaces (hacklabs, hackerspaces, fab labs, makerspaces and after-school academies) and the growth of each type since the 1990s. The development of these types of spaces is reflected against the commodification and commoditisation of DIY in Spain. The article argues that the removal of the political layer of the early Spanish DIY techno-tactical movements allowed a higher degree of dissemination within society in general, while reducing the emancipatory potential of these new spaces. However, the analysis of the degree of commodification and commoditisation of types of spaces in relation to the amount of spaces per type shows an anomaly for makerspaces. The authors reflect upon this anomaly and whether a data set enlargement could correct it. For their analysis, the authors constructed a data set of events of the Spanish DIY history through the design of an ad hoc mixed method. Tracing events and spaces could not be done in a simple way due to the long time span of the study: older spaces existed in the pre-social network days, and new ones exist only in dedicated platforms for niche communities of practice. This method of tracing events and spaces is another contribution of the article as it could be used to make similar causality analyses of historical data in other case studies.

Keywords: hacklab, makerspace, hackerspace, fab lab, commodification, commoditisation, Spanish DIY history

Introduction

Spain's spaces dedicated to host Do-It-Yourself (DIY) activities have evolved since the late 1990s – there were hacklabs, hackerspaces, makerspaces, fab labs and after-school activities in *making and coding*. Each type of these spaces emerged at a different moment in time over the course of the last 30 years, and all of them still coexist. The different types of spaces address participants with similar interests. They align themselves with the values of open-source/free software development and later open-source hardware, generating social change by collaboratively developing alternative forms of material culture, embodied in objects such as Reprap 3D printers or Arduino boards. Shared machine shops emerged to distribute the costs of acquiring and operating machines (Troxler 2011), enabling more people to participate. As Van Holm (2015) observes, there is a thin line separating the definitions of what constitutes a hackerspace, a makerspace, and a fab lab. This article asks the question if the various types of spaces dedicated to DIY activities in Spain underwent a double transformation – commercialisation of the culture or the experience (commodification) and a loss of values (commoditisation), which resulted in opening more locations than the previous ones and translated into attracting larger audiences.

The Techno-socio-economic Context of DIY in Spain

DIY cultures are strongly dependent on the techno-socioeconomic context in which they grow (Sun et al. 2015). In this study, we focus on the different techno-social movements, or as Hess calls them technology- and product-oriented movements (2005), departing from the Spanish hacker groups in the 1990s and analysing their coexistence with other cultures like *makers*, or *fabbers* (participants in the fab lab activities), all the way towards the end of the second decade into the 21st century. We established a timeline of different historical events that serves as a background to the arrival of each one of these communities of practice to Spain.

Science and Technology Studies (STS) literature looks at technologies in interaction with society and economy (Williams/Edge 1996: 893; Hess 2005). In this context, technologies are described as *inclusive*, going beyond the mere idea of *equipment* (Williams/Edge 1996: 875). Knowledge and expertise do not only create technologies, but also technologies "generate new environments" (ibid). We suggest looking at spaces as technological "boundary objects" rather than as organisations since they are "plastic enough to adapt to local needs […], yet robust enough to maintain a common identity across sites" (Star/Griesemer 1989: 393). We feel these spaces lack the representation of multiple worlds (Guston 2001) and later revisions of the concept (O'Mahony/Bechky 2008; Parker/Crona 2012; Leith et al. 2016) that would qualify them as "boundary organisations", although we acknowledge that many spaces have meta-structures constructed around them of various categories that could be considered organisations.

DIY culture in Spain has evolved greatly in the last three decades spanning from the early communities at hacklabs, passing by the temporary meeting spaces established in various LAN parties in the 1990s where Free Software advocates met P2P (Peer to Peer, here referring to the computer users joining file-sharing networks) aficionados. The emerging Internet infrastructure served as a backdrop for the first hackerspaces, recurrent face-to-face events, and experimental centres about digital culture such as Medialab-Prado.

In the period from 2005 to 2006, several important events kickstarted the "maker movement" as we know it: the Arduino platform was born (Arduino Team 2005); the RepRap project, on self-replicable machines, managed to produce its first replica using 3D printing (All3DP 2016); Maker Faire San Mateo launched its first edition (Maker Media 2018) and fab lab users would start hosting yearly "FabEvents" (Fab Foundation 2019). All these in-person gatherings served to materialise some of the online conversations around open-source initiatives. As ephemeral as they were, these meetings accelerated knowledge transmission, built trust and tried to open some of the technological black boxes to the general public.

The timeline (Figure 1) shows new spaces emerging in 2006–2007. Encounters and conferences fostered a sense of community with a strong focus on Arduino. It would take more than four years for new permanent spaces to appear, mainly linked to institutions.

Events on Free Libre Open Source Software (FLOSS) technology evolved from specialised to mainstream, targeting the general public. At the same time, new independent makerspaces appeared in several large cities. It would take those spaces 18–24 months to mature and start launching their own activities and gatherings to exchange best practices in Gijon and Ourense.

In the late 2010s, STEM (abbreviation for Science, Technology, Engineering and Math, used to name the collective body of knowledge covering the mentioned fields) education was introduced into the Spanish official curriculum in technology for schools

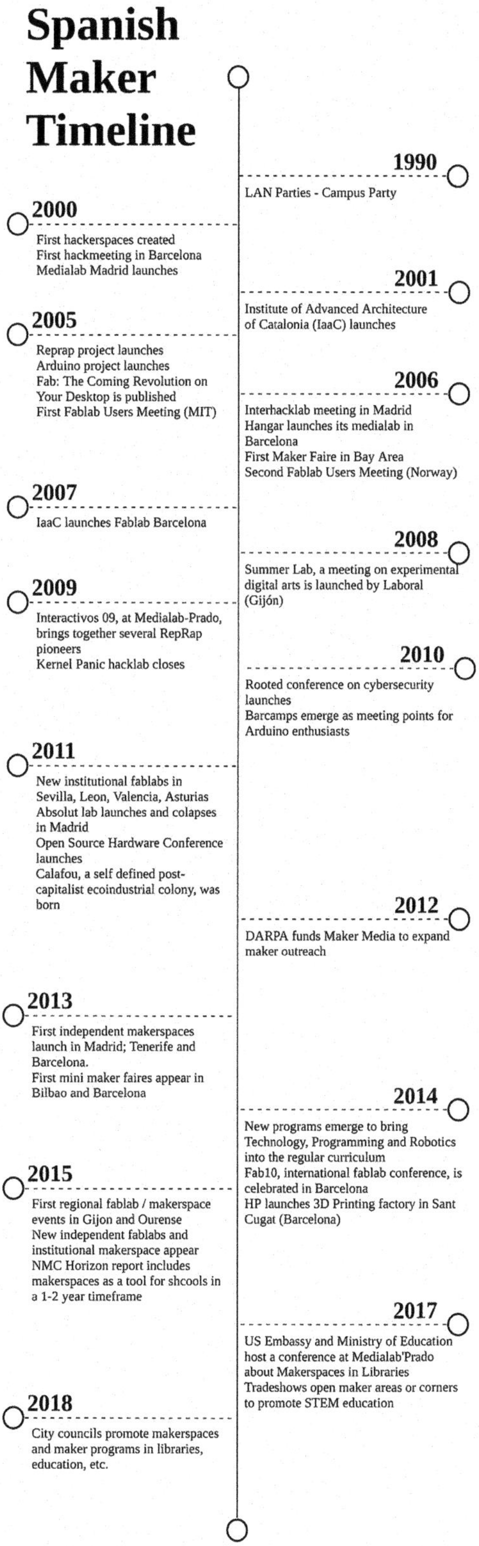

Figure 1: Timeline for the Spanish DIY culture (including international contextual events).

Spanish Maker Timeline

1990
LAN Parties - Campus Party

2000
First hackerspaces created
First hackmeeting in Barcelona
Medialab Madrid launches

2001
Institute of Advanced Architecture of Catalonia (IaaC) launches

2005
Reprap project launches
Arduino project launches
Fab: The Coming Revolution on Your Desktop is published
First Fablab Users Meeting (MIT)

2006
Interhacklab meeting in Madrid
Hangar launches its medialab in Barcelona
First Maker Faire in Bay Area
Second Fablab Users Meeting (Norway)

2007
IaaC launches Fablab Barcelona

2008
Summer Lab, a meeting on experimental digital arts is launched by Laboral (Gijón)

2009
Interactivos 09, at Medialab-Prado, brings together several RepRap pioneers
Kernel Panic hacklab closes

2010
Rooted conference on cybersecurity launches
Barcamps emerge as meeting points for Arduino enthusiasts

2011
New institutional fablabs in Sevilla, Leon, Valencia, Asturias
Absolut lab launches and colapses in Madrid
Open Source Hardware Conference launches
Calafou, a self defined post-capitalist ecoindustrial colony, was born

2012
DARPA funds Maker Media to expand maker outreach

2013
First independent makerspaces launch in Madrid; Tenerife and Barcelona.
First mini maker faires appear in Bilbao and Barcelona

2014
New programs emerge to bring Technology, Programming and Robotics into the regular curriculum
Fab10, international fablab conference, is celebrated in Barcelona
HP launches 3D Printing factory in Sant Cugat (Barcelona)

2015
First regional fablab / makerspace events in Gijon and Ourense
New independent fablabs and institutional makerspace appear
NMC Horizon report includes makerspaces as a tool for shcools in a 1-2 year timeframe

2017
US Embassy and Ministry of Education host a conference at Medialab'Prado about Makerspaces in Libraries
Tradeshows open maker areas or corners to promote STEM education

2018
City councils promote makerspaces and maker programs in libraries, education, etc.

and universities (Comunidad de Madrid 2018). This new discourse about technology had been brewing in other spaces different from schools for decades in Spanish society, digital technology having just reached after-school learning-by-doing programmes.

Commodification and Commoditisation

We selected the events on the timeline in Figure 1 to highlight the increasing commodification and commoditisation for every newly arriving category of spaces. We found it useful to separate both terms as a way to create a visualisation of a possible classification of spaces.

Boltanski and Chiapello define *commodification* as the "transformation into 'products' [...] of goods and practices" (2005: 441). The commodification of the DIY culture is therefore a transformation into a means of consumption: for example, hackers become chief data officers of large telecommunication networks (El Mundo 2016) or making and coding become common pedagogical tools for teachers at schools (Halverson/Sheridan 2014; O'Brien/Hansen/Harlow 2016; Chan/Holbert 2019). The *commodification of authenticity* describes how any real-life experience – also described as the authenticity of practice (Kohtala/Bosqué 2014) – is a good to be sold (Boltanski/Chiapello 2005: 441). In the case under study, after-school programmes use kits, artefacts with a pedagogical intention, but with a structured execution plan (Cuartielles 2018) that somehow commodifies and commoditises the idea of *project*. Since kits respond to a recipe – a sequential programme that participants execute for maximal success and optimal outcome, they do not make sense when conceptually run through the basic values of hacklabs. As Raymond puts it: "No problem should ever have to be solved twice [...] Anyone who can give you orders can stop you from solving whatever problem you're being fascinated by [...]" (2001). In a sense, a kit at an after-school is no solution to a problem, what in Raymond's terms is keeping you from learning by doing something interesting to you. In addition, from that perspective, why should anyone document a project that has been copied from a step by step tutorial?

In the discourse of commodification by Williams and Edge this is known as a "black-boxed solution" (1996: 874). The same concept can be applied to the tools, hardware or software, used at the DIY spaces. The more a technology is used, whether open or not, the more it succeeds among less technical people, who perceive it in terms of attributes and not its constituting parts (ibid). Consequently, openness stops being a relevant value for the tools or the experiences, increasing the possibility for those technologies to become proprietary. As a matter of fact, the higher the degree of commodification and commoditisation in a category of spaces, the less observance towards using open source/free software tools, as will be explained later. If the work to be performed is about features and not social transformation, why care about using software tools that might offer a higher resistance?

There is also a *commoditisation* of the culture itself. Molist – the documentarist of the Spanish hacker culture – highlights how the moment the hacker culture went mainstream, people detached the experience from its values and saw only the possible profits, which quickly killed the culture (2012: 259). From a value-analysis perspective, the Spanish hacker scene turned into cybersecurity consultants around 2002, disregarding the sharing of information among members, who focused on their companies instead (ibid).

Research Methods and Data Collection

Williams and Edge mention how "SST [social shaping of technology] specialists investigating contemporary technologies could be [...] actors shaping technological development" (1996: 892). Both authors of this article are or have been part of one or more of the communities of practice under scrutiny in this current article. One of us is involved in documenting the maker community through a podcast (with over 200 available audios and videos) (García 2014–2020), articles, articles for the Spanish Foundation for Innovation, Cotec, as well as reports for the Orange Foundation (García 2016); the other is co-founder of the Arduino open-source hardware platform and community (Cuartielles 2014), who is involved in the creation of open-source educational tools and programmes through making and coding. We both are actively involved in the creation of DIY activities and events, lecture on the topic at universities and perform research in the field.

There are different academic traditions looking at the involvement of researchers in the techno-social situations they study. In this article, we departed from a participatory activist research perspective as a methodological tool that helps grasp the techno-social context in first person (lisahunter/Emerald/Martin 2013), "acting as the catalyst in the conversation among actors" and yet gives space for reflection through the comparison of multiple cases side by side (Cuartielles 2018: 176). This work done as researchers implies an attitude of "commitment to social transformation, challenging power relations, [...] building spaces for critical dialogue" as much as it involves "the other" through the participatory action (Chatterton/Fuller/Routledge 2007: 8).

Data Collection

While participatory activist research as an ongoing research activity offered an entry to the world of makers and DIY spaces, we had to complement our methodological repertoire with other tools like surveys and web scraping (Rogers 2017). We reviewed different studies dedicated to the mapping of DIY spaces in Spain to compare data capturing approaches. Maxigas used the registration of names for web properties for hacklabs (2012). Recent studies, like the one studying maker cultures through Twitter by Menichinelli (2016), use social networks to take snapshots of social situations at a specific moment in time.

None of those methods were satisfactory for providing all the data for the period presented here. The different categories of spaces emerged at different times, and the available tools for communication as well as Internet platforms used by those spaces differed. For example, hacklabs existed before there were social networks and search engines and therefore looking for information on those requires yet another approach such as using the Wayback Machine at archive.org which started archiving the internet in 1996 (Internet Archive 1996).

Therefore, we built the timeline of events in a double process of harvesting data from written and online sources while surveying different communities of practice. The starting point for the data set was mapping existing spaces from specialised public directories. Data from hacklabs was constructed starting from Hackstory's website directory (Molist 2012). Regarding hackerspaces in Spain, the collection came from the *official hackerspace wiki* (HackerspaceWiki 2017). The *fablabs.io* website offered a curated list of registered fab labs in Spain and around the world (2013). Most makerspaces in Spain are registered in one of the previous directories, as there is no dedicated listing for this category of spaces. For each space, we tried documenting their opening and closing dates using primary and secondary sources. Whenever the data was not collected by us in first person (e.g. when collecting data with an open survey on the Internet), we made a second check through whatever sources were at hand.

Additionally, we launched an online survey in the first half of 2019. The survey consisted of an online form disseminated through social media and specific community channels. The main goal of the survey was to capture data that were relevant for participants in different Spanish DIY culture groups, such as which events they had personally experienced and found relevant in the building of the national makers' community. This brought new data from meet-ups, barcamps, or conferences, to dates when spaces – yet unknown to us – were created. We thereby constructed a data set with over 450 data points for which we registered different attributes in order to establish the Spanish DIY culture timeline: the opening and closing of spaces, the publication of media of any kind (print, video, blog, etc.) relevant to any of the communities, conferences, workshops, seminars, the visit of relevant members of the international DIY community to Spain or the presence of Spanish community members in international events.

Challenges in Data Capture

The different types of spaces presented different operational challenges when collecting data, as not all of them were listed in open directories. We defined a process to survey different Internet platforms following a specific protocol. When possible, the process included the mapping of the opening of a new space by searching through press releases or a dedicated website. If that failed, we looked for the existence of the space's website on the Internet Archive (https://archive.org/web/). If that information was not clear, the registration of social media accounts and even the domain name registration date were taken into account. There is room for failure using this mechanism for data collection, but given the goals of this research, there was no need for higher precision on the time axis.

In the specific case of the fablabs.io website, it was not straightforward to determine which fab labs were actually open. As van der Heijden et al. (2014) alleged, fab labs follow a long bootstrapping life cycle. The time from the conception of a space until it is operational can take over two years. Spaces are registered at the time of their conceptualisation and not when they open to the public, which cannot be inferred through the website or an Application Programming Interface (API), the set of tools that allow programs to communicate with other programs or the operating system. We had visited several fab labs in previous years, so they could verify whether they were open or not. For those without a public physical address at *fablabs.io*, we sent an email to the available public contact, 36 emails in total. We received 19 responses: six fab labs were in fact open, four were preparing their spaces to open in the following year, two were ready to open imminently, two were currently lacking a space but remained active through regional maker activities, one was running but closed to the public, two others were running but open only to students, one recipient offered an inconclusive response, and one email bounced as the contact email was unavailable.

Regarding the after-school academies and our lack of personal involvement in these businesses, we resorted to other tools like online search and web scraping. To gather a significant sample, we constrained our search to the first 100 results found in Google and the first 100 results found on a platform specialised in after-school programme searches in Spain (https://buscaextraescolares.com). We found that there existed franchises for some of these after-school academies – there could be as many as 20 franchises of one brand across the country. For practical reasons, we decided to count each academy only regardless of the number of franchises – given the time frame to produce the initial data set and the complexity of reaching out to all of the academy operators and the amount of data we wanted to collect, such as whether academies were currently open, for how long they had been offering their services, etc. We deemed this approach appropriate for a first approximation of the matter.

The Appearance of DIY Spaces in Spain

To address the article's research question of establishing a relation between the different types of spaces and the increase of the people partaking in the space's activities, we mapped the types of spaces in two ways, first plotting the amount of spaces opened per year against a timeline and second categorising them in terms of commodification and commoditisation.

Types of Spaces

We classified the spaces following definitions and criteria extracted from literature, narrowing down those definitions where needed, to make sure each space belonged to just one category. Our data showed that spaces were sometimes listed in more than one thematic repository, like fablab.io or wiki.hackerspaces.org. Some spaces are listed as hackerspace, makerspace, and even fab lab. We decided that spaces should have a primary category which would be determined via a specially defined process. The primary criterion for classifying a space was its own definition in any available public records: registration documents, official website, press release, or any other material. When spaces did not include any hints to whether they were part of any of the categories mentioned above, we made an in-depth analysis of the data looking for values, outcomes, political stances, and audience types to sort a space into one of the categories.

Hacklabs and *hackerspaces* are the oldest categories. These spaces differ in their "ideological and historical roots" (Maxigas 2012). Hacklabs usually come from an anarchist tradition, showcasing strong political implication around resistance and tech-sovereignty. In Italy and Spain, hacklabs emerged at the so-called CSOA (in Spanish "Centro Social Okupado Autogestionado") or self-managed, occupied social centres (Wright 2000), which are "radical left-wing spaces, often anarchist, that host a range of events open to the public such as gigs, talks, workshops, films and parties" (Dee 2016: 111).

Hackerspaces appear to have a more libertarian background, starting from the Chaos Computer Club (CCC) in Germany. According to Smith et al. (2016: 111), in August 2007, a group of American hackers called Hackers on a Plane visited German hackerspaces and hacklabs. They attended the Chaos Communication Camp and learned about hackerspace design from CCC activists Thorsten Haas, Jens Ohlig and Lars Weiler who created a known-in-the-field manual on how to create such a space (2007). After the visit, several of the most prominent US-based hackerspaces launched, like San Francisco's Noisebridge or NYC Resistor. These new hackerspaces adopted a more pragmatic approach to technology, missing the strong political stances of hacklabs (Smith et al. 2016: 112), and levitated towards a project-based approach (Maxigas 2015). Self-organisation and governance remained as a common original trait for both kinds of spaces. This contrasts with hacklabs in Spain that have become further depoliticised in the last decade, mainly through institutionalisation processes that include entrepreneurship-focused initiatives like the case of Remolacha Hacklab by the public project Zaragoza Activa (2017). The creation and dismantlement of the different Spanish hacklabs has been captured in the data set.

Fab labs (fabrication laboratories) originate from the Center for Bits and Atoms at MIT (Gershenfeld 2005). One of the goals for fab labs is being able to reproduce any digital design at any of the spaces. To achieve this, all spaces must share a common digital fabrication inventory and practices. This requirement is covered in the Fab Charter, a set of principles all fab labs must adhere to. Other principles include open access for individuals, shared operations and documentation, safety for people and machines, non-secrecy for designs and processes for individuals, and the goal of serving as incubators for new businesses (Center for Bits and Atoms 2012). Given their academic origin, fab labs are usually related to larger institutions. On the other hand, grassroots fab labs emerged – operating under a paradigm similar to the hackerspaces – and generated new paradigms much more embedded in the local communities (Kohtala/Bosqué 2014). In terms of values, the Fab Charter mandates that spaces should be open to everyone. Designs and processes could be "protected and sold, [...] but should remain available for individuals to use and learn from" (Center for Bits and Atoms 2012). We can contrast this position with some principles of the hacker ethos: "Access to computers – and anything which might teach you something about the way the world really works – should be unlimited and total. [...] All information should be free" (Levy 1984: 27). While hackers make a clear statement about openness and freedom of information, fabbers' view on the matter is more ambiguous.

Makerspaces are a relatively new kind of space. The term was coined in 2011 "when Dale [Dougherty] and MAKE Magazine registered *makerspace.com* and started using the term to refer to publicly-accessible places to design and create, often in the context of creating spaces for children" (Cavalcanti 2013). Other authors such as Rosa et al. (2017: 8) explain that the term has evolved since its origin to now include "any generic space (often also including fab labs and hackerspaces) that promotes active participation, knowledge sharing, and collaboration among individuals through open exploration and creative use of technology (i.e. through tinkering and making)". For the purpose of the classification of spaces, we are not using Rosa et al.'s broad definition of makerspace since it turns it into an umbrella term flattening any differences between categories of spaces. Rather, we use a more precise definition: makerspaces as any generic space (excluding fab labs and hackerspaces) that promotes active participation, knowledge sharing, and collaboration among individuals through open exploration and creative use of technology (i.e. through tinkering and making) that self-identifies as a makerspace (*espacio maker* in Spanish). Makespace Cambridge was one of the first spaces that self-identified as such and served as inspiration to the foundation of Makespace Madrid, the first makerspace in Spain since 2013.

After-school academies for STEM (or STEAM) learning appeared in Spain as spaces for extracurricular activities – covering topics like robotics or coding – to promote vocations in Science, Technology, Engineering (Arts) and Mathematics. These topics were later introduced as formal subjects in the official educational curriculum covering Technology, Programming and Robotics (Comunidad de Madrid 2015). Most academies follow project-based learning pedagogies, resembling the practices of previously existing DIY spaces. However, the relationship between the initiatives and their participants differs from their predecessors.

Finally, spaces not corresponding to any of the expected categories – for example, the Absolut lab in Madrid that disappeared after only one month, or the Ateneus in Barcelona that are inspired by fab labs but functioning like institutionalised makerspaces – were excluded from the analysis.

Timelines by Space Category

Figure 2 shows a common timeline that indicates space appearances per year grouped by category, a snapshot of how different types of spaces have arrived in Spain over the years. Each colour represents a category (from bottom to top): hacklabs, hackerspaces, fab labs, makerspaces and after-school academies.

The total numbers of spaces can be better compared in Figure 3 where the aggregated amounts of each category of space is depicted over time; this is particularly useful to visualise the size of each one of the categories in comparison to the others.

Along the time axis, we can perceive a shift in the types of spaces launched through the years. A few independent hackerspaces opened in 2017. In 2019, at the time of writing, no new hacklabs were launched. The number of makerspaces in the graph seems low. A reason for this could be that makerspaces within schools are not part of the data set. After-school academies, working mostly on robotics, were opening all around Spain with an aggregated volume (84) that dwarfs all other alternatives. The graphs hint that the amount of DIY spaces was reaching something of a plateau when it comes to the creation of spaces of any of the categories under study.

Commodification and Commoditisation of DIY Spaces in Spain

Mapping types of DIY spaces according to their degree of commodification and commoditisation served the purpose of establishing whether the younger types of spaces present higher commodification and commoditisation than their predecessors.

Hacklabs are the least commodified spaces given that most activities are offered to anyone for free. Furthermore, these spaces are also explicitly de-commoditised: members are expected to support each other through mutual aid practices and to actively participate in the initiative's governance. In *hackerspaces*, members are required to participate in the governance of the spaces as well as in maintaining the spaces. In *fab labs*, the Fab Charter requires that fab lab users should engage in the maintenance of the space, like cleaning or documenting the use of tools, yet it establishes no participation in the governance of labs. This translates to an increasing commoditisation among the three, where hacklabs see comrades, hackerspaces see participants, and fab labs see users.

Makerspaces are more heterogeneous than any of the previously mentioned spaces. On one hand, they have been depicted as linked to different forms of

Figure 2: New spaces per year by category.

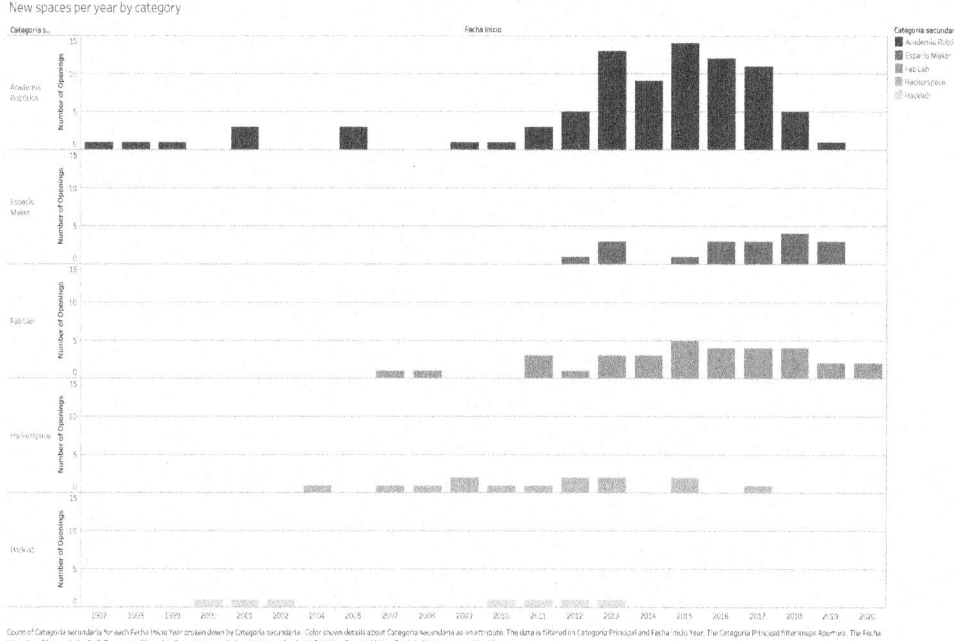

Figure 3: Aggregated amounts of new spaces per year.

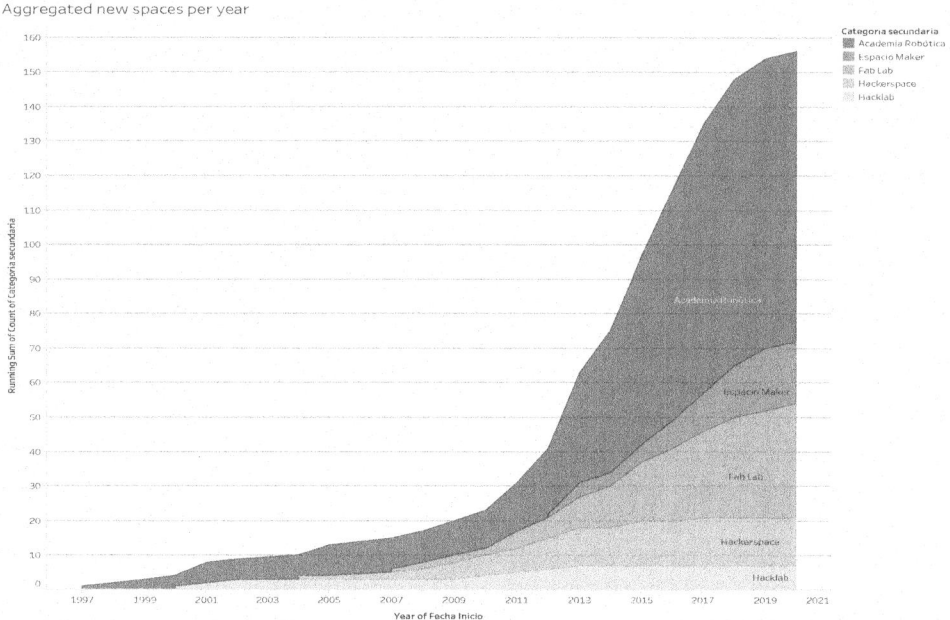

entrepreneurship (Anderson 2012; Hatch 2017). At an institutional level, President Obama announced the National Week of Making in 2016 as a way to promote local production of goods. This professionalisation of the "maker movement", also known as "maker pro" (Baichtal et al. 2014), indicates a strong commodification of the DIY culture at this point. On the other hand, Spanish makerspaces such as Makespace Madrid or MADE Makerspace Barcelona are incorporated as non-for-profit organisations, fostering open communities for learning and production. They are open to professionals but also to amateur musicians, artists, and hobbyists in general. It is this mix of potential audiences that seems to be the origin of the lack of definition of the makerspaces' values: does an entrepreneur in the need of a shared workspace have the same ethos as a family willing to spend some time building something together?

The values of makerspaces and the Maker Movement are the source of a series of academic controversies. The Maker Movement Manifesto is a compilation of shared values and practices put together by Hatch in 2013, former CEO and co-founder of TechShop, a now-defunct network of for-profit shared machine shops. Grassroots initiatives such as the Deconstructing Maker Movement Manifesto (Martínez/Mestres/Hinojos 2017) or Critical Making (Hertz 2012) have contested Hatch by directly revisiting each one of the values originally proposed by him. One of the criticisms stresses the lack of analysis about the relationship of the makers with the spaces (Martínez/Mestres/Hinojos 2017: 151). Menichinelli explores the idea of the maker identity, made of different narratives that together constitute the individual identity of each maker (2017). Another foundational document is the Maker Bill of Rights by Phil Torrone, focused on openness from a very pragmatic perspective (2006). Hertz looked critically into this document and published an alternative bill of rights, centred instead on social aspects (Hertz 2018).

The original description of Makespace Cambridge includes no reference to values: "Makespace is a space with various bits of manufacturing and prototyping kits to help you make things, with places to design, build and meet, accessible to members 24/7 via swipe card. Members pay a monthly subscription and need to take a training course and sign a membership agreement before they can use the space. On occasion the space will be open to the public for events" (Makespace Cambridge 2013). This pragmatic definition focused on the opportunities that the space could provide to a community of inventors. The British space differentiated itself also from fab labs: their users need not abide by the non-secrecy clause. They could use the space without having to give back anything to the community in terms of knowledge production. Another point of departure from hackerspaces is clearly stated as they plan to be "inclusive through being insured and safe and friendly". The governance model of the spaces is however derived from hackerspaces, with strong connection to projects and less so to the political aspects of making.

Finally, *after-school academies* offer kit-centric content under a tight schedule rather than free forms of peer to peer learning. They replace the participatory aspects with properly crafted user experiences, mediated by the payment of professional teaching services. Some of the robotics academies support themselves through licencing their kits to third parties or even through a franchise model, where they could be creating new spaces or delivering maker programmes to schools. It is probably this model that allowed for a massive expansion in the number of spaces from 2005 onwards, as the data set shows.

Figure 4 maps the types of DIY spaces against the qualities of commodification and commoditisation, estimated in relative form. We did not make a quantification of the data, but an estimation of whether one type was more or less or commodified or commoditised than another one. Thus, the boundaries of the types of spaces in the graph should not be interpreted as sharp delimitations, but as areas of higher probability for a space to belong to a certain type. Of course, if new types of spaces were to be evaluated, they could follow the same systemic analysis and "occupy" new areas of the two-dimensional representation space.

Figure 4: Types of spaces mapped in terms of their degree of commodification and commoditisation.

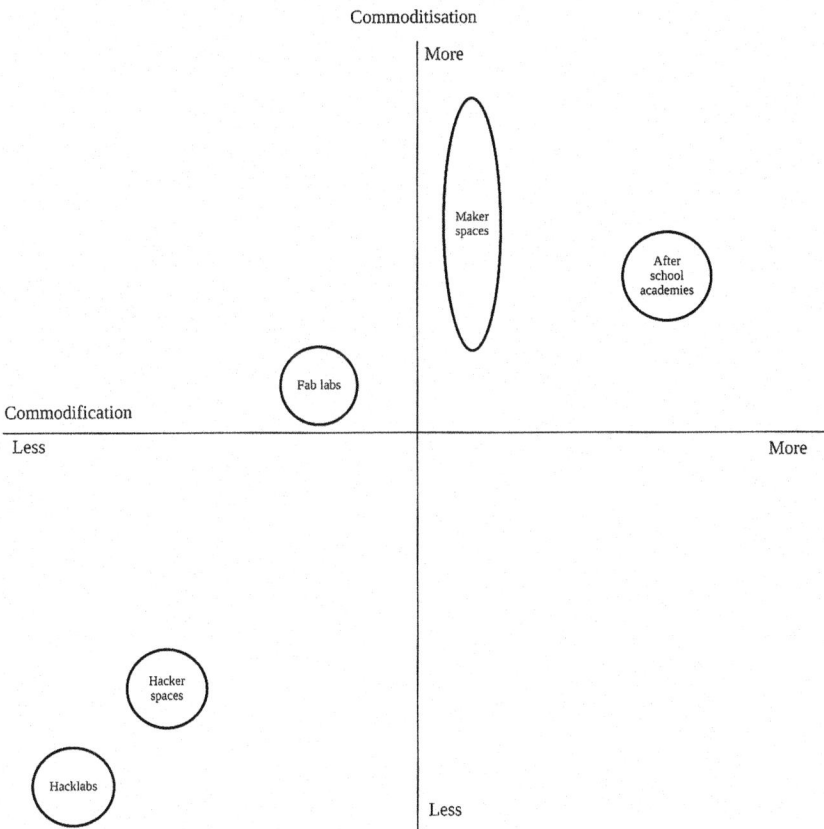

Interpreting Commodification and Commoditisation

Firstly, keeping in mind the chronological appearance of types of DIY spaces in Spain, from hacklabs and hackerspaces through fab labs and makerspaces to after school academies, Figure 4 shows a steadily increasing degree of commodification over time.

However, secondly, looking at the commoditisation axis, makerspaces present an abnormality: the values in the makerspace are stretched over a large vertical area due to a lack of definition of the makerspace ethos. In that sense, we understood makerspaces as the most liberal category, with lower demands for members in terms of knowledge sharing and community engagement. After-school activities do have a pedagogical intention towards their "clients" that makerspaces do not have towards their members; this gives after-school academies a much more specific set of values.

Thirdly, this graph is the point of departure for our following analysis questioning whether a higher degree of commodification and commoditisation would also mean a larger participant base in the activities of a certain type of space. We therefore compared and cross-related the commodification and commoditisation mapping of Figure 4 with the amounts of spaces from Figure 3. By looking at the horizontal axis of Figure 4, there is a correlation between the degree of commodification and the amount of spaces per type in Figure 3 – with the notable exception of makerspaces. However, as mentioned above, makerspaces seem to have moved into public institutions (Ministerio de Educación y Formación Profesional 2017), an extent that is not reflected in the data set and that could easily explain the mentioned abnormality.

To summarise this section, we observe that the commodification increases as new categories of spaces emerge, just as we expected. Newer categories capitalise more on selling the experience of authenticity to always younger audiences. Attendants to after-school spaces (clients) cannot take ownership of the spaces, thus reducing their emancipatory potential. While the removal of the political layer of hacklabs has allowed a higher degree of dissemination within society in general, commoditisation presents some challenges that can only be partially explained and that will require further research.

Reflections and Limitations

Evaluating the type of a space required ad hoc solutions for data analysis and classification. There was no standard mechanism in existing literature, leaving an open door to define how to classify spaces and even whether a space is part of more than one type. While fab labs adhere to their official charter, makerspaces have a certain degree of freedom to define their values, if participants are interested in such an activity at all. The problem of classification requires additional ethnographic research to properly map out how each one of the spaces deviate from the Fab Charter, Maker Manifesto, or any other principles that might have been established for a specific category. For instance, Wolf et al. reflected about how in fab labs "knowledge sharing is far from the norm, despite the high claims of the Fab Charter [...] fab lab users often do not find or do not take the time to document in a way that they feel is good enough to be shared online and globally" (2014).

But the classification challenge is just one of the methods that must be revisited. Data collection is also a relevant challenge for research. When dealing with some of the older pioneering spaces, there was limited information to be found. Most of the hacklabs were never formally incorporated to the public registry and their websites were hosted on platforms that no longer exist. Original hacker groups circulated information within circles of trust, communicating towards the outside world using fanzines. This reflected their political stance, confronting the status quo by setting up their own autonomous communication mechanisms.

Later spaces operated from a much more commodified scenario. This offered us more reliable methods to determine the timestamp of events. For example, in Spain, once an organisation falls into a standard registration scenario (non-for-profits must be registered either at national or at regional level, companies need to be incorporated), it becomes much easier to gain access to public records regarding their foundation and closure, the membership status, etc. It was also possible to obtain plenty of information through web scraping. However, there was a lesson to be learnt in optimising the process of cleaning and verifying the information.

Therefore, we defined an ad hoc (yet systematic) methodology for tracing events and spaces based on surveying the community and establishing a prioritisation to determine the validity of information. For example, primary sources like the answers from members of a space to a survey or the inclusion of a space in the public registry are considered first compared to press releases, press releases on official press were considered before personal sites reporting about a space and so on. This way of establishing the validity of sources has been key to creating the visualisation of the data set and we consider it to be a methodological contribution for us and others to continue researching on the topic, or even to apply it to similar causality analyses of historical data in other studies.

It should be possible to open new lines of research by adding new fields to the data set. Each field presents a separate problem of categorisation and classification. For instance, we have detected at least five different scenarios to set the opening date of a space: official opening by authorities, opening to the general public, internet domain registration, social media registration and official registration validation in platforms like fablabs.io. A standardisation of such data would allow developing new lines of research as follows: What is the average time from domain registration to public opening for fab labs in Spain? Could one learn patterns or best practices from the outliers to accelerate space development?

In this article, we presented a visualisation of the chronological evolution of the categories of spaces out of a snapshot of the data at the time of writing. Data was cleaned from inconsistencies and properly referenced after capture.

The application chosen to create the visualisation of the data is the commercial software Tableau (https://www.tableau.com).

The data set exceeds the informational needs for the analysis in this article. It was a methodological decision to focus on the opening of DIY spaces making use of digital tools. Thus, spaces like artisan associations, spaces dedicated to traditional arts and crafts, or companies working in the field of digital tools like 3D printing enterprises were left out of the analysis.

Conclusion and Further Work

In this study, we have explored five different categories of spaces related to digital DIY cultures with presence in Spain: hacklabs, hackerspaces, fab labs, makerspaces, and after-school academies. By mapping their occurrence over time, it was possible to observe how types that were more commodified and commoditised such as makerspaces and after-school academies grew in numbers as years went by. Other coexisting spaces like fab labs and hackerspaces slowed down their growth, while the opening of new hacklabs was residual.

To construct this kind of analysis, we had to solve the problem of the categorisation of spaces. We used a definition of makerspace as a distinct category. However, for the type of makerspaces, we discovered a misalignment in the relation between the degree of commodification and commoditisation of types of DIY spaces and the amount of spaces opened. The misalignment could be explained for commodification, but not fully for commoditisation. The values of makerspaces range from none – where as long as participants pay their quota, there is no perceived obligation towards the community – to full ethical charters. One could claim that the article's original hypothesis cannot be fulfilled.

The experience of being part of one of the DIY communities of practice is exposed to hard commoditisation processes, evolving from guilds – to acquire knowledge and skills as tools for personal expression – to a mere commercial experience that heavily limits any application of the hacker ethos. The fact that some after-school academies are offering a franchise model is the ultimate expression of the commodification process happening in parallel. As the data shows, once a successful formula has been tested and replicated, it enables faster growth rates compared to their non-commodified counterparts.

The commodification of the authentic is constantly fed by the coexistence of spaces of different categories. It is still possible to find non-commoditised and non-commodified practices like the ones characterising *Hacksturlab*. This hidden hacklab in the north of Spain has no public address; in order to access it, visitors have to meet up with the space's members at a bus stop. No money is requested to join the space. The existence of hacklabs like this one augments the idealisation of the guild. This increases the desire to belong and sustains the commodification of the authentic manifested at other spaces different from hacklabs. There is an opportunity for hackerspaces, fab labs, makerspaces, and even after-school academies to offer a "get back to your roots" experience.

By focusing on the opening of spaces, we were looking at the birth of sites for creation and learning. Spaces are boundary objects bringing together those promoting the activities with those partaking in them. Therefore, a higher commodification degree of a certain space implied the potential exchange of money for experiences. We did not see these potential economic exchanges as indicators of a sustainable model, nor the longevity of a space. While the data set contains information to further elaborate these topics, we consider such discussion worthy of a publication on its own and is not further discussed in this article.

Open Data

We have released the data set based on these criteria that might foster new research following similar classification strategies. This data set is publicly available for anyone to test their own hypotheses against the data, submit their comments or to check the validity of the facts supporting the research question in this paper (https://bit.ly/hackingtomaking).

References

All3DP. (2016): "The Official History of the RepRap Project." Retrieved from https://all3dp.com/history-of-the-reprap-project.
Anderson, C. (2012): Makers: The New Industrial Revolution. New York, NY: Crown Business.
Arduino Team (2005): Arduino Board – Serial Interface. Arduino.cc. Retrieved from https://www.arduino.cc/en/Main/ArduinoBoardSerial.
Baichtal, J./Tremayne, W. J./Huang, A./Kravitz, S./Altman, M./DiResta, J./Gentry, E./Jankowski, T./Dyba, A./Krumpus, M./Solarz, S./Klingberg, R./Meno, J./Gauntlett, D./Hord, M./Wolf, A. (2014): Maker Pro: Essays on Making a Living as a Maker. Sebastopol, CA: Maker Media.
Boltanski, L./Chiapello, E. (2005): "The New Spirit of Capitalism." International Journal of Politics, Culture, and Society 18(3–4), pp. 161–188.
Cavalcanti, G. (2013): "Is It a Hackerspace, Makerspace, TechShop, or FabLab?". Retrieved from https://makezine.com/2013/05/22/the-difference-between-hackerspaces-makerspaces-techshops-and-fablab.
Center for Bits and Atoms (2012): "The Fab Charter." Retrieved from http://fab.cba.mit.edu/about/charter/.
Chan, M. M./Holbert, N. (2019): "Exploring Modalities of Reflection Using Social Online Portfolios for Maker-Oriented Project-Based Learning." Proceedings of FabLearn 2019. New York, NY: ACM, pp. 172–175.

Chatterton, P./Fuller, D./Routledge, P. (2007): "Relating Action to Activism: Theoretical and Methodological Reflections." In: S. Kindon/R. Pain/M. Kesby (eds.), Participatory Action Research Approaches and Methods: Connecting People, Participation and Place. London: Routledge, pp. 216–222.

Comunidad de Madrid (2015): "Implantación de La Nueva Asignatura 'Tecnología, Programación y Robótica' En Los Centros Educativos de La Comunidad de Madrid." Consejería de Educación, Juventud y Deporte. Comunidad de Madrid. Retrieved from http://www.madrid.org/cs/Satellite?blobcol=urldata&blobheader=application%2Fpdf&blobheadername1=Content-Disposition&blobheadervalue1=filename%3DPRE.

Comunidad de Madrid (2018): "¿Qué Es STEMadrid?." Retrieved from http://educacionstem.educa.madrid.org/?page_id=74014.

Cuartielles, D. (2014): "How Deep Is Your Love? On Open-Source Hardware." In: P. Ehn/E.M. Nilsson/R. Topgaard (eds.), Making Futures: Marginal Notes on Innovation, Design and Democracy. Cambridge, MA: The MIT Press, pp. 153–170.

Cuartielles, D. (2018): "Platform Design: Creating Meaningful Toolboxes When People Meet". PhD diss., Malmö University, Faculty of Culture and Society. Retrieved from https://doi.org/10.24834/2043/26130.

Dee, E.T.C. (2016): "Squatted Social Centres in London: Temporary Nodes of Resistance to Capitalism." Contention: The Multidisciplinary Journal of Social Protest 4, pp. 109–127.

El Mundo (2016): "Telefónica Nombra al 'hacker' Chema Alonso como Jefe de Datos." Retrieved from https://www.elmundo.es/economia/2016/05/26/5746920e268e3efe4d8b4646.html.

Fablabs.io (2013): "Welcome Page." Retrieved from https://www.fablabs.io.

Fab Foundation (2019): "FABx Event." Retrieved from https://fabevent.org/.

García, C. (2014–2020): "La Hora Maker." Retrieved from https://lahoramaker.com.

García, C. (2016): (Casi) todo por hacer: una mirada social y educativa sobre los Fab Labs y el movimiento maker. Madrid: Fundación Orange.

Gershenfeld, N. (2005): FAB: The Coming Revolution on your Desktop – From Personal Computers to Personal Fabrication. New York, NY: Basic Books.

Guston, D.H. (2001): "Boundary Organizations in Environmental Policy and Science: An Introduction." Science, Technology, & Human Values 26(4), pp. 399–408.

Haas, T./Weiler, L./Ohlig, J. (2007): "Building a Hacker Space." 24C3. Retrieved from https://wiki.hackerspaces.org/Design_Patterns.

HackerspaceWiki (2017): "Spain – HackerspaceWiki." Retrieved from https://wiki.hackerspaces.org/Spain.

Halverson, E.R./Sheridan, K.M. (2014): "The Maker Movement in Education." Harvard Educational Review 84(4), pp. 495–504.

Hatch, M. (2013): The Maker Movement Manifesto: Rules for Innovation in the New World of Crafters, Hackers, and Tinkerers. New York, NY: McGraw-Hill Education.

Hatch, M. R. (2017): The Maker Revolution: Building a Future on Creativity and Innovation in an Exponential World. New York, NY: John Wiley & Sons.

van der Heijden, P./Juarez, B./Bassi, E./Hernamdt, K./Menichinelli, M./Vreeswijk, D./Waldman-Brown, A. (2014): The Fab Lab Life Cycle Report of the FAB10 Workshops. Fab Lab Paramaribo (Suriname), Sofos Consultancy (Amsterdam, The Netherlands), Fab Lab Lima (Peru).

Hertz, G. (ed.). (2012): Critical Making. Hollywood, CA: Telharmonium Press.

Hertz, G. (2018): The Maker's Bill of Rights by Garnet Hertz. Neural, Summer 2018 (8 September 2018). Retrieved from http://neural.it.

Hess, D. J. (2005): "Technology- and Product-Oriented Movements: Approximating Social Movement Studies and Science and Technology Studies." Science, Technology, & Human Values 30(4), pp. 515–535.

Internet Archive (1996): "Internet Archive: About IA." Retrieved from https://archive.org/about/.

Kohtala, C./Bosqué, C. (2014): "The Story of MIT-Fablab Norway: Community Embedding of Peer Production." Journal of Peer Production 5. Retrieved from http://peerproduction.net/issues/issue-5-shared-machine-shops/peer-reviewed-articles/the-story-of-mit-fablab-norway-community-embedding-of-peer-production/.

Leith, P./Haward, M./Rees, C./Ogier, E. (2016): "Success and Evolution of a Boundary Organization." Science, Technology, & Human Values 41(3), pp. 375–401.

Levy, S. (1984): Hackers: Heroes of the Computer Revolution. Garden City, NY: Anchor Press/Doubleday.

lisahunter/Emerald, E./Martin, G. (2013): Participatory Activist Research in the Globalised World: Social Change Through the Cultural Professions. New York, NY: Springer.

Maker Media (2018): "Maker Faire. A Bit of History." Retrieved from https://makerfaire.com/makerfairehistory.

Makespace Cambridge (26 February 2013): "The Makespace Guiding Principles." Retrieved from https://web.archive.org/web/20130226180129/http://makespace.org/space/principles/.

Martínez, O./Mestres, A./Hinojos, M. (eds.) (2017): Deconstruyendo el Manifiesto Maker. Barcelona: Transit Projectes – MakerConvent.

Maxigas (2012): "Hacklabs and Hackerspaces: Tracing Two Genealogies." Journal of Peer Production 2. Retrieved from http://peerproduction.net/issues/issue-2/peer-reviewed-papers/hacklabs-and-hackerspaces/.

Maxigas (2015): "Organising Flexible Working Spaces Through Techno-Social Networks: The Case of Door Systems in Hackerspaces." IN3 Working Paper Series. Retrieved from http://www.in3wps.uoc.edu/in3/ca/index.php/in3-working-paper-series/article/view/2488.html.

Menichinelli, M. (2016): "Mapping the Structure of the Global Maker Laboratories Community Through Twitter Connections." In: C. Levallois/M. Marchand/T.

Mata/A. Panisson (eds.), Twitter for Research Handbook 2015–2016. Lyon: EMLYON Press, pp. 47–62.

Menichinelli, M. (2017): "Deconstruyendo y rehaciendo las identidades de los Makers." In: O. Martínez/A. Mestres/M. Hinojos (eds.), Deconstruyendo el Manifiesto Maker. Barcelona: Transit Projectes – MakerConvent, pp. 18–33.

Ministerio de Educación y Formación Profesional (2017): "Makerspaces en bibliotecas públicas: Las bibliotecas públicas como lugares de producción de conocimiento y comunidad." Retrieved from http://www.educacionyfp.gob.es/mecd/cultura-mecd/areas-cultura/bibliotecas/novedades/jornada-makerspaces.html.

Molist, M. (2012): "Hackstory.es. La historia nunca contada del underground hacker en la Península Ibérica." Retrieved from http://hackstory.es/ebook/Hackstory.

O'Brien, S./Hansen, A. K./Harlow, D. B. (2016): "Educating Teachers for the Maker Movement: Pre-service Teachers' Experiences Facilitating Maker Activities." Proceedings of the 6th Annual Conference on Creativity and Fabrication in Education. New York, NY: ACM, pp. 99–102.

O'Mahony, S./Bechky, B. A. (2008): "Boundary Organizations: Enabling Collaboration Among Unexpected Allies." Administrative Science Quarterly 53(3), pp. 422–459.

Parker, J./Crona, B. (2012): "On Being All Things to All People: Boundary Organizations and the Contemporary Research University." Social Studies of Science 42(2), pp. 262–289.

Raymond, E. S. (2001): "How to Become a Hacker." Retrieved from http://www.catb.org/esr/faqs/hacker-howto.html.

Rogers, R. (2017): "Doing Web History with the Internet Archive: Screencast Documentaries." Internet Histories 1(1–2), pp. 160–172.

Rosa, P./Ferretti, F./Pereira, Â. G./Panella, F./Wanner, M. (2017): "Overview of the Maker Movement in the European Union." Publications Office of the European Union, Luxembourg. Retrieved from http://publications.jrc.ec.europa.eu/repository/bitstream/JRC107298/jrc_technical_report_-_overview_maker_movement_in_eu.pdf.

Smith, A./Fressoli, M./Abrol, D./Arond, E./Ely, A. (2016): Grassroots Innovation Movements. Abingdon, Oxon: Routledge.

Star, S. L./Griesemer, J. R. (1989): "Institutional Ecology, 'Translations' and Boundary Objects: Amateurs and Professionals in Berkeley's Museum of Vertebrate Zoology, 1907–39." Social Studies of Science 19(3), pp. 387–420.

Sun, Y./Lindtner, S./Ding, X./Lu, T./Gu, N. (2015): "Reliving the Past & Making a Harmonious Society Today: A Study of Elderly Electronic Hackers in China." Proceedings of the 18th ACM Conference on Computer Supported Cooperative Work & Social Computing. New York, NY: ACM, pp. 44–55.

Torrone, P. (2006): "The Makers Bill of Rights." Retrieved from https://makezine.com/2006/12/01/the-makers-bill-of-rights/.

Troxler, P. (2011): "Libraries of the Peer Production Era." In: B. van Abel/L. Evers/R. Klaassen/P. Troxler (eds.), Open Design Now: Why Design Cannot Remain Exclusive. Amsterdam: BIS Publishers, pp. 86–95.

Van Holm, E. J. (2015): "What Are Makerspaces, Hackerspaces, and Fab Labs?" SSRN Electronic Journal. Retrieved from https://doi.org/10.2139/ssrn.2548211.

Williams, R./Edge, D. (1996): "The Social Shaping of Technology." Research Policy 25(6), pp. 865–899.

Wolf, P./Troxler, P./Kocher, P.-Y./Harboe, J./Gaudenz, U. (2014): "Sharing is Sparing: Open Knowledge Sharing in Fab Labs." Journal of Peer Production 5. Retrieved from http://peerproduction.net/issues/issue-5-shared-machine-shops/peer-reviewed-articles/sharing-is-sparing-open-knowledge-sharing-in-fab-labs/.

Wright, S. (2000): "'A Love Born of Hate': Autonomist Rap in Italy." Theory, Culture & Society 17(3), pp. 117–135.

Zaragoza Activa (2017): "Zaragoza Activa refuerza su comunidad de emprendedores con un nuevo proyecto: La Remolacha HackLab." Retrieved from https://zaragozabuenasnoticias.com/2017/04/24/zaragoza-activa-refuerza-comunidad-emprendedores-nuevo-proyecto-la-remolacha-hacklab/.

Entering the Field

Tracing the History of DIY and Maker Culture in Germany's Open Workshops

Regina Sipos and Kerstin Franzl

Abstract

This article presents preliminary research findings on the history of Do-It-Yourself (DIY) and maker culture in Germany. It aims to identify historical, political, economic and societal shifts that have led to the existence of approximately 1000 makerspaces of various kinds in Germany today. The article summarises the beginnings of DIY in the 20th century in West Germany and East Germany. It focuses on how infrastructures supporting DIY were created out of necessity and economic considerations, how tools and spaces were offered as public service, the influence of counterculture movements and expression of political views through DIY and finally the use of DIY as a meaningful way to spend newfound leisure time and the phenomenon of state-funded vocational educational spaces. It aims to inspire further research elucidating the connections between broader societal contexts and DIY throughout the past century and its effects on maker culture today.

Keywords: history of DIY, makerspaces, counterculture, vocational training, open workshops

Introduction

The current discourse around the so-called "digital fabrication movement" or "maker movement" highlights actions originating in the United States that contributed to its worldwide success. In order for digital fabrication to become a broader societal phenomenon, awareness, access and engagement were needed, and these prerequisites seem to be discussed mostly in institutionalised and branded forms, such as Make and Fab Labs, seemingly forgetting about the diversity of "maker culture". *Make* magazine and Maker Faires have been crucial in the "maker movement" reaching millions of people worldwide, as people learned about and found sources of inspiration for Do-It-Yourself (DIY) projects. *Make* magazine has been a crucial medium, publishing articles and instructions for DIY projects that people can make themselves. Additionally, under the same brand, Maker Faire events allow makers to showcase their creations and learn about new tools and gadgets. Maker Faires have been organised in around 100 countries and have attracted millions of visitors (Dougherty 2012; Burke 2015). What could demonstrate the political and societal influence of Maker Faires better than the fact that, in 2014, a Maker Faire was hosted by the White House (Fried/Wetstone 2014)?

The revival of DIY through digital tools was given great stimulus by a course at the Massachusetts Institute of Technology, which teaches students "How to Make Almost Anything" (Gershenfeld 2012). The course inspired what eventually evolved as the international Fab Lab (fabrication laboratory) Network, which provided a blueprint of low-cost fabrication laboratories (today approximately 1750 in 100 countries) accompanied by a set of values that emphasised the Fab Lab as a laboratory allowing individuals to share space and tools. Basic tools, in addition to those not available in every home, such as 3D printers and laser cutters, are commonly offered in Fab Labs as well as in many other types of workshops worldwide, such as makerspaces, hackerspaces or repair cafés. Education provided to all age groups from young children to grown adults on how to use tools was also necessary, and a version of the original course under the name Fab Academy is offered to provide this education (Martin 2015; Peppler et al. 2016; Blikstein 2017). Many other spaces also offer workshops and training tailored to the needs of their communities. Thus, a number of recent developments took place that built on each other and occurred in parallel, giving people access to spaces with tools, educating them on how to use the tools, and providing inspiration to tinker on projects as well as opportunities to join a community and showcase these projects. Many of these developments are outside of the mainstream discourse.

What the discourse described above also rarely mentions is that people have been engaging in DIY activities for a long time and in very diverse ways, and how historical developments also contributed to the range of open workshops we are seeing today. In Germany, the number of non-profit open workshops is estimated to be around 1000, many of which have existed for decades and can be found in smaller cities and rural areas (VoW 2019). Aside from Fab Labs, there is a compelling diversity in the global as well as the German open workshop landscape, including not only hackerspaces and makerspaces, but also DIY/Do It With Others (DIWO) spaces, biologist and feminist spaces, repair cafés, mobile makerspaces and Fab Labs. In German, such spaces are called "offene Werkstätten" or open workshops. For the sake of simplicity, we will be referring to these as makerspaces throughout this article.

When we set out to research this phenomenon, the high number of makerspaces and variety in their specialisation seemed to indicate that the history of DIY culture and maker culture goes further back than is often suggested. We were surprised to discover that the history of German makerspaces had barely been documented. DIY culture, especially in community settings, seems to have only gained visibility in recent years due to its technologically inspired revival (Richterich/Wenz 2017). While DIY and low-tech maker culture created most of the necessary setting for the movement to become what it is today, any oral history depicting relevant experiences and perspectives of stakeholders involved from the beginning is scarcely recorded.

Rather than presenting a complete history, the current article is a first attempt to explore potential research questions. It also aims to present key experts and available resources on which researchers can draw to explore the topic. We traced back the influences and driving factors in the growth of the movement, with the goal of revealing the interplay between theoretical, political and technological developments, as well as the distinct historical socio-cultural currents that inspired the founding of long-standing makerspaces in Germany decades ago. This article aims to be a starting point: there are other long-standing makerspaces that deserve exploration with diverse individual histories that provide context for their unique circumstances, and the histories of the makerspaces discussed herein only provide a glimpse of this vast and diverse movement.

The methodology applied encompassed secondary research, document analysis and semi-structured interviews. The secondary research focused on a literature review on the history of DIY and grassroots political movements, including alternate spaces and communication methods such as citizen journalism, pirate, free and HAM radio movements (Soley 1999; Pinseler 2001; Kahl 2013); punk, squat and zine culture (Furian/Becker 2000; Hoekman 2011; Klingenberg 2012; Bennett/Guerra 2018); and community spaces for handicraft activities (Bredereck 2014). Information regarding DIY in Germany was gathered from a newspaper article "Die Axt im Koffer" documenting the beginnings of the movement (Spiegel 1965), a podcast with a stakeholder in German (Schramm/Thorhauer/Fischer 2013), websites of long-standing makerspaces, such as Haus der Eigenarbeit (House of Self-directed Work, HEi) in Munich and Stations of Young Naturalists and Technicians in Weißwasser and Lübbenau.[1] Semi-structured interviews were conducted for the sake of primary research with stakeholders, including Oliver Kurz, Frank Thorhauer and Christoph Popp. Kurz researched the beginnings of German DIY for an exhibition on the history of makerspaces in 2017, as well as an exhibition on the history of self-directed work and repair in 2018. Thorhauer has been an active member at the Station Lübbenau and shared with us the history of his home institution and a more general reflection on the historical settings of its founding and development over time. Popp, an artist from Nuremberg, whose parents were active members of the "Soziokultur" movement, gave us information about the origins of the school subject Economy, Work Study, Technology (Wirtschaft-Arbeitslehre-Technik, WAT). Some information they shared with us was based on personal research and some parts on personal memories and oral history. Simultaneously, the topic turned out to be so extensive, significant and

---

1 These were originally called Station Junger Naturforscher und Techniker. The Lübbenau Station was renamed Technikschule clever inside Lübbenau (Technology school clever inside Lübbenau) after the reunification of Germany.

multidimensional (e.g. with each institution having its specific, scarcely documented history) that we decided to use this as an opportunity to recommend more comprehensive research in order to fully trace back the historical development of the German DIY movement.

Finally, we would like to mention that we chose to describe the development chronologically and structured along the inner East German and West German border. This presents how West German makerspaces were influenced by necessity, DIY in the US and later counterculture, and East German makerspaces by state policies. In all contexts, an important role is played by the politics of the time as well as the functionality which is attributed to DIY and its spaces.

The Beginnings of DIY

Our focus in this article is on the beginnings of the DIY movements in the 20th century, as this time frame allows us to identify direct links between early movements and maker culture today. Earlier cases of communities engaging in handicrafts can be found, such as the creation of the Ladies' Society Gowanda, NY, established in 1873, a community of women "quilting, knitting, sewing, socialising, and discussing books" (Keengwe/Bull 2016). The term Do-It-Yourself can be traced back to the beginning of the 20th century, appearing in the American magazine *Suburban Life* in 1912. The magazine encouraged people living in the suburbs to do smaller renovations themselves, including painting their own walls instead of hiring tradespeople. It did not take long for the idea to spread to Germany (Gold et al. 2011), mainly with a focus on home renovations. Kurz pointed out that during and after World War II, DIY became popular in Germany because of general poverty and the lack of construction materials and craftspeople. People started creating basic commodities for themselves out of leftover military materials, including stoves from airplane metal sheets and cutting blades from shrapnel. In some places, these activities also had a community-oriented and sharing-economy character: when it was possible to purchase tools (e.g. with the financial support of the mayor), these were shared among citizens to overcome the common shortage.

In the late 1950s, through the availability of practical DIY literature, the American trend was introduced to West Germany and shortly after the industry of DIY tools helped the market grow. With the emergence of leisure time and the question of how to spend it meaningfully, educationists delivered an ideological framework for what the DIY industry had already started: to import the DIY culture to Germany (Voges 2017). With this, a new cultural inspiration was born. During the time of "economic miracle", West Germany rose from the destruction brought on by World War II and became the world's third largest economy. The overall situation changed fundamentally: a lack of resources was no longer a problem. Capitalism as the ruling economic model led not only to industrial and economic prosperity, but also to the birth of counter-movements that were seeking freedom from a profit-oriented way of living and individual streamlining for increased production. DIY was part of these sociocultural changes and developed a political character.

DIY as Community-based Open Services

In the 1960s DIY, repairing and crafting became an act of liberation from a strictly organised capitalist society – in economic, political and emotional terms. DIWO in affordable citizen centres and DIY, enabled by the first specialised hardware stores, were thriving. "Bürgerzentren", or citizen/community centres, were established in many places based on a public service model. These were shared, affordable spaces where citizens could meet to work together on their hobbies, without any pressure to produce something professionally.

Heinz Georg Baus opened the first German hardware store called "Bauhaus" and as Kurz found other businesses followed rapidly. An open workshop which, based on our definition today, could be called the first makerspace, was established in 1961. As described in 1965 in *Spiegel* magazine, in their issue entirely dedicated to DIY, the Centre for Information and Instruction on DIY[2] opened in Hainburg, offering DIY courses to educate people on tools and techniques. Founded by the publisher of the popular DIY magazine *Happy Leisure Time*,[3] it brought together 186 German and international companies. Their courses on soldering, welding, car repair and maintenance were visited by 15,000 participants in the first four years, and the exhibition rooms with "foolproof" machines were visited by 70,000 people. Soon, a similar space was set up in Stuttgart (Spiegel 1965).

In 1965, the mass movement of DIY was set in motion by "the notorious lack of tradespeople, high prices of services, and the lack of willingness of vocational practitioners to do smaller repairs" (Spiegel 1965), and people with lower and middle incomes started to learn how to do smaller repairs in their own homes, to, for example, fix faucets or mount parquet flooring. The public sector continued to engage in DIY projects, more and more local authorities offered courses, spaces and tools for rent, and publishers published books on DIY and "artisanal self-help" (ibid). As Kurz explained, in many towns, communities of shared interests, clubs and associations were founded, for example, the Association of Practically Oriented People.[4] DIY was supported by churches, unions and the public sector in many cities. In Hesse, almost every village community centre had a DIY den, and adult educational centres set up their own DIY workshops. The mayor of Schongau started a hobby centre and acquired tools and educational materials, including a

2   Aufklärungs- und Instruktionszentrum der Heimwerkerei.
3   Frohe Freizeit.
4   Verein der praktischen Leute.

wood and ceramics workshop, model building, HAM radio and a physics experiment workshop, as well as weekly expert advice sessions.

DIY as Political Act and Counterculture

In the late 1960s, Christoph Popp's parents were engaged in the movement known as Soziokultur, based in the criticism of rigid, inflexible structures in social and school education. "Soziokultur" (social culture) was an umbrella movement of the group KEKS (Art, Education, Cybernetics, Sociology[5]), advocating for free culture groups, centres, youth art schools, cultural and art youth work, workshops, etc. Various forms of creative making were promoted, connecting art and education to everyday life. Their aim was to improve people's living, working and learning conditions with the means of art and culture (Baar 2014). The association of German Art Teachers published a manifesto for reforming the German school system (KEKS 1971 in Baar 2014). The approach was successful: in the 1970s, the school subject Economy, Work Study, Technology (WAT) was established (Cortina et al. 1994).

DIY and self-education became part of other types of counterculture, such as the birth of punk culture in the 1970s, which included setting up bands, creating media such as (fan)zines and alternative radio stations, and developing unique fashion, sales and marketing structures. Bennett and Guerra (2018) describe the emergence of punk as an organised DIY (counter-)culture phenomenon. Cheap and accessible reproduction methods such as photocopying, copying music cassettes and screen printing became tools of a new alternative movement building on DIY to express political views (Furian/Becker 2000). As a reaction to economic and political issues that caused employment crises, the political manifesto "For a Right to Self-Directed Work" (von Weizsäcker/von Weizsäcker 1978) was published. This manifesto emphasised the value of unpaid work and feminist attempts to make housework visible. "The publication had a huge impact", commented Kurz. Subsequently, he summarised, self-organised shared spaces and alternative economies were established, such as citizen centres,[6] self-organised day cares,[7] community-supported agriculture,[8] low-tech makerspaces and repair cafés.[9]

In 1982, the association "anstiftung" was founded in Munich by a Jens Mittelsten Scheid in order to create establishments that enabled, supported and guided artisanal, cultural and social self-directed work to solve the problem that social work did not develop autonomy in beneficiaries, but rather enmeshed them in

---

5   KEKS stands for Kunst, Erziehung, Kybernetik, Soziologie.
6   Citizen centres were called Bürgerzentrum in West and Kulturhaus in East Germany.
7   Kinderläden.
8   Solidarische Landwirtschaft.
9   Kurz, O. (researcher at Haus der Eigenarbeit), in discussion with the authors, 3rd July 2019.

dependence. Thus, one of the founding goals of "anstiftung" formulated an alternative model: to support exemplary projects that strengthened the autonomy of people, i. e. they should define their own needs and choose and put to the test their own ways of fulfilling these needs, both individually and collectively. Kurz pointed out that these programmes were made accessible in a permanent space in 1987, when HEi opened in Munich. The space, still operational today, included a makerspace with courses for woodwork, metal, textile, children's workshops, as well as community-supported agriculture programmes and an eco-farmers' market.

DIY as Education of the Future Workforce

In East Germany, the political, economic and societal situation was fundamentally different from the West German economic miracle. It was a struggle to keep citizens from emigrating and, by the mid-20th century, there was a serious lack of skilled labour. At the same time, East German citizens were expected to be active members of society, including children and youth, for example, as pioneers (Jeanrenaud 1951).

In 1953, one of the first Stations of Young Naturalists and Technicians opened in Weißwasser and at least 141 other stations were set up in the following years (ND-Archiv 1983) in every large city affiliated with local education authorities. Such spaces helped fulfil the societal expectation that youth had to take part in activities after school. They offered further education in science such as tinkering, electrical engineering, computer science, astronomy, photography, nature and environmental protection, woodwork and beekeeping. As we learned from Thorhauer, who has been working with Station Lübbenau for decades and has conducted research on its history, stations were very similar in their set-up, available equipment and interior. "Local economies and institutions served as lenders or providers for tools and material", Thorhauer explained, "and gained, in turn, pre-skilled labour forces."[10] Thus, depending on the local enterprises and industry, stations were focused on different subjects but were often stepping stones for apprenticeships. Thorhauer highlighted that, in Lübbenau, the equipment was a permanent loan from the local power plant, which also aimed to inspire youth to work for them when they entered the workforce. This institutional relationship had a strong influence on the gender balance in stations. Frank Thorhauer said that most of the participants were male, reflecting the gender segregation in work fields. The DDR government distributed apprenticeships and pushed men into more technical occupations and women into the fields of educational and retail (Falk 2005). Through this, when the Lübbenau power plant invested in future employers by sponsoring the Station, they focused on men and not on women as Station participants. The stations were open to both genders; however, only

---

10   Torhauer, F. (active member at the Station Junger Naturalisten und Techniker, Lübbenau), in discussion with the authors, 1st August 2019.

seldom did it happen that women overcame the cultural barriers that came along with biased spaces.

Schramm, who has worked with Station Lübbenau since 1976, explained in a podcast that stations employed teachers as well as others with a background in vocational education to lead working groups. In Lübbenau, these working groups focused on biology, model construction, electrical engineering, metal construction, automobile technology and photography. Projects were based on the interests of the participating youth and free of charge. "Participation was voluntary, however, students were strongly encouraged by the school to join such activities" (Schramm/Thorhauer/Fischer 2013). Until 1990, Station-Festivals (which strongly resemble Maker Faires today) were organised annually, were localised within the districts and were common events covering all stations in East Germany. The Fair of Tomorrow's Master Craftspeople[11] was a popular youth competition and fair, organised to encourage young people to become engineers, attracting 2–3 million participants every year (ibid).

Maker and Hacker Landscape Today

After the reunification, most stations closed because of the public sector's financial burdens, Thorhauer explained in our interview with him. "In the region where I worked brown coal was at the centre of the local economy. When mining discontinued after the reunification and the power plant closed down, the municipality could not afford financing the Station. We were lucky – some of the former members became volunteers in Lübbenau and Weißwasser. After the governing structure of the Station officially became an association, they helped continue. And we managed to negotiate with the municipality the continued usage of the buildings. They have become important community spaces."[12] As they rely on volunteers, the stations seem increasingly difficult to maintain today: employers used to encourage and support volunteering in DDR times, but today this is no longer the case. Youth have different extrinsic motivations and are no longer obliged to become apprentices.

At the same time, with the emergence of and access to digital tools, computers and the Internet, new kinds of makerspaces arose. In the mid-1990s, the Chaos Computer Club, a German hacker association founded in 1981 (Wieckmann 1989; ZDFinfo 2016), started branching out and hackerspaces all over Germany were founded, some of which also have hardware workshops.

Since the 2000s, German makerspaces are booming again: partially because, as demonstrated above, many DIY communities and spaces have existed for a long time, but also due to the internationally growing interest in maker culture. The combination of a heterogeneous, vivid history of DIY in Germany with new inter-

---

11 In German: Messe der Meister von Morgen.
12 Torhauer, F., in discussion with the authors, 1st August 2019.

national inspiration led to a novel differentiation of makerspaces. As Kurz put it in the interview, "On the one hand, technology-based, economically oriented workshops with a focus on self-empowerment and start-up culture became successful. On the other hand, (ultra-)low-tech activities are maintained by communities, serving as community spaces to fulfil people's need for closeness. Somewhere in between are communities that are concerned with the scarcity of natural resources and thus see DIY as part of a necessary survival strategy".[13] This division can surely be discussed; however, it points out some interesting steps that are understandable when they are read against the history that has been sketched here. Profit orientation might well have emerged not only out of inspiration for entrepreneurship and a new start-up spirit, but also from the hard learning that voluntary work is not a reliable foundation for a maker space. In Germany, makerspaces and DIY communities received governmental support several times – in the West in the 1950s, as part of the reconstruction and in the East as part of the vocational training policy – and, when these discontinued, they were left without financing structure. These experiences might well have led to an openness for new financing models, including profitable activities and start-up-like business models. In this light, profit orientation in makerspaces and DIY is more a question of how to achieve sustainability in their infrastructures.

Conclusions

During our exploratory research, it became clear to us how far-reaching the complex political, societal and economic developments of the past 60 years are in today's German makerspace landscape. The broad adoption and popularity of DIY, hardware stores, open workshops, self-directed work and Stations in German society historically evidently contributed to the high number and diversity of historical, established makerspaces and the instant acceptance of new makerspaces across the country. Decades of development under various political influences have inspired different communities to generate their respective versions of makerspaces. This makes the German maker movement a broad and inclusive movement, instead of a segregated phenomenon that serves only small segments of society.

It was highly valuable for us to learn about the differences and similarities of DIY emergence and development in East Germany and West Germany, as this difference is still visible, for example, in Stations still operated by volunteers, where the importance of the community is fundamental, compared to the idea of self-directed work as empowerment that is prominent in HEi. However, not only the larger socio-political picture has had a strong influence. Locally specific histories particular to each case seem to have shaped the physical characteristics

---

13   Kurz, O., in discussion with the authors, 3rd July 2019.

and ideological backgrounds of spaces. Single personalities, an ambitious circle of people, or even geographical circumstances have also been driving factors in this process. It would be of interest to understand how lasting such factors are: for example, do major differences remain between makerspaces in East Germany and West Germany? Interviews could be conducted with stakeholders to collect more oral history in order to identify how ideological, historical, political, cultural, societal and geographic factors influenced them, how these feed into their development over time and, if they still exist, their current practices.

This leads to the compelling point of the sustainability of makerspaces, which has been a struggle for most spaces over time. At first glance, it seems that the local cultural-political backgrounds have also shaped the strategies for ensuring sustainability. However, a deeper analysis would be helpful to show clearly what kinds of sustainability strategies do exist, how they were formed over time and whether there are correlations to local or national histories or other factors such as ideological backgrounds.

Acknowledgements

We would like to thank Max Voigt (Verbund Offener Werkstätten), Oliver Kurz (Haus der Eigenarbeit, Munich), Frank Thorhauer (Station Junger Naturalisten und Techniker, Lübbenau) and Christof Popp (LIPOPP) for the rich information they provided us. Also, we would like to thank the experts involved in the review process of the journal for their extremely valuable recommendations and hints as well as Owen Wooden for English language and grammar corrections.

References

Baar, T. (2014): "Die Gruppe KEKS – Aufbrüche der Aktionistischen Kunstpädagogik." In: Kontext Kunstpädagogik Band 39. Munich: kopaed Verlags-GmbH.

Bennett, A./Guerra, P. (2018): "DIY Cultures and Underground Music Scenes." Routledge Advances in Sociology. London: Routledge.

Blikstein, B. (2017): "The History and Prospects of the Maker Movement in Education." In: M.J. DeVries (ed.), Handbook of Technology Education. Cham: Springer Verlag, pp. 419–437.

Bredereck, M. (2014): "Warum treffen sich Menschen zum gemeinschaftlichen Handarbeiten?" In: Stricken zwischen Individualisierung und Social Support. Hamburg: Diplomica Verlag GmbH.

Burke, J.J. (2015): "Makerspaces. A Practical Guide for Librarians." In: Practical Guides for Librarians, no. 8. Lanham, MD: Rowman & Littlefield.

Cortina, K. S./Baumert, J./Leschinsky, A./Mayer, K. U./Trommer, L. (eds.) (1994): "Das Bildungswesen in der Bundesrepublik Deutschland." Strukturen und Entwicklungen im Überblick. Reinbek bei Hamburg: Rowohlt Verlag.

Dougherty, D. (2012): "The Maker Movement." Innovations: Technology, Governance, Globalization 7(3), pp. 11–14.

Falk, S. (2005): "Geschlechtsspezifische Ungleichheit im Erwerbsverlauf." Analysen für den deutschen Arbeitsmarkt. Wiesbaden: VS Verlag für Sozialwissenschaften.

Fried, B./Wetstone, K. (2014): "The White House Maker Faire: "Today's D.I.Y. Is Tomorrow's 'Made in America'"." Retrieved from https://obamawhitehouse.archives.gov/blog/2014/06/18/president-obama-white-house-maker-faire-today-s-diy-tomorrow-s-made-america. Accessed on 10 May 2020.

Furian, G./Becker, N. (2000): Auch im Osten trägt man Westen. Punks in der DDR – und was aus ihnen geworden ist. Bad Tölz: Thomas Tilsner Verlag.

Gershenfeld, N. (2012): "How to Make Almost Anything, The Digital Fabrication Revolution." Foreign Affairs 91 (6), pp. 43–57.

Gold, H./Hornung, A./Kuni, V./Nowak, T. (2011): "Do It Yourself." Die Mitmach-Revolution. Ausstellungskatalog, Bd. 29. Mainz: Museumsstiftung Post und Telekommunikation.

Hoekman, G. (2011): Pogo, Punk und Politik. Münster: Unrast Verlag.

Jeanrenaud, W. (1951): "Inhalt und Methoden der Pionierarbeit." Ost-Probleme 3(47), pp. 1457–1463.

Kahl, J. (2013): "Elektronische Presse und Bürgerjournalismus." In: Schriften zum Medien- und Informationsrecht, Bd. 7. Baden-Baden: Nomos Verlag.

Keengwe, J./Bull, P. H. (eds.) (2016): Handbook of Research on Transformative Digital Content and Learning Technologies. Advances in Educational Technologies and Instructional Design (AETID) book series. Hershey, PA: IGI Global.

KEKS (1971): "Eine Dokumentation. Mitteilungen des Bundes Deutscher Kunsterzieher e. V., Otto Mayer Verlag Ravensburg." In: Baar, T (2014): Die Gruppe KEKS – Aufbrüche der Aktionistischen Kunstpädagogik. In: Kontext Kunstpädagogik Band 39. Munich: kopaed Verlags-GmbH.

Klingenberg, A. (2012): Keine Zukunft für immer – Das Punk-Lexikon. Meine: Verlag Andreas Reiffer.

Martin, L. (2015). "The Promise of the Maker Movement for Education." Journal of Pre-College Engineering Education Research (J-PEER) 5(1), Article 4.

ND-Archiv (1983): "Unterrichtsbeginn nach erlebnisreichen Ferien." In: Neues Deutschland, 16. May 1983, p. 2. Berlin: Neues Deutschland Druckerei und Verlag GmbH.

Peppler, K./Halverson, E. R./Kafai, Y. (2016). Makeology: Makers as Learners (Vol. 2). New York NY: Routledge.

Pinseler, J (2001): "Sprechen im Freien Radio. Eine Fallanalyse zu Möglichkeiten alternativen Hörfunks." M & K Medien & Kommunikationswissenschaft 49(3), pp. 369–383.

Richterich, A./Wenz, K. (2017): "Introduction: Making and Hacking." Digital Culture & Society 3(1), pp. 5–21.

Schramm, V./Thorhauer, F./Fischer, M. (8 June 2013): "Vom Forscherdrang, Wechselblinkern und nächtlichen Bastelrunden." 2013. Retrieved from https://www.staatsbuergerkunde-podcast.de/2013/06/08/sbk022-station/. Accessed on 15 August 2019.

Soley, L. (1999): Free Radio: Electronic Civil Disobedience. Boulder, CO: Westview Press.

Spiegel (1965): "Die Axt im Koffer." In: Do It Yourself: Geschäft mit der Freizeit. Der Spiegel 17/1965, 21 April 1965, p. 48. Retrieved from https://www.spiegel.de/spiegel/print/d-46272317.html.

Voges, J. (2017): "Die Axt im Haus. Heimwerken – die "Verbürgerlichung" des Selbermachens in den 1960er Jahren." In: N. Langreiter/K. Löffler, (eds)., Selber machen: Diskurse und Praktiken des "Do it yourself". Bielefeld: transcript Verlag, pp. 35–56.

VoW (Verbund offener Werkstätten): "List of 'Open Workshops' in Germany." Retrieved from https://www.offene-werkstaetten.org/werkstaetten. Accessed on 15 May 2019.

von Weizsäcker, C./von Weizsäcker, E. (1978): "Für ein Recht auf Eigenarbeit." In: Duve, Freimut: Technologie und Politik. Band 10. Reinbek bei Hamburg: Rowohlt Verlag, pp. 185–189.

Wieckmann, J. (1989): "Das Chaos Computer Buch. Hacking Made in Germany." Reinbek bei Hamburg: Wunderlich Verlag.

ZDFinfo (2016): "Hacker, Freaks und Funktionäre: Der Chaos Computer Club. 2016." Retrieved from https://www.zdf.de/dokumentation/zdfinfo-doku/hacker-freaks-und-fuktionaere-der-chaos-computer-club-100.html. Accessed on 22 August 2019.

"What You Can Invent over the Weekend" and the Recurring History of Corporate DIY

Samantha Shorey

Abstract

At the emergence of the contemporary American maker movement, O'Reilly's Make: magazine positioned making as a method of innovation beyond the system of industrial research and development. These narratives emphasised the value of hands-on, material engagement for inspiring novel ideas and building inventive minds. This Do-It-Yourself (DIY) spirit was positioned as inherently oppositional to the corporate groupthink of "do as you're told". Today, dominant public discourses tend to emphasise the power of digital fabrication tools – collapsing much of the innovative potential of the maker movement into a single set of material practices and thus limiting the analytic field of making research.

In this "Entering the Field" format article, I explore two maker texts: early issues of Make: magazine (published between 2005 and 2007) and a collection of pamphlets produced by the General Motors Information Rack Service throughout the 1950s. These pamphlets were distributed for free in order to inspire and advance General Motors (GM) employees. Through connecting these collections, I both extend and complicate an industrial history of making as a source of innovation. I argue that, more than any particular set of tools, it is DIY practice that defines the core of Make: magazine's vision of making. However, as the pamphlets at GM illuminate, these practices are never fully outside of industries that benefit from the betterment of makers. Taken together, these stories reveal DIY as alternately challenging and contributing to corporate logics – a cyclical process that yields a current cultural moment in which makerspaces are installed in the ground floor of offices at Google, Facebook and, unsurprisingly, GM.

Keywords: Do-It-Yourself, maker, corporate culture, innovation, General Motors, *Make:* magazine

Overview

Since the emergence of the American maker movement, O'Reilly's *Make:* magazine has put Do-It-Yourself (DIY) practice at the centre of what it means to make. The cover of their inaugural issue touts "181 pages of DIY technology". The coffee table book commemorating their first year of publication celebrates "the creativity and the resourcefulness of the DIY movement" ("Maker's Corner" 2005: 183). While proponents and critics of making increasingly focus on the digital fabrication tools that have become the movement's most visible symbols, the hands-on and material practice of DIY is at the core of the maker movement's potential for innovation.

DIY can occur through a variety of materials and practices. More of an orientation than a specific set of skills, DIY is defined through "creative activities in which people use, repurpose and modify existing material to produce something" (Buechley et al. 2009: 4823). How might bringing our attention to DIY open the boundaries of what we recognise as making? DIY activities like fixing, tending and home improvement occur in domestic space. They can be both sustaining and productive of something new. This expansive definition of DIY represents an opportunity to open the analytic field, allowing researchers to recognise an array of innovative practices that occur beyond ubiquitous makerspace tools like 3D printers.

At least since the era of *The Whole Earth Catalog*, DIY culture has championed the perspective that basic tools and empowered action are transformative on a personal, local and global level (Turner 2006; Sivek 2011). Projects like these have, at their core, the ethos of DIY. Yet, their successful integration into high-tech industries suggests that DIY is also compatible with corporate logics. Previous histories of DIY reveal a complementary relationship between DIY culture and businesses that benefit from capable and creative employees. For example, throughout the 1950s ham radio hobbyists were recruited by the emerging electronics industry, in part because their self-taught status was seen as a sign of personal dedication and practical knowledge (Haring 2007). General Motors (GM), in particular, began blurring the boundary between at-home hobby and career training as early as the 1930s with "model coach" kits that groomed young men for the future work force (Oldenziel 1997).

In the following article, I connect these currents in DIY history by tracing early narratives of *Make:* magazine and positioning them alongside a set of mid-twentieth century DIY manuals produced by GM for their employees. Taken together, these stories highlight DIY as a site for producing multiple orientations to innovation, both contributing to and challenging corporate goals.

The General Motors Rack Service

Throughout the 1950s and 1960s, General Motors Information Rack Service printed hundreds of thousands of DIY booklets for the men and women employed in GM production plants and offices (IPA Review 1956). The thin, colourful guides were stocked in reading racks alongside a range of other self-improvement and informational guides. They were staple-bound and light: free to take, easy to bring with you and very popular. A field report from a pro-business think tank praised their success (and their potential as company propaganda) stating, "GM puts out more booklets than automobiles" (ibid: 10).

By 1956, GM had produced more than 500 titles on various subjects – about a quarter of them about "home and family" (ibid: 10). Many of the booklets in this series were DIY guides that would not be out of place in *Make:* magazine. Titles included the following: *What You Can Invent over the Weekend, Rugs You Can Make, 125 Simple Home Repairs* and *Transformagic: How to Make Old Furniture into New*. In their introductory pages, many of the booklets emphasise that the guides are meant for beginners, amateurs or at-home hobbyists. "There are many things you can make out of concrete without being an expert and at very little cost", assures H. Wood (1953), author of the booklet *Concrete Ideas* (2). Inside, the instructions use common, inexpensive tools and proportions are measured by the shovel-load.

In GM's Rack Service booklets, practical knowledge acquired through experience is emphasised over theoretical, textbook expertise. There is also an assumed level of competence in booklets like the *ABC's of Hand Tools* (1943), which was originally published for the maintenance staff of the armed forces. Adapted for the GM audience, the foreword explains, "it was thought it might be equally helpful to other people – the civilian mechanic, high school student, or amateur repairman found in most households". Tellingly, each of these audiences is described as having "years of practical experience in the shop" (ibid: 3). They address a wider American culture replete with DIY knowledge.

Today, the key figures of the contemporary maker movement speak nostalgically of the time when America was a nation of makers (Frauenfelder 2010). In higher education, especially, making is framed as a way of reclaiming and reteaching students basic material competencies that have disappeared due to our digital and consumer-driven world (Shorey 2019). Seen alongside the *Make:* magazine narratives that follow, it becomes clear that DIY is valuable because it helps makers develop material skills sets and develop new product ideas. Yet, neither of these completely captures why GM would encourage employees to pursue DIY. Because the DIY guides were distributed at GM plants, a fair number of the recipients were certainly people who were manufacturing car parts on industrial production lines. These workers were handy. And, opportunities for enacting new ideas are limited in Fordist systems that focus on the batch producing of standardised parts (Vidal 2015). Why then might GM have invested in DIY?

A call for submissions in the 1958 *Writer's Market* provides some clues for the intentions of the rack service booklets: "The main theme is service; to inspire or to make the reader want to advance" (Writer's Digest Books 1958: 409). DIY was as much about self-improvement as it was home improvement, and the rack service charted the direction of growth. The DIY booklets were published alongside others that educated readers on American enterprise, civic responsibility and the power of positive thinking. This contextualisation gestures towards the way that DIY, like making, is embedded in larger cultural projects of professionalisation and socialisation, which are often gender normative. Especially demonstrative of this point is the series of pamphlets titled _____ *Men Like* which includes *Soups Men Like, Pies Men Like, Cakes Men Like* and the spin-off *Meats for Men*. The GM rack service booklets were published during the time when DIY was established as an ideal in American culture, specifically as a method to define separate spheres of masculine and feminine domestic work (Gelber 1997). With these realisations comes a renewed attention to the subjectivities that are developed by makers and doers of any creative practice.

Contemporary Corporate DIY

Today, DIY still has a place at GM. GM's "careers" page on Facebook recently posted a video of a group of GM employees building a 3D printer for their new makerspace. "Our makerspace is about collaboration and bringing new ideas to life", they write enthusiastically, ending the post with hashtags for "automotive", "innovation" and "technology". Technologies like 3D printers allow engineers to quickly create physical models of potential components or devices. Rather than sending out specs and computer aided design files for prototype production, employees can DIY on site. Creating a makerspace that supports these activities makes a lot of sense for a company like GM that manufactures automobiles. Although modern cars contain more than a hundred million lines of code, they are inescapably material. Makerspaces have been key in spurring innovations at the nexus of software and hardware.[1]

Yet, makerspaces are also becoming a fixture of technology offices for companies whose primary products are digital. In the ground floor of Google's Seattle office is a keycard-accessible workshop. Hammers, pliers and rolls of duct tape hang on a wall of peg-board above a station with a computer monitor and 3D printer. Workshops like these can easily be seen as just another Ping-Pong table

---

1   The most famous example of this is probably the company "Square", co-founded by Twitter's Jack Dorsey. Square is a digital payments app but their key innovation was material: a small plastic card reader that can be plugged into the audio jack of a smart phone. The card-reader was prototyped at a TechShop makerspace in San Francisco (Schwartz 2011).

or nap-pod: spaces meant to bring a spirit of fun and restorative leisure to what is ultimately professional life. However, makerspaces have a more direct line to the productive and creative goals of technology companies. Founders of the first Google workshops described them as an effort to inspire the "verve and creativity" of the garage workshop where the company was famously founded (Liedtke 2011; see also Turner 2018). As technology companies grow, they increasingly resemble the large firms they once disrupted. Remaining on the cutting edge requires connecting workers to the entrepreneurialism and innovation that brings about new ideas. Corporate makerspaces are, at least in part, an attempt to encourage and capture the spontaneous creativity of DIY practice.

How Making Became Innovative

Throughout their early issues, *Make:* magazine positions DIY as their central intervention into technology culture. Magazine contributors build new creations from raw materials and they engage existing technologies in acts of personalisation, modification, experimentation and repair. Much of the maker movement's value is generated through a narrative that points to DIY as a neglected source of innovation. For example, in a design brief discussing the potential of open source cars, the author posits as if speaking to GM. "Do you want to see innovation in the hybrid electric automobile market? There's an R&D department composed of millions of people in millions of garages around the world" (Griffith 2005: 46). This instantiation of the corporate abbreviation for research and development (R&D) legitimises the knowledge produced by those tinkering with old cars and sharing information in auto-tech chat groups. DIY practice becomes a source of product development, of innovative ideas.

DIY practice is also valued within *Make:* magazine as a source of innovative thinking. For professional engineers and designers, DIY can light the creative spark that is dimmed by the structures of technology corporations. In its inaugural issues, *Make:* magazine puts forth a perspective on technology industries that frames them as slow, unwieldy and risk-averse. Alternately, DIY is a hands-on and imperfect creative process (Sterling 2006: 18). These material engagements are framed as incredibly productive for innovation because they help designers let go of the minor, iterative improvements that define industrial design processes (Lidwell 2005: 32). From their perspective, corporate R&D will only ever lead to outcomes that are similar to what already exists – rather than something new, divergent and truly innovative.

Both of these narratives position DIY as the driving spirit of the maker movement and a challenge to corporate ideals. It is DIY that disrupts the tired habits of engineering and design to inspire innovation. It is DIY that takes the inadequate solutions produced by technology companies and uses them as the basis for something new. Without DIY, users and engineers can never become *makers*. Yet, central narratives about the maker movement mobilise a limited definition of DIY. Rather than being framed as an approach or mindset, commentary has increasingly centred digital fabrication tools as the impetus for innovation (Upbin 2008; Tierney 2015). Electronics and robotics are naturalised as the de facto methods of making, narrowing who is recognised as a maker along racial and gendered lines (Buechley 2013; Faulkner/Mcclard 2014).

Maker movement narratives that centre digital fabrication further the perspective that it is tools – not designers, orientations, goals and collectives – that are the drivers of change. These discourses rest upon a "technosolutionist" point of view in which technology is treated as the solution to social problems (Lindtner/Bardzell/Bardzell 2016). Technosolutionist visions of the maker movement centre artefacts and devices. Garnet Hertz (2018) critically summarises this perspective in his manifesto *The Maker's Bill of Rights*, declaring "the world's key problems won't be fixed by simply adding 3D printing, open source, and the Arduino". Digital fabrication tools like these are lauded as empowering and democratising because of their "open" design. They make the tools of production, and their associated instructions and schematics, readily available to users. Yet even this type of expertise is not widely distributed. As Shoshanna Zuboff (2019) argues in *The Age of Surveillance Capitalism*, the concentration of technical knowledge in contemporary society creates a small, powerful and privatised labour pool driven by economic imperatives.[2] Research that locates making through the presence of digital fabrication tools will mostly find this type of maker: where corporate logics bleed into creative practice, constraining paths for action.

The maker movement has long advocated for a democratised view of innovation in which amateurs and enthusiasts are seen as a wellspring of new ideas. Inspired by (and sometimes directly referencing) the research of Eric Von Hippel (2005), early explanations of the maker movement emphasised the creative power of "lead users" and "alpha geeks" (Dougherty 2005: 7; O'Reilly 2009). By using a word like democratisation, Von Hippel invokes a vision of innovation that occurs beyond the elite purview of professional engineering. Yet, design researchers Björgvinsson, Ehn and Hillgren (2010) observe that Von Hippel's notion of democratised innovation almost always has novel products as its end goal.

Product-centric notions of innovation limit our ability to recognise other outcomes, processes and participants as part of making. As Debbie Chachra (2015) writes in her article *Why I'm Not a Maker*, the maker movement's emphasis on the production of artefacts reinscribes value into some labour processes, at the expense of others. An activity becomes "making" if it is public, profitable and performed by men. This delineation constrains our field of view to the most visible sources

---

2   Zuboff (2019) actually makes this point by comparing modern tech-giant Google to GM at the peak of their success. When GM reached its highest market capitalisation in the mid-1960s, it employed nearly *ten times* more people than Google did in 2016 (312, emphasis added).

of new technology: makerspaces, hackathons, incubators and start-ups. Here, the methods of design are heavily influenced by the goals of industry and Silicon Valley (Avle/Lindtner/Williams 2017). They produce a corporate orientation to technology that emphasises action over deliberation and scalable solutions for communities who may not be included in the design process (Irani 2015; Costanza-Chock 2020). Recognising DIY as the engine for innovation in the maker movement provides a new agenda for making research – one that may be capable of recognising innovation done differently and as something separate from high-tech tools.

A Future for DIY

The GM Rack Service booklets first came to my attention in a one-page article printed in the inaugural issue of *Craft:* magazine (the short-lived sister publication to *Make:*). Under the winking title "A Crafty Worker is a Happy Worker", the founding editor of *Make:* Mark Frauenfelder (2006) describes the stack of booklets he found at the thrift store. "Can you imagine any major corporation today handing out booklets to its workers titled *There's Magic in Clay?*" he asks (18). Yes, I nod. I can.

DIY – as both a site of self-improvement and a site of innovation – is productive for technology companies. Decades of cultural studies scholarship demonstrates that the cultural industries have long been parasitic on the creative activities of everyday people. Yet, in *Understanding Popular Culture,* John Fiske (2010 [2001]) calls for a renewed research agenda. "Instead of tracing exclusively the processes of incorporation [...]", we must investigate the "vitality and creativity that makes incorporation such a constant necessity" (18). Bringing our attention, as researchers, to DIY practice opens our field of vision to forms of making beyond those that are predefined by corporate culture. Yet, perhaps more importantly, it refocuses our attention on the ethos of DIY – the "vitality and creativity", in the words of Fiske – rather than digital fabrication tools and their outcomes. From this perspective, it becomes clear that mindsets, ways of doing and subjectivities are the most significant products of DIY practices, including making. It is here that we find *both* the radical and the reproductive potential of DIY.

In localised design communities – organised around both practical interventions and more overtly political projects – we see innovation activity that challenges rather than reproduces corporate logics. Activities like these are what Matt Ratto and Megan Boler (2014) have termed "DIY citizenship". DIY citizenship projects often involve outsider innovators who leverage the skills of home improvement to reimagine public space for collective good (DiSalvo 2014; Light 2014). Though many examples are speculative or ephemeral, similar projects are also widely evident in the everyday. For example, the curb cuts that are now a common part of neighbourhood plans were originally designed by disability activists who altered concrete to improve sidewalk accessibility (Hamraie 2017). In this and other forms of "DIY urbanism", individuals and small groups that are not often recognised as innovators are nevertheless innovating to improve their immediate communities and address structural failings (Douglas 2018). Here, participants develop new subjectivities and political orientations through making and doing together (Dunbar-Hester 2014).

To be sure, DIY cultures face many of the same challenges as maker culture. There is a long history of DIY movements that have also fallen prey to a kind of technosolutionism that Langdon Winner (1986) calls "build a better mousetrap" theory (78). Like their more corporate counterparts, utopian technological projects also place invention – of albeit more sustainable and more culturally responsive artefacts – as impetus enough for social change. Gender inequality is reproduced even in DIY communities that explicitly seek to disrupt structures of dominance (Dunbar-Hester 2014). And, those who already possess various types of social power have greater resources for enacting DIY in their environments and fewer consequences for doing so (Douglas 2018). DIY is rife with contradictions. As an analytic category, artist Florian Cramer has questioned "whether DIY is still a useful term at all" because of its ability to describe "extremely opposite" creative forces and political agendas (2019). Contradictions like these make DIY a site of ideological struggle rather than discursive closure.

Reconstituting DIY as the core of making has the potential to open the analytic field, casting the glow of innovation onto practices and participants who are too often overshadowed by the dominant discourses of making. In exploring the corporate history of DIY, it also becomes clear that DIY practice holds the same potential for co-option, dominance and exclusion. As Lucy Suchman observes, discourses of design have hegemonic power. They centre a singular mode of future-making – defined by specific locals and material practices – which minimises our ability to see how innovation can be done otherwise (Suchman 2018). However, Dennis Mumby (1997) reminds us that hegemonic control is never complete. It is animated by the *struggle* for meaning, holding the capacity for dominance and resistance, at once. Mumby observes that acts of resistance against corporate systems often fail because workers build shared identities based in other forms of structural dominance, like patriarchy. How might alternate histories of DIY help us to see the way that the gendering of creative practice constrains the radical possibility of DIY and of making?

References

"ABC's of Hand Tools" [booklet] (1943): General Motors Rack Service pamphlet series. Detroit, MI: General Motors Corporation.

Avle, S./Lindtner, S./Williams, K. (2017): "How Methods Make Designers." CHI '17 Proceedings of the 2017 CHI Conference on Human Factors in Computing Systems. New York, NY: ACM, pp. 472–483.

Björgvinsson, E./Ehn, P./Hillgren, P. (2010): "Participatory Design and 'Democratizing Innovation.'" PDC '10 Proceedings of the 11th Biennial Participatory Design Conference. New York, NY: ACM, pp. 41–50.

Buechley, L. (2013): "Making is Mostly Marvelous" [Keynote presentation]. FabLearn: Digital Fabrication in Education Conference, Stanford University, Palo Alto, CA, 27–28 October. Retrieved from http://edstream.stanford.edu/Video/Play/883b61dd951d4d3f90abeec65eead2911d.

Buechley, L./Rosner, D. K./Paulo, E./Williams, A. (2009): "DIY for CHI: Methods, Communities and Values of Reuse and Customization." CHI '09 Extended Abstracts of the CHI Conference on Human Factors in Computing Systems. New York, NY: ACM, pp. 3823–4826.

Chachra, D. (23 January 2015): "Why I'm Not a Maker." The Atlantic.

Costanza-Chock, S. (2020): "Design Practices: Nothing About Us Without Us." In: Design Justice. Cambridge, MA: The MIT Press, pp. 69–102.

Cramer, F. (2019): "Does DIY Mean Anything?" [Blog Post] Retrieved from http://cramer.pleintekst.nl/essays/does_diy_mean_anything/.

DiSalvo, C. (2014): "The Growbot Garden Project as DIY Speculation Through Design." In: M. Ratto/M. Boler (eds.), DIY Citizenship: Critical Making and Social Media. Cambridge, MA: The MIT Press, pp. 237–248.

Dougherty, D. (2005): "Maker Friendly." Make: (3), p. 3.

Douglas, G.C.C. (2018): The Help-Yourself City: Legitimacy and Inequality in DIY Urbanism. New York, NY: Oxford University Press.

Dunbar-Hester, C. (2014): Low Power to the People: Pirates, Protest, and Politics in FM Radio Activism. Cambridge, MA: The MIT Press.

Faulkner, S./Mcclard, F. (2014): "Making Change: Can Ethnographic Research about Women Makers Change the Future of Computing?" Ethnographic Praxis in Industry Conference Proceedings 2014 (1), pp. 187–198.

Fiske, J. (2010 [2001]): "The Jeaning of America." In: Understanding Popular Culture. London, UK: Taylor and Francis, pp. 1–18.

Frauenfelder, M. (2006): "A Crafty Worker is a Happy Worker." Craft: (1), p. 18.

Frauenfelder, M. (2010): Made by Hand: Searching for Meaning in a Throw Away World. New York, NY: Portfolio.

Gelber, S.M. (1997): "Do-It-Yourself: Constructing, Repairing and Maintaining Domestic Masculinity." American Quarterly 49(1), pp. 66–112.

Griffith, S. (2005): "The Open Source Car: A Design Brief." Make: (1), pp. 44–46.

Hamraie, A. (2017): "Sloped Technoscience: Curb Cuts, Critical Frictions, and Disability (Maker) Cultures." In: Building Access: Universal Design and the Politics of Disability. Minneapolis, MN: University of Minnesota Press, pp. 95–135.

Haring, K. (2007): "Amateurs on the Job." In: Ham Radio's Technical Culture. Cambridge, MA: MIT Press, pp. 78–89.

Hertz, G. (March 2018): "The Maker's Bill of Rights." ConceptLab. Retrieved from http://makermanifesto.com/.

IPA Review (January–March 1956): "Understanding Free Enterprise." The Institute of Public Affairs, pp. 9–10.
Irani, L. (2015): "Hackathons and the Making of Entrepreneurial Citizenship." Science, Technology and Human Values 40(5), pp. 799–824.
Lidwell, W. (2005): "The Dean of Engineering." Make: (4), pp. 28–37.
Liedtke, M. (2011): "Google Replants Its Garage Roots in Tech Workshops." In: USA Today, 26 March. Retrieved from http://usatoday30.usatoday.com/tech/news/2011-04-26-Goolge-garage-workshops.htm.
Light, A. (2014): "Citizen Innovation: ActiveEnergy and the Quest for Sustainable Design." In: M. Ratto/M. Boler (eds.), DIY Citizenship: Critical Making and Social Media. Cambridge, MA: The MIT Press, pp. 259–268.
Lindtner, S./Bardzell, S./Bardzell, J. (2016): "Reconstituting the Utopian Vision of Making: HCI After Techosolutionism." Proceedings on the 2016 CHI Conference on Human Factors in Computing Systems. New York, NY: A, pp. 1390–1402.
"Maker's Corner." Make:, Volume 4 (2005), p. 183.
Mumby, D. K. (1997): "The Problem of Hegemony: Rereading Gramsci for Organizational Communication Studies." Western Journal of Communication 61(4), pp. 343–375.
Oldenziel, R. (1997): "Boys and Their Toys: The Fisher Body Craftsman's Guild, 1930–1968, and the Making of a Male Technical Domain." Technology and Culture 38(1), pp. 60–96.
O'Reilly, T. (3 February 2009): "Where Real Innovation Happens." Forbes.
Ratto, M/Boler, M. (2014): "Introduction." In: M. Ratto/M. Boler (eds.), DIY Citizenship: Critical Making and Social Media. Cambridge, MA: The MIT Press, pp. 1–23.
Schwartz, A. (13 September 2011): "TechShop's Mark Hatch is Building a Place Where You Can Build Your Dreams." Fast Company. Retrieved from https://www.fastcompany.com/1678519/techshops-mark-hatch-is-building-a-place-where-you-can-build-your-dreams.
Shorey, S. (2019): Handmade Future: A Field-based Inquiry of Innovation Through Making and Craft. PhD diss., Seattle, WA: University of Washington.
Sivek, S. C. (2011). "We Need a Showing of All Hands": Technological Utopianism in Make Magazine. Journal of Communication Inquiry 35(3), pp. 187–209.
Sterling, B. (2006): "Hands On: Elegant Innovation." Make: (6), pp. 16–17.
Suchman, L. (29 March 2018): "Design." Theorizing the Contemporary. Fieldsites.
Tierney, J. (17 April 2015): "How Makerspaces Help Local Economies." The Atlantic.
Turner, F. (2006): "The Whole Earth Catalog as Information Technology." In: From Counterculture to Cyberculture: Stewart Brand, the Whole Earth Network, and the Rise of Digital Utopianism. Chicago, IL: University of Chicago Press, pp. 69–102.
Turner, F. (2018): "The Arts at Facebook: An Aesthetic Infrastructure for Surveillance Capitalism." Poetics (67), pp. 53–62.

Upbin, B. (13 August 2008): "Grass-roots Innovation Takes Root." Forbes.
Vidal, M. (2015): "Fordism in the Golden Age of Atlantic Capitalism." In: S. Edgell/H. Gottfried/E. Granter (eds.), The Sage Handbook of Sociology of Work and Employment. Thousand Oaks, CA: Sage Publishing, pp. 283–303.
Von Hippel, E. (2005): Democratizing Innovation. Cambridge, MA: MIT Press.
Wood, H. (1953): "Concrete Ideas" [booklet]. General Motors Rack Service pamphlet series. Detroit, MI: General Motors Corporation.
Winner, L. (1986): "Building the Better Mousetrap." The Whale and the Reactor: A Search for Limits in an Age of High Technology. Chicago, IL: University of Chicago Press, pp. 61–84.
Writer's Digest Books. (1958): Writer's Market. Cincinnati, OH: F&W Publications.
Zuboff, S. (2019): "A Coup from Above." The Age of Surveillance Capitalism: The Fight for a Human Future at the New Frontier of Power (first edition.). New York, NY: Public Affairs, pp. 309–325.

In Conversation with ...

Makers and Design in South Africa
Technology and Craft Cultures and their Antecedents

Felix Holm and Suné Stassen in Conversation with Cindy Kohtala and Yana Boeva

Felix Holm is co-founder of the Maker Station makerspace in Cape Town, South Africa, a coordinator of the Cape Town maker movement, and contributor to a pan-Afrikan makerspace founders' network. Suné Stassen is founding director and custodian of Open Design Afrika (ODA), a festival and activation platform that advocates, demonstrates and educates how design and creativity should be used for social, environmental and economic transformation. Over many years these two organisations have made significant contributions to reposition the roles of design, making, creativity and innovation within the greater ecosystem and helped build a healthier and more prosperous South Africa. Some of these efforts also contributed to Cape Town's proposal, submitted before the city was eventually crowned as World Design Capital in 2014. Maker Station and Open Design Afrika believe that fostering people's ability to become more active and responsive global citizens is key to increasing impact, improving more lives and initiating work towards achieving the UN Sustainable Development Goals as a collective effort to design our new preferred futures. Their efforts bring to light contributions to DIY making and hacking and alternative histories less addressed in academic research.

Felix (FH) and Suné (SS) spoke to Cindy Kohtala (CK) and Yana Boeva (YB) about their passions and the recent histories of South African DIY making over video-conference, mere days before South Africa went into lockdown due to the COVID-19 pandemic, for this issue.

CK: Felix, can you tell us about your makerspace and how it started?

FH: I studied design – product design, industrial design – about twenty years ago, and then did a lot of work in various design fields. But I also did a lot of development work over the years, rural job creation related work, and in that journey kept an eye on the whole maker movement over the last twelve to fifteen years as it was growing – Maker Faires, all those online platforms. In development work we've always looked at *tools* to use in the field. So, I've always had an eye on makerspaces since they started coming up.

And then the opportunity came along about eight years ago, when my brother and myself both needed a workshop, and I bullied him into having our studio in a makerspace. We basically rented a building ten times bigger than we needed and started running a makerspace. That's our origin story. When I was in development, during the big financial crisis, we had to zig and zag a little bit with our international donors, especially around getting infrastructure stuff funded in rural communities. Our workaround back then was to convince them to do shared workshop space in mobile units like shipping containers. Our sell to them was that the investment could be redeployed if a project failed, because their argument was that they didn't want to put money into anything except consultants. That started off my makerspace journey.

When we needed workshop space for our own studios, we started the Maker Station in Cape Town. I think we were about the third makerspace in South Africa. There were a few fab labs that came and went before us, because they popped up at about the time MIT started going international. What used to be called the Cape Craft & Design Institute had a very small fab lab. That was the first "makerspace-y" shared workshop. Since 2013 there are about six makerspaces in South Africa now. Many of them have evolved a lot.

And now we've just taken a second building. Our original building is about 750 square metres and the new building is another 600 square metres. In the first building, we've kept all the makerspace *light* stuff, 3D printing, electronics, laser cutting, sewing – the sort of *clean* stuff – and we've got mainly tenants in the rest of the space with cubicles and studios. The new building is our makerspace *heavy*, it's about 200 metres down the road, and that's where we're moving the wood shop, the metal shop, my studio has a foundry in it and an engineering shop that we run, an art foundry. So all the big, heavy, dirty stuff is now in Maker Station "Heavy" down the road. The lease might run out in this first building so we might have to reassess what we're going to do with this one. But then we might move everything to the new space.

YB: What kind of profile do you have as a makerspace? What is your identity?

FH: We've booked about 700 members over the six years. Half of those are international people who mainly come in for concerts, big events like AfrikaBurn[1] and some of the big music festivals. They come in and use our facilities, sign up as members, and some of them have been coming back for a couple of years. Out of the balance, out of 300 members, we have about 40 to 50 regulars, and an average of ten tenants. The other 200 to 250 people are sort of seasonal migrants, people who come into town for the film festivals, also people who come from the rest of

---

1   AfrikaBurn is an annual regional Burning Man festival in the Tankwa Karoo, located in the Northern Cape Province of South Africa, since 2007.

South Africa for things like the big events. During the year we've got a few waves of people coming in and using this space.

The big problem we have with makerspaces in South Africa and Afrika[2] is that our demographics, the proportion of the population that has the disposable income to support makerspaces, that has the education, the cultural background, the sense of innovation – those things are all there, but proportionally to a western society, it's really hard to sustain makerspaces. There's often a very big mismatch between what people offer in makerspaces versus the market. We put our makerspace in pretty much the Soho of South Africa. The area we are in, Woodstock, is *the* design centre. It's where all the film studios are; all the design schools are around us. It's the art centre, one of two or three hubs in the Western Cape where there are a lot of artists; we literally have about a dozen sculpture studios within a street block of us. So we purposefully placed ourselves here. My brother and myself come from analogue backgrounds, we're too old for all these geeks! When starting, we therefore had a bias regarding our art and artisanal backgrounds, but also strategically we had to look at that. I had ten years of looking at makerspaces, looking at best practice and business models and figuring out what works, seeing what the Cape Craft & Design Institute did, and what failed. We knew that if we wanted to run a makerspace in the European or American model, we had to find the demographic that fits that.

We did start a pilot two years ago with Vaal University of Technology (VUT). And they started a project they called I2P Lab, the Ideas to Products Lab, it was pretty much a copy of the Fab Lab model. They've got a big additive manufacturing centre at VUT and want to spread their gospel of additive manufacturing which is basically their mission. They approached us about three years ago to run a pilot for an I2P Lab and they wanted to give us 30 printers, which was stupid in our opinion; we said no, you can't have a toolbox full of hammers. You know, we need other tools as well. We're not running a training centre so it's not for us. Then they came back about six months later and told us they'd come up with this brilliant idea of an I2P Plus Lab. We can have some 3D printers and with part of the budget we could pick equipment of our own choice. We got some 3D printers from them and then we added electronic equipment, laser cutters, CNC and a bunch of other tools, just to give us a bit of diversity.

I come from design and I've pretty much been a carpenter my whole life. And my brother is a grease monkey. We are both quite curious about technology stuff. But we also decided to make a very multidisciplinary space, also from the need of our members. We've therefore got all the analogue facilities, woodwork, metalwork. And then we've also got all the tech stuff.

---

2   As more than 2000 languages on the continent refer to "Afrika" with a "k", we too refer to Afrika in this article to express solidarity with Afrikan pride and a decolonised acknowledgement of Afrikan ownership of Afrikan futures.

CK: And Suné, can you tell us about yourself and how Open Design Afrika came into existence?

SS: I also studied design as well as education – two fields I am very passionate about and that became a driving force in everything I do. Early on in my career when I was still teaching design at secondary school level, I realised the underlying skills children develop because of their exposure to creativity and any "making" environment, might it be in art, design, music, dance or drama. These skills are human skills and life skills that should be a priority for every child to develop. For example, skills like complex problem solving; holistic, entrepreneurial and innovative thinking skills; critical thinking, empathy and even the ability to negotiate and collaborate with others are all skills that can and should be developed in each child if we want them to be successful and thrive in the future. Today we also refer to the same skills as future-skills.

In the early 1990s a few of us approached the National Department of Basic Education. Our goal was to convince them of the value of Design with regards to crucial skills development and that Design should be introduced as an independent subject at secondary school level. This became a delicate dance and an unexpected long journey, but after nine years we finally succeeded and in 2006 the very first design curriculum was introduced into a number of South African schools as a choice subject. At the time we had no idea that South Africa was the first country in the world to include Design as a school subject.

Due to the lack of appropriate resources like textbooks to support and guide the educators with this new subject, I decided to look for additional support elsewhere and joined forces in 2005 with Woolworths so we were able to develop support material. In 2006, just in time for the introduction of the new Design curriculum, our collaborative effort resulted in the launch of the "Making the Difference Through Design" programme which we originally introduced to 121 schools in the Province of the Western Cape. Within a year the programme was rolled out to additional schools in another two provinces, bringing our total to 400 schools and exposing the world of design to more than 18 000 learners. The programme also included an important resource manual that was distributed to all educators, featuring more than 80 case studies that focused on the work and design processes executed by South African designers, makers and crafters. The case studies amplified a diverse selection of local and iconic designers, makers and crafters who were leaders in their field, which in itself also helped us to develop local role models and local pride in South African Design. A few years later and to our biggest surprise, the "Making the Difference Through Design" programme was nominated and eventually a finalist in the 2009 INDEX Award, the biggest design award in the world.

Shortly thereafter I was approached to help develop the first textbooks and teacher manuals for grades 10–12 which are still being used today. We had a super team of writers and contributors – people who I highly respect for their knowledge and expertise in Design Education. As a team we were also determined to make the content as relevant and accessible as possible in order to encourage full participation of educators and learners from marginalised communities where the lack of basic resources like water and electricity is a daily reality. In the end these were all great achievements, but I soon realised that it was again very exclusive, because only learners who believe they are creative will choose Design as a subject. So how and where are the rest of the learners supposed to develop these vital life and future skills?

CK: Design and designer-making is often seen as an elite and consumerist activity that only serves industry, in many regions.

SS: Yes. That became our big challenge: how can we democratise these learnings and creative experiences also beyond the classroom so that we can start to develop a society of problem-solvers and change-makers that can collectively add value to socio-economic development? If you look at a developing country like South Africa, the scale of change that we need to execute is overwhelming. Yes, there are a lot of incredible projects and organisations that do amazing work to create change, but at the same time we also have to recognise that we need platforms and find alternative ways to democratise knowledge and experiences that are also accessible for marginalised communities so that we can impact and create change on a broader scale and for the greater good. Most design, innovation and technology related events are still very exclusive, as potential opportunities available for participation still comes with high price tags.

So how do we create a platform that is more inclusive and accessible? How do you create a platform where everyone feels they belong and have the right to participate, learn, share and network? How do we educate the masses about the value and impact of creativity, design and making across diverse sectors like education, healthcare, mobility and transport and social development? And how do we develop role models and Afrikan pride that can ignite hope and inspire the youth to aspire to greatness?

These questions really drove our new agenda, which eventually inspired the creation and the launch of the first Open Design Cape Town Festival and platform in 2013. The festival format itself is perfect, as it not only allows you to develop a diverse programme, but this is also an easy way to extend your reach and impact to a broader audience and to get the media to focus on reporting on the relevance, value and impact of creativity and design-led innovation within a variety of context and sectors. The philosophy of Ubuntu ("I am because you are") therefore really resonates with us because we strongly believe in the power of the collective. It is important for us to also include the participation of marginalised communities in order to reach that broader and more diverse audience and in this way have a better chance at effecting change in a more systemic way.

This also guided us to mindfully create interesting and engaging experiences that ignite greater social cohesion. With our focus on basic human needs instead of a focus on any particular design sector and through demonstrating how creativity, design-led innovation and the act of making can add value within a broader context proved to be a great approach as our topics for talks, workshops and other experiences are indeed more accessible to a diverse audience.

This is where I want to come back to the importance of "making" and the role that Felix and the Maker Station has played over the years. In South Africa, our education system has a huge focus on technology to develop digital and other related skills. Creative subjects like Art and Design are seen as a "nice to have" and therefore absent in most schools. These subjects are completely undervalued and not recognised as a necessity to help develop the "future-skills" I mentioned. Subjects like Woodwork that encourage learners to make, explore and experiment have been deemed unimportant, and therefore alternative makerspaces disappeared from the education agenda.

So, at Open Design we understand the importance of creating different "maker experiences", which is why our Family Makers Weekend is a core part of our festival programme. It not only creates a playful and fun learning environment for young and old, but these experiences also inspire and teach crucial skills and develop new knowledge. They stimulate and ignite a different mindset and a level of confidence in people to jump in, get their hands dirty, make and experiment. For innovators and entrepreneurs, this freedom to just "make" often unlocks new ideas and solutions. For us it's way more than just a one-off "makers" experience. It's also really important to understand that each experience have a powerful ripple effect and how it can add value and impact on people's lives beyond the event itself, might it be in a professional or personal capacity.

For this reason, Felix and the Maker Station has been an important partner of Open Design since our inception in 2013. It's a great way to integrate relevant technology as part of the creative and maker experience and thus also expose participants from marginalised communities to technology like stop-motion animation, augmented and virtual reality for the very first time. This is when the magic happens and new aspirations especially for the young is realised.

That gives you an overall idea of where and how the maker community fits into our space.

CK: What kinds of things in South Africa would have preceded your endeavours in the same area of development, accessibility and technology? Were there things like innovation centres?

FH: Yeah, there was one spinoff from the design school at CPUT (Cape Town University of Technology), the Cape Craft & Design Institute, now called the Cape Design Institute (CDI). Basically, they were set up to assist small-scale entrepreneurs in the development context with design, prototyping, business development, market access and machines, and they had the first fab lab. There were some other fab labs that popped up in the universities; most of them have died quite quickly.

SS: I have a question for Felix. I heard that the fab lab concept did not work at all in Cape Town, but it did survive a little bit longer in other provinces. Do you understand why that is?

FH: The fab lab came from quite a strict recipe. MIT had their Fab Lab model and from their context and point of view it was very technology-based, so it was very much lasercutter, mini CNCs, electronics orientated, a lot of PC software.

It's a little more engineering-, hackerspace-orientated, and I think that's why in Europe it's taken off so well. There are a lot of fab labs all over Afrika, but they all thrive in a university context. They're normally attached to an engineering department or in a hackerspace. They are very technology-, innovation-focused, in Kenya – Nairobi, in Ghana, they're very much in the hacker environment. And very successful, they do amazing innovations.

All those spaces that were more a makerspace environment, like CDI, their mission statement originally was to deal with the craft sector. And that was a very big mismatch. They ended up designing for the tool most of the time and not for the problem that the customer, the crafter off the street, needed. You ended up with everything from bead workers to weavers getting lasercut jigs to make their stuff.

There were a couple of makerspaces that popped up five or six years ago, when we started, there was one that was a year old and the other about two months old. There was one fab lab in Bloemfontein, and one in CPUT, the one at CDI, I know there was one in Namibia that closed down about a year ago now. I think there was one in Zimbabwe for a while. Someone's taken up that project of the fab lab in the meantime. So that's about technology centres and makerspaces. There's a bunch of hackerspaces and hacker groups, doing the classic work out of garages and meet-at-coffee-shops thing. If you tally all that up, there's probably about 20 spaces and get-togethers. At last count there's definitely five well-established makerspaces and there's one or two that is closed every other month or move buildings.

SS: If I could add my two cents, what I find interesting and why I think fab labs don't really work, especially in an Afrikan context, is that there's a very big division between the engineering side of things and the special qualities you find with hand-made products and craft. Afrika prides herself with a rich heritage of cultures, each coming with their own indigenous knowledge, systems, materials and well-designed and hand-crafted products. So I am actually not surprised that the Fab Lab concept did not initially take off because the environment itself was not creative and inviting enough for a broader audience. What really works well here at the Maker Station is that it is not a sterile fab lab environment. It's a messy and creative space, yet it also avails a variety of technology and tools to its members – the same you would traditionally find in a fab lab. It's the combination that works really well that also appeals to a broader client base. In this way they manage to get a diverse group of people and expertise to work in the same space.

It's no surprise that people love working at the Maker Station to build their mutant vehicles and sculptures for AfrikaBurn, for instance. It's a space that not only boosts your own creativity, but you are also surrounded by people with diverse skillsets to assist or bounce off ideas and at the same time you also have access to a variety of tools and technology you might potentially need. The Maker Station creates a melting pot where art, design, craft, engineering and technology can thrive. I think that's why Felix's space is so different.

YB: That means a makerspace oriented to art, design, artisans and education works better in the Afrikan context?

FH: Per capita Afrika has very few makerspaces. Maybe half of the countries have one makerspace, per country. A few places like Ghana, Nigeria, Tanzania – like South Africa, they have a couple, but they are few and far between. Egypt has got a couple hackerspaces and makerspaces, but they're quite thinly spread. I think it's back to the demographics: the need is huge, and the makerspace as a tool – to *do* things – is great. That's why we also look at the education side of makerspaces, as the education space is much more of an equaliser. The outcomes that we need to achieve in an education space are a lot more universal, so when it comes to the whole problem of packaging the makerspace and creating access, it makes it an easier problem from a business, structural or product-offering point of view. Here at Maker Station, we originally had the ambition of being the McDonalds of makerspaces and roll out the solution to Afrika, and every new makerspace has those ideas, but the reality, the business point, is that there isn't the demographic to carry it, the interest, the disposable income or the education, never mind the awareness – those are the things that make it quite hard.

That's why our relationship with Open Design has been so strong, because of their education expertise in that project. That's where we see one could actually build a franchise or a model that is more universally scalable. Education systems across Afrika are very similar, the outcomes are set, the curriculums are very similar. And you have captured audiences all tiered for you at skill levels or access levels already. It makes much more sense to look at bringing in makers' tools. Especially when they basically wiped the slate clean when it comes to any of the artisanal subjects at school. Everything got tossed out. Woodwork, metal work, needlework, home economics, agriculture.

SS: Felix and I have been friends for many years – too many to really remember how and where we originally connected, but because of our shared vision and passion for design and education, it's always been an easy and mutually supportive friendship. Lately we have been exchanging exciting ideas around his new dream, and that is to develop a Maker School for kids.

FH: The advantage of all the technology is that we suddenly have a huge push, a huge demand from the school sector. All the kids want, and all the parents want their kids, to be involved in technology, robotics and coding. Some schools are now building robotics labs, art centres and makerspaces as facilities to put on their prospectus. And that's what we've been saying for years should happen.

CK: Do you see this phenomenon related to past initiatives that I'm sure were happening in the 1980s and 1990s regarding the digital divide, access to technology, access to the Internet, access to different kinds of communication technologies, in southern Afrika then?

FH: Yeah, definitely. Back in the 1980s and 1990s, what typically happened was that every school put up a computer lab, and it was the rage to have Internet cafes and computer labs in school. Everybody had to have one. They put them all up and then there was normally no backup support, no teacher training, curriculum, nothing. So you ended up with these dusty, dead computer labs sitting at every second school. That has all settled down and now everybody's using all the tech, and there are more advanced schools using all the latest, greatest digital whiteboards and educational technologies. But I think now, with the new wave of robotics and 3D printing, that is like the new computer lab of the 1980s. It worries me a bit, how every second school is now needing a 3D printer and a makerspace. But like Suné said, there's this huge gap. It's like we lost twenty-plus years of teachers who had any background in practical subjects or design or making of any sort. That's been cleaned out of our system. I think we're doing a second wave of technology now. Hopefully we can dissect it a bit, with what we're trying to do, and actually create capacity with teachers, curriculums and skills development, and get the schools to actually integrate these spaces and these technologies with the curriculum in the school. A lot of them are only putting up a makerspace because it's the new *it* thing. It's the strength or the negative thing that's happening. We get a lot of calls from schools that got donated equipment by overly enthusiastic parents and don't really have the capacity to deal with it, don't know what to do with it or how to use it. And we've even had a few schools put up facilities, but they completely disconnect with actually integrating it into the education they are offering, into the curriculum. They treat it as an extramural, the same as how a chess club, makerspace and rugby are things you can sign up for. They don't use it as *we* would like to see it, as a tool for education and vital skills development.

SS: I think what our country has been guilty of for many years is to not believe in our own abilities to develop our own appropriate and local solutions. Instead we rather scout the world for successful solutions, trends or education systems and use a cookie-cut approach without considering that the context it was originally designed for is vastly different from our own local context. Of course there is nothing wrong with learning from others and exploring different solutions and systems, but what is really crucial is to understand why and how to adopt and change it so that it is appropriate for our local context in order to have a successful execution with more sustainable results that is also beneficial and relevant for our own people. And we really need to start investing more in local talent and believe in the ability of our own people to come up with our own appropriate and relevant solutions.

Another concern is the *misinterpretation* of the Fourth Industrial Revolution. In the National Development Plan for South Africa the inclusion of the "Fourth Industrial Revolution" (4IR) *only* focuses on technology and the development of tech related skills. There is a vast difference between the 4IR and the ones that came before. What really sets the 4IR apart from the rest is the realisation that humans matter and that a symbiotic relationship between the machine and humans is key in order to reach and impact on a scale that has never been possible before. To make this future a reality, there needs to be equal investment in technology and tech skills, as well as in creativity in order to optimise the development of relevant human qualities and skills (future skills) – otherwise that symbiotic relationship will just stay an idea and we won't be able to press the reset button and design a just society where people, business and our environments can thrive in.

FH: It's basically saying that putting a robotics lab in a school is now as good as having the first rugby team in the province. We're in the same space as the 1980s–1990s computer romance with all the accessible tech now. The CDI making a mistake in understanding what they were getting out of the fab lab, ending up with a bunch of very glamorous, glitzy toys and then trying to work everything they did into that space. We literally had *years* of lasercut everything-you-can-imagine craft with a lasercut template and jig armature because they *had* to use the toys.

And 90 percent of their demographic weren't skilled up to use the equipment, half of them can't even read and write. You end up having this disconnect between the romance with the toys and the Fourth Industrial Revolution, and actual real implementation or real use, usefulness. There's a huge romance that the government and a lot of companies are exploiting. You can never throw the baby out with the bathwater, there is good in all these things, but I think at the moment it's very skewed. I already know of half a dozen schools that got a pile of 3D printers that are in the cupboard or the broom closet. In a day-to-day schooling environment, it's a useless piece of equipment, because they don't have any way to match the teacher and the equipment to curriculum outcomes. And at the end of the day, if a tool or facility doesn't fit in there, it will get relegated to the backburner because the teachers are all so overwhelmed, with thirty to forty kids to a class. That becomes really hard. I think in a couple of years we're going to have a bunch of 3D printer labs standing with dust covers on. And people with no skills, at the end of the day.

YB: Felix, are there connections to other makerspaces across South Africa and Afrika? What kind of exchange do you have with them?

FH: With the other makerspaces here, we've got a South African makerspace founders' network. We share and connect quite a lot with each other and bounce off each other, about business and management, but also about memberships, we share a lot of information. There are a couple of us who are also connected across Afrika, in a pan-Afrikan makerspace founders' network. We're looking at other ideas related with technology, the way things are going now, we're trying to see how we as Afrikans can turn the idea of a makerspace on its head. How can we hack what we've copied as best practice and had to tweak and change from Europe and America, what's happening there, and how can we hack it to suit this market? Because there are obviously things that work, things that are needed. Running a commercial makerspace in Afrika is near impossible. And in a lot of places there is also not support from government or from education. A lot of people survive off grants, donations, sponsorships from corporates and things like that.

One idea we're looking at is a dispersed makerspace, a space where we can use all kinds of digital platforms to connect what we think the three things are that make a makerspace – the people, workspace and access to equipment. Access to people that know stuff is probably the most important thing that people take away from the makerspace. The fraternity is probably 50 percent, and then 25 percent is access to somewhere to work and 25 percent access to tools that they need to share, like a laser cutter. We work quite hard as a makerspace to build those networks of makerspaces. We treat all our suppliers as networks of makers and manufacturers as an extension of our space. We deal with all our members in that way as well. If there is something that is not available, we have a network of spaces and places and people, that idea of a dispersed makerspace. Somewhere down the line we almost would like to be without a building, being able to adjust to being a more virtual makerspace. Sometimes the resources are there, but the users are so thinly spread you can't justify a physical space. But you can still connect the resource and the maker, even if it's by some other platform or system then you still have the same effect. So, we try and think in those ways as well.

CK: Do you think that is that one direction that the South African maker scene is going? Localising production?

FH: Because I'm coming out of the development world and specialised in rural areas, I've worked all over southern Afrika, in very deep rural areas, so I've got a bit of a bias to decentralise stuff and create accessibility. When all the makerspace founders sit around a table, there's the "McDonald's" guys, and then everyone in the spectrum, and I'm probably far left when it comes to democratising the makerspace idea. Also, a lot of the makerspaces run dual businesses. They either run a laser cutting business and a makerspace or an engineering workshop, and a makerspace to subsidise, especially if they don't have a lot of outside funding. So sometimes it's hard to divorce the ideas of running the business and providing the service. To our own detriment, we spend a lot of time trying to do good rather than trying to do business. The reality is, there is a huge opportunity and a huge need, for whatever makerspaces can bring in a development situation. But to make it sustainable is a big problem. That's partly why we started looking at makerspaces and trying to figure out how one could make them available in a business-like way, where you actually make it sustainable or self-sustain. Technically our space won't work, we realised, anywhere outside our little cocooned western environment in the CBD (Central Business District), heavily laden with artists and artisans and crafters and designers, here where we are.

CK: Is that why the "maker" label also works for you? I was wondering if there has been any regional resistance to Make as a brand, Maker, Fab Lab, and Maker Faire, coming from the United States.

FH: It took a couple of years for people to associate because it wasn't a strong concept, the maker idea, the maker movement. We were very familiar with artists and crafters. That was pretty much the general terminology, you were either an artist or a crafter and maybe if you had a little bit of education you might know about design. But we didn't bundle all those disciplines under making. It took a while. We were also the founders of the Cape Town design network that eventually got the Cape Town Design Capital going and then spun off a bunch of things like Open Design. All that terminology, makers and maker movement, now it's a little more known and commonly used. I think there really was a direct connection with Make Media and Maker Faires that way.

SS: Don't you think, it's probably the same in other countries? Even still today people are looking down at crafters. They acknowledge them with less importance. People have a lot more respect for designers. So even in that context I don't think people value crafters and artisans, in the same way they do makers. Felix is obviously, because of his work, keeping a keen eye on the maker movement and Maker Faires. Unfortunately, I think "making", or being called a maker or referring to an actual makerspace carries more credibility than being called a crafter because of the link with technology and the related perception people have. The crafters are simply perceived as people who make things by hand and not really valued for their skills, knowledge and expertise. Even though master basket-weavers and beaders from South Africa and Afrika are great examples of people with valuable indigenous knowledge, they are more acknowledged and famous for their craft and expertise internationally than locally. This is very sad because instead of us celebrating our own masters on an international stage, we are not even familiar with their names or their work locally. Don't you think again it's the maker movement's connection with technology that fuels this perception?

FH: Most of the community out there are very detached from technology or even access to education. Ninety per cent of people in Afrika or South Africa won't know what a hackerspace is, unless maybe they're millennials. Even the term makerspace, almost every day we have to explain, it's pretty much a shared workshop. That's the default explanation. Shared tools and workspace, that's what a makerspace is and we're all makers. It's not as strong a brand or name as it is in the States.

The other thing that is quite different from Europe and the States is that when we talk about crafters, we have definite layers or strata of crafters. We've got huge numbers of people that are in craft. When I was in the development world, we used to call them masters of a product, not masters of a craft. A typical European craftsman would become a master weaver or strive to becoming a master woodcarver. Because craft is a low barrier of entry industry, a lot of people here use it to make a subsistence living. They literally pick up just enough skills to make one version of a product, like a soapstone turtle or a wooden giraffe or a beaded lizard. If you then go ask that guy to make a beaded crocodile, it doesn't work. They can make that one product, or one or two products really well, and they literally just do it for subsistence; they're not a passionate true artist in that sense. If that person literally got a cleaning job the next day for ten cents an hour more, there's no loyalty to the trade, they'll switch immediately. The motivation for ninety percent of people being in craft is subsisting or supplementing their income, compared to someone who actually does craft or making as a proper career, as a master crafter or does it as a hobby.

When we worked in rural areas, it took us a long time to get NGOs and funders from overseas to understand that. The other term we coined was a multi-income survival strategy. There the economics runs around the household. So you have half a dozen people bringing income into the household, it'll be the chickens, the sheep, the seasonal maize, it'll be the granny knitting jerseys for the school, the dad on the mine sending money, pension from grandpa, somebody making beads. And that also changes what and when and how people do stuff, and what they are prepared to do, to access makerspaces for their craft. They'll make as many beaded lizards as they need to for the week and sell them on the highway for a bit of cash. Their motivation for dabbling in making is completely different. And if a crop needs to come in, all production stops. That's really hard then for those people to plug into a normal economic world, like a retail buyer coming in to buy a thousand lizards a week scenario. That all bounces back to makerspaces and what role we have in that environment. It's very different to the role that we have with the fifteen art studios and sculptors in our area, dedicated artists that sculpt and create 24 hours a day and will access the resources they need when they need no matter *what*. And there are the exceptions, the master basket-weavers in the Okavango Delta, or the master woodcarvers in the Koffie bay Forest. It creates a lot more layers, but the rule of thumb is that a lot of the people, the majority, per capita, is in it for subsistence. Which plays havoc with what *we* try to do.

CK: So, being some kind of free intersection space, also educationally, with access to equipment where you bridge art and technology, would offer more people more options and more resilience in their livelihood?

FH: Yes. At the beginning, as a makerspace we made a list of things that we *do* and a *long* list of things that we *don't*. Because of where we are: when we started here, within a three-kilometre radius of us, I counted about thirty-two design-related training institutions, the design schools, colleges, private design schools, music schools, film schools, and all that. That's also the reason we picked this suburb. One thing on our list of things that we *don't* do is training: we don't put ourselves up as a training facility. We very much stick to our three services: space, tools and expertise. That doesn't mean that training doesn't happen. People come and run workshops. We do run workshops, training by osmosis.

Because we took on the mindset of the dispersed makerspace, so as not to be competing with our partners or extended facilities, we do not offer any accredited training, we do not offer design services, we do not offer any fabrication. It doesn't mean you can't come to a member and ask them to fabricate or teach you something. On the teaching side, that's also where we didn't sit at the same table with I2P Lab when they came. As a university, they've got a training outlook on everything. They wanted to give us piles and piles of 3D printers and they had visions of a lecture theatre, lots of students pouring in here. And we had to tell them that's not what we're about. Training is not our core function. We don't teach in that sense.

SS: Then you also have your other business, right? Flat Rock Studio where you as a designer can really exercise your own creativity, design products and get creative with innovative solutions.

FH: Because we also run our own studio out of the space, we're the anchor tenant. In a way, that's also the reason we can sustain it, and probably about two-thirds or now half of our total floor space is tenants or members that book cubicles and studios. From our studio's point of view, we treat them also as sort of extension of our studio, which allows us to do all kinds of exotic projects. We would have done wood furniture and foundry work, but now we do everything from road markings to film props, because there's somebody in the family that we can count on. But because of the type of space we've got, it's more like an art studio than a lab.

SS: Yes, it's indeed a great creative and messy space that connects many different disciplines of making!

FH: (laughs) And it makes it more accessible. We do have a bunch of crafters. There's a couple of people that would typically book a couple of hours in the workshop on a Thursday, to make stuff for their markets on a Saturday, and just pop in for an odd tool, so on the craft survival, subsistence crafter level, we've got those guys. And then on the other end of the spectrum, we have meet-ups, tech start-ups that use the space as well. And everything in-between. We try and be more accessible and multidisciplinary for many reasons.

YB: Because you brought up craft and mentioned Indigenous local practices, the master weavers and their tradition of crafting, are there any idiosyncratic, typical South African design, craft, making traditions that are shaping overall South African design and innovation today? Something that would have been brought from the past into what's going on now, in this kind of culture?

SS: Because we have a melting pot of cultures which presents us with an incredible, vibrant canvas of endless inspiration, I think South African design is more recognised for its eclectic, brave and bold qualities – there is a vibrant energy about South African design that appeals to a diverse audience. But if I have to highlight one South African designer that very successfully integrated indigenous knowledge in a modern and appropriate way, then it will be one of our iconic designers called Laduma Ngxokolo, the founder of the internationally known brand MAXHOSA.[3] In my opinion he is a great and very inspirational example of integrating local craft and local materials (in this case mohair – South Africa is the second biggest exporter of raw mohair) while at the same time celebrating his cultural heritage and customs with a modern twist, which makes his products very unique and therefore desirable beyond its own cultural relevance. Being born into the Xhosa culture, Laduma was inspired by his desire to design suitable knitwear for "amakrwala"[4] (i.e., an initiation ritual). As someone who has already undergone this initiation process, Laduma had a great understanding of this market and successfully launched his first range of premium knitwear that celebrates traditional Xhosa aesthetics. And the rest is history! His bold and vibrant designs and authentic approach quickly elevated him to international fame and today he works with international brands like Ikea to develop modern yet authentic and vibrant Afrikan products.

South Africa is very rich in Indigenous knowledge, but I don't believe we are creating enough noise around its uniqueness and we don't make enough effort to celebrate local role models like Laduma to develop local pride and to inspire our young designers to celebrate and preserve their unique heritage.

FH: There is also now the new crafts, like craft made out of recycled materials. There are tribe-specific things, like patterns and meanings, that you can recognise. There are nodes of basket-weaving, and nodes of woodcarving, and nodes of stone

---

3 MAXHOSA is a South African knitwear brand that was founded in 2012.
4 As part of the Xhosa tradition, boys have to participate in an initiation school when they come of age before they emerge as men and return back to society.

carving. If you go to Zimbabwe and the north-eastern parts of South Africa, stone carving and woodcarving is big. There's also a lot of cultural movement around southern Afrika, so there's a lot of trading. And now that people are so much more mobile, much has blurred quite a lot. Eight or ten years ago I was working in Swaziland on a project, and we tried to track certain basket patterns and basket making techniques. We could, for instance, plot a certain basket pattern and weaving technique all the way through Mozambique to Madagascar and all the way up almost to India. And in some places there was a typical palm-frond weave, which is not the same weave that you use with grass. Then in areas like in Swaziland, where there's not a lot of palms, as you would have in Mozambique or Madagascar, they switched to plastic packaging materials and still had the same weaves. So it's very hard to say that there's a specific craft technique or culture that has now percolated into design. There's a lot of fluidity, horizontally, culturally. And sometimes also it has to do with the resources. A lot of these things are now percolating into design and makerspaces, like everywhere in the world.

There are also natural patterns that form out of the weaving process, out of basket-weaving, which is a universal cultural practice. Patterns come through crafts into design and making, and even via the new crafts with waste materials. There are a couple of designers, people who have moved from subsistence craft, or waste-material craft, and are now moving to the professional design world. So it's hard to give a specific answer, but it seems a very fluid and very nice space. Very rich.

SS: There are of course a number of South African designers who don't just design products for the sake of, for instance, designing another chair. Yes, of course they creatively respond to the very rich and eclectic canvas around them, but they are also conscious that there are more pressing issues that need our attention like the high rate of unemployment and lack of opportunities for skills development in order for many more to make a decent living and restore their dignity. A great designer and maker will consider much more than their own desire to design another chair. They will also consider how their work can create opportunities to transfer skills and to increase employment – so the design process and outcome is also influenced by this collective effort that not only delivers another product, but also has a social impact, create significance and meaning and improve lives. I think there is something very special and unique in the way these designers work – and a quality and depth that is very difficult to mimic for instance in a first world context. For us it's all about how we design to include, how we design for change and how we design so that more than an exclusive few can benefit and prosper.

CK: And maker culture can contribute to this increased accessibility?

SS: Yes, for sure, as the maker and creative culture will contribute to the development of much needed skills and qualities in people which in itself opens new doors and creates accessibility to new opportunities for them to actively participate and contribute to the dynamic future that's ahead. I believe that COVID-19 is certainly amplifying the scale of change that's needed in this world. We are globally faced with the harsh reality that we have to change our ways. The current situation is presenting us with a once-in-a-lifetime opportunity to wipe the slate clean, press the reset button and design a different world, a just society and sustainable environments that create equal opportunities for anyone to thrive in. And this change needs to happen on all levels – it's a new value chain and ecosystem that needs to be designed and the first pillar of this design brief is to start with education, as this will have a ripple effect on the type of society, business, environments and governments that develop in the future. Going back to business as usual is not an option. But as mentioned before, there is a lot of work to be done and the clock is ticking.

This is why we will continue our work and advocacy for creativity and the makers community, as it can greatly contribute to the development of this new world. And we will continue to explore alternative ways to use the Open Design Afrika platform to create accessible opportunities so that we can democratise new knowledge, technology and experiences and make our contribution towards igniting new mindsets, change of behaviour and help to develop new aspirations, trust and pride in what we as South Africans and Afrikans deliver. Of course, the current pandemic is also forcing us to relook and evaluate our own value, so at the moment it is difficult to foresee what the immediate future of Open Design Afrika will look like.

CK: We live in uncertain times at the moment.

SS: Very much so. But we'll survive. We'll get through it. And this again creates new opportunities, right?

CK: That's for sure. Thank you for introducing us into the histories and the originality of South Afrikan craft, design and making. We really appreciate your time.

SS, FH: Thank you for involving us.

The Exhibition of People's Technology, 1972

Peter Harper in Conversation with Simon Sadler

At the periphery of the landmark June 1972 United Nations Conference on the Human Environment (UNCHE) in Stockholm, in the Skeppsholmen Annexe of the Moderna Museet, the Exhibition of People's Technology proposed that environmental crises could be addressed through the low-tech solutions of alternative technology. Alternative Technology (AT) was a term in use since the eponymous conference at the Bartlett School of Architecture the previous February. It was a de-industrialising movement which extolled the small-scale, decentralised, labour-intensive, energy-efficient, environmentally sound and locally controlled. One of a number of UNCHE fringe events sponsored by the Swedish "PowWow" group, the Exhibition of People's Technology was organised by the UK editors of a new magazine *Undercurrents: The Journal of Radical Science and People's Technology*, launched that same year.[1] In 1976, its founder Godfrey Boyle coedited a major and widely read survey of alternative technology, *Radical Technology*, with Peter Harper, to whom the term "alternative technology" is attributed (Boyle/Harper 1976). Harper, a student of biology and experimental psychology, was a key organiser of the Exhibition of People's Technology and in 1983 joined the pivotal Centre for Alternative Technology (CAT) in Wales, of which he had been a frequent visitor and occasional teacher since 1974.[2]

This article begins with Harper's recollections of the exhibition and then moves to a record and discussion by Harper of its contents. It concludes with a more free-ranging conversation between Harper and design historian Simon Sadler about the exhibition's philosophical and scientific context and implications, transcribed by Iris Xie.

---

1   *Undercurrents* was published for the next 12 years (when it was merged into *Resurgence*). On the events around the 1972 Stockholm conference, see Chapters 3 and 4 in Scott (2016).

2   Harper remarks: "As everybody else said, 'I didn't mean to stay'". He was there for 30 years.

Peter Harper's Recollections

I had many friends in Sweden, having been visiting since 1967.

The UN Conference on the Human Environment (UNCHE) was the first major recognition of the significance of the global environment and a Great Event.[3] Naturally every young environmentalist and her dog wanted to be there, and I was no exception. I took part in a series of meetings in Scandinavia earlier in 1972 to plan various fringe activities.

My friend Björn Eriksson, an engineer, knew Pär Stolpe, an official of the Modern Art Museum in Stockholm, who was in charge of the "Filialen" or Annexe of the Museum of Modern Art on the island of Skeppsholmen, walking distance from the city centre. Stolpe saw the function of the Filialen as experimental, to address cutting-edge topics, and he wanted to do something related to the theme of the UN conference. Björn and I conceived the idea of an exhibition of "alternative technology", although in Swedish it was called "För en Teknik i Folkets Tjänst" which translates as "towards a technology to serve the people" (For a Technology in the Service of the People 1972).

In the months before, Björn and I drew up plans for what we would like to display and started to collect materials. We had no money or institutional resources to draw on, so we "begged, borrowed and stole", leaning on friends and acquaintances and our own research and imaginations. Even so, the exhibition was a bit thin when we started, and we decided it just had to be a "work in progress" that would gradually bootstrap itself into something tangible by the end. This was very much in the grain of the age and in the improvisatory spirit of the subject-matter.

I arrived in Stockholm with my colleague Chris Ryan[4] (Figure 3) and our partners Lyn Gambles and Barbara Hammond. Together with Björn, the architect Varis Bokalders[5] and many other local contributors, we started to assemble pieces of equipment, models and explanatory texts. People would drop in from absolutely

---

3   It led to the setting up of the permanent UN Environment Programme in Nairobi and was followed by further important conferences in Rio 1992 (when the United Nations Framework Convention on Climate Change, UNFCCC, and the Convention on Biodiversity were signed by almost all major governments) and in Johannesburg 2002.

4   Chris Ryan was a physicist who moved into design and town planning, eventually becoming Professor of Design at the University of Melbourne, with visiting posts in Sweden, Italy and the Netherlands. He was a founder of the alternative technology demonstration centre "Ceres" in Melbourne in 1975, a cousin, as it were, of the Centre for Alternative Technology in Wales (see Figure 3).

5   Varis became a distinguished architect and the author of many books including the magisterial *Byggekologi*, translated into English as *The Whole Building Handbook* (Block/Bokalders 2010).

anywhere and spend a few days with us. I remember Godfrey Boyle[6] arrived with some other members of the *Undercurrents* team, and set up floating inflatables around the island, allowing us to "walk on water" (see Figure 6). Richard Coon drove from London on his propane-powered motorbike – which was itself intermittently on display.

The eventual layout was something like the plan shown below (Figure 1), with "exhibits" around the outside and space in the middle for discussions, chatting and for visitors to make their own contributions. There was a landscape model of a traditional village that you could visit at full scale just across the bay in Skansen. Unfortunately, very few photographs have come to light, except some embarrassing images of myself with the ubiquitous and infinitely hirsute "1970 eco-face".

Figure 1: Exhibition layout, Exhibition of People's Technology.

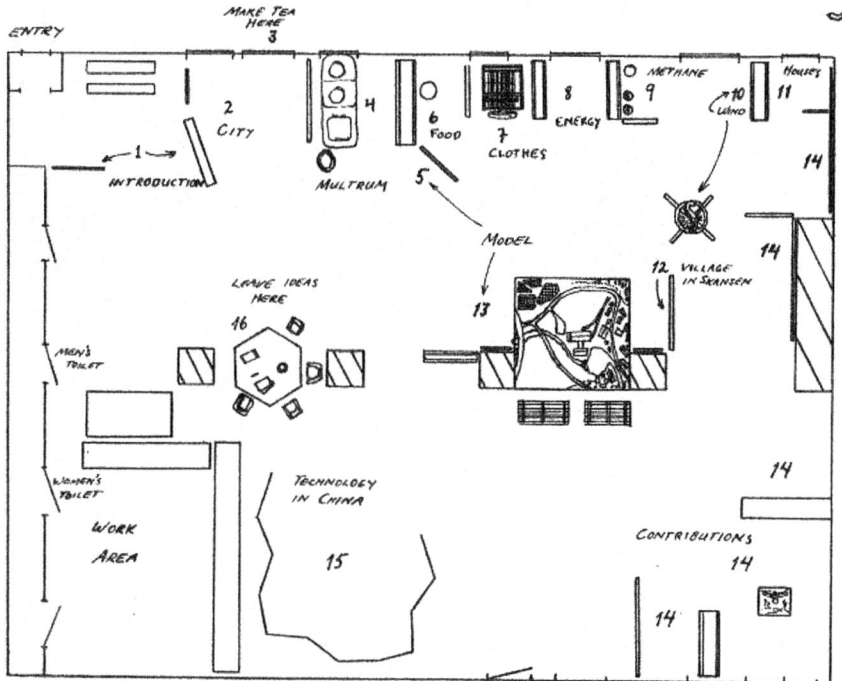

We were there all the time of course, and visitors could see everything being assembled, written, argued over, pasted up and (often) hastily modified. But it meant that we got to engage with them and often enough they stayed to help.

---

6   Godfrey Boyle founded the alternative science magazine *Undercurrents* in 1971 and co-edited *Radical Technology* (Boyle/Harper 1976). He later became Professor of Alternative Energy at the UK's Open University. Sadly, he died in July 2019.

The image in Figure 2 tells something of the place and the process. Yes, that is the younger me with the 1970 eco-face. I am obviously showing something to two young women, who perhaps just dropped in to see what was going on. The floor is tiled, and the walls are bare, but there are semi-circular alcoves. There is a blank display board in the background. It was severe but functional and we liked being there.

Often, we would work till very late and then just curl up in sleeping bags on the floor, to start again the next morning.

Figure 2: Peter Harper, left, working on the Exhibition of People's Technology, Moderna Museet, Stockholm, in 1972, with unknown. Photograph: Björn Gustafsson.

Figure 3: Peter Harper (right) and Chris Ryan preparing for the "Olympics of Pollution", a street-theatre event organised by PowWow during UNCHE. Photograph: Björn Gustafsson.

Before the exhibition, there were around two dozen separate ideas for exhibits, grouped into functional categories (food, transport, etc.). Most of these were based on already existing projects, many of an experimental nature, or on tangible pieces of equipment. The idea was that in each case we would have something to show, photographs, plans, objects and possibly results. It did not always work out so neatly, but it is surprising how "realistic" and prescient some of our choices were (see Figure 4).

As a broad generalisation, our greatest mistakes were about scale. Lots of the principles are sound, but they only become worthwhile on a large enough scale,

Figure 4: Sample of the exhibition proposal, an unpublished mimeograph sheet available to visitors. Printing and photocopying were very expensive at the time, and the mimeograph process (also called cyclostyling, roneoing, gestetnering, depending on model) was the default method of reproducing text, or even line-drawings, as shown in Figure 1.

ALTERNATIVE TECHNOLOGIES EXHIBITION
People's Forum - Alternative Technology Group
Details of exhibition projects

Incroduction

The selection of projects for the exhibition is meant to sample various species of the genus Alternative Technology. Perhaps "alternative" is not a very good generic name to use, but it is the only one vague enough to cover the wild zoo of gadgets, materials, processes, skills, principles and philosophies that we feel to be groping in roughly the right direction. Some of the diverse trends can be discerned from other names that have been used:

    New Alchemy
    Soft Technology
    Counter-Technology
    People's Technology
    Ecologically-based Technology
    Biotechnics
    Natural Technology
    Utopian Technology
    Independent Technology
    Self-Help Technology
    Radical Hardware
    Appropriate Technology
    Intermediate Technology
    Living Technology
    Community Technology   ...etc

Each of this has a different goal as its primary focus, variously emphasising, for example:

    Workers' control
    Resource conservation
    Low specialisation
    Reform of work-roles
    Environmental quality
    Local self-sufficiency
    Recovery from industrial collapse
    Community cooperation
    Low energy use
    Subversive activity
    Independent economic development   ...etc

It is hard to claim that these add up to a coherent philosophy, but never mind. The intent of the exhibition is exploratory. The examples are deliberately picked to serve different ends and if they appear to contradict each other - or themselves, so be it. They range from the immediately practicable, through the somewhat revolutionary, to the frankly Utopian. And some are just for fun. Revolution? Yes! But start now. It is necessary for us to show what alternatives would be possible...if only they were possible. The purpose of the exhibition is to show both old and new ways of doing things which are liberating and non-exploiting, and "to celebrate our joint power to provide all human beings with the food, shelter and clothing they need to delight in living." (Ivan Illich).

and we had strong bias against mass scale, favouring instead small local communities and households. We assumed that small is *always* beautiful, but actually it is only *sometimes*. This mistake is still being made!

Here are the candidates, with comments.

FOOD

- Aquaculture-horticulture rotation system
- Indoor fish-culture unit
- Hydroponics

I have grouped these together because they demonstrate a willingness to accept quite complicated systems, provided they can yield well on a smallish scale. We had a strong belief that "self-sufficiency" – self-provision in food – was not only desirable, but could be readily achieved without too much labour, and on less than a "fair allocation" of land. In the UK of the time we had about 1 acre (0.44 ha) per head, but not all is good growing land, so that suggests systems that (a) use less land area and (b) are independent of the quality of the land. Hence these intensive "ponics" systems.[7]

The aquaculture systems were based on those pioneered and reported by the New Alchemy Institute in North and Central America. We simply took their word for it. But they never really worked, either for the New Alchemists or in attempts to copy them at the Centre for Alternative Technology (CAT) in Wales. Later, commercial "aquaponics" systems were more successful in recycling nutrients to optimise growth of both plants and fish, including crustaceans. But as far as I know, it has never been adopted as a community-scale food system and certainly not at the single-dwelling level, as the New Alchemists attempted to demonstrate in their "Ark" project on Prince Edward Island. It simply failed: the yields were far too low relative to the capital cost and maintenance effort.

Hydroponics (soil-less growing) using cheap mineral fertilisers is much more reliable and is now used at vast commercial scales to produce salad crops. In the early days of AT, the hope was that minerals could be replaced by waste products like wood ash and urine, or fish manure from aquaculture. Well, they can to some extent, but the system is too fiddly and capital-intensive for a household to maintain, and it only produces vegetables, not staples with starch, protein and fats.

Having said this, if you really *have* to do it and you have the right equipment and very large amounts of money, it can be done, as witness the Biosphere 2 project in Arizona. Eight "Biospherians" survived for two years on what they could grow on an area of about 300 m² a head, partly using data from the New Alchemy experiments. Remarkable, but dazzlingly expensive. (See Allen/Nelson/Alling 2003.)

---

7   The suffix '-ponics' (from the Greek for cultivation) was used by its inventor, William F. Gericke, to distinguish his strictly soil-less system from 'aquaculture' (Gericke 1937). Since then the suffix has been adopted for other systems such as 'aquaponics'. Hydroponics is growing plants without natural soil, using an inert solid medium such as gravel or sand, irrigated with a solution containing soluble plant nutrients.

- Three-dimensional agriculture in New Guinea

This was derived from the systematic research and quantities measured by the anthropologist Roy Rappaport (2000 [1967]). To the western eye, it does not look like agriculture, but yet it keeps its practitioners fed on a few hours' work a day. I think this was one of the inspirations behind Holmgren and Mollison's notion of "Permaculture" that first emerged around 1978 (Mollison/Holmgren 1978). They noted that in the tropics, western-style plough agriculture usually fails catastrophically, and much subtler, multi-layered plantings work better, using mostly perennial species. This idea has been widely imitated in temperate areas like the UK under the banner of Permaculture, but for the most part has performed poorly. Just as Western systems often fail in the tropics, so tropical systems tend to fail elsewhere. In fact, the New Guinea system is not very "efficient" in terms of land, so it does not lend itself to intensive self-sufficiency.

Having said this, the notion of "forest gardens" is now widespread in temperate areas and could encourage dispersed production of tree-crops including high oil- and protein-yielding items such as nuts. (The *locus classicus* is *Forest Gardening* by Robert Hart [1996].)

- Soy culture as a source of protein

This is strangely prescient, because now, many decades later, soya production is big business and causing substantial deforestation in the tropics. But this is largely used to provide high-protein feed for livestock, not people. The point of the Exhibit was to show that soya beans could be grown in temperate areas and provide their own nitrogen. They produce meat-equivalent protein on only one-tenth of the land used by (say) cattle, so are excellent for intensive production – and are a staple crop.

At the time, a temperate-adapted soybean variety had just been introduced, but it generally performed poorly, and it is almost certainly better to grow "genuine" temperate legumes, of which there are many kinds. They are easily available to householders and are being used as the basis for all manner of high-protein foods and meat substitutes, largely on grounds of low carbon emissions, an issue we were unaware of in 1972.

HOUSING

- Traditional building materials

The rationale given was that these had been displaced by "modern" materials for commercial reasons, which we regarded as distasteful. The displacement is indeed a market effect, because modern materials are much cheaper per unit of service: usually stronger, more durable, easier to apply and so on.

Having said this, we can now note that many modern high-performance materials also generate high carbon emissions, while "traditional" materials are much better. As a result, there is growing interest in using low-carbon natural materials such as wood and "engineered wood" such as glulam, plywood and oriented strand board.

There are also many modern buildings that use low-carbon materials (earth, wood, bamboo, stone, slate, straw and reed) for the bulk of the construction, plus a small proportion of "industrial vitamins"[8] (plastic membranes, steel ties, screws, glass, plumbing and wiring) that bring performance up to modern standards. The WISE Building at CAT in Wales is a good example. (Further examples can be found in *Vegetarian Architecture* [Bocco Guarneri 2020].)

I think many Swedish visitors had been attuned to our strange messages by the publication that year of Gösta Ehrensvärd's *Före-Efter* ("Before and After") (1972) which painted a picture of how life might be after the collapse of civilisation – widely discussed at the time.

- Non-western house forms

In the febrile 1970s, there was much criticism of the "nuclear family" and the dwellings produced to house it. If families could be non-nuclear, what patterns might be more suitable? These are reasonable questions, although subsequent experience suggests that the nuclear pattern is the overwhelmingly preferred form in modern societies.

Still, social experimentation continues, for instance in the form of co-housing and "ecovillages" (Gilman 1991), and these have engendered new patterns of physical layout to accommodate multi-generational communities while maintaining the "nuclear" unit to a large extent. These remain rational solutions to many modern problems.

The famous "autonomous terrace" (drawn by anarchist illustrator Clifford Harper, no relation) shown in *Radical Technology* (1976) suggested thoroughgoing collectivisation, but had a nuclearised equivalent in the re-purposed double terrace at Spencer Street in the British city of Milton Keynes (Figure 5).

- Construction materials using industrial waste

Well of course, who wouldn't want this? If source materials are cheap and can be made into something useful, what's not to like? Unfortunately, waste materials are often in the wrong form, in the wrong place, arising erratically and perhaps contaminated. And material inputs are usually only a small fraction of the total cost

---

8   Peter Harper introduced the phrase "industrial vitamins" to describe common practice at CAT, but the term was never published or carefully defined.

Figure 5: "Autonomous Terrace" illustration by Clifford Harper, Radical Technology *(Boyle/Harper 1976). Based on indicative sketches by Peter Harper.*

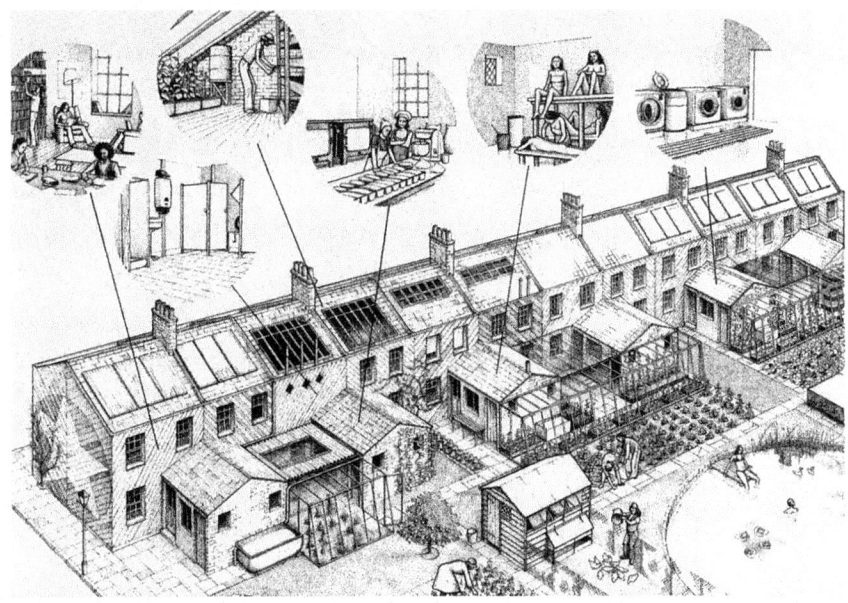

of a product, so the industries concerned usually prefer to get clean raw materials whenever they can.

Although the notion of "industrial ecology" became very fashionable, with the Danish city of Kalundborg as its poster-child, in practice it proved much more difficult and never became common practice.

From today's perspective, we relate this question to recycling of household waste, the "zero waste" movement and the so-called "circular economy". Great improvements have been made, but they are not driven by plain market forces: they require "ideological" intervention. As, perhaps, they did in 1972.

- Autonomous servicing

This was astonishingly fashionable in the early 1970s. It fitted our decentralised, self-sufficiency vision. Most of the technical ideas, however, came from a group at the University of Cambridge around the architect Alexander Pike, who looked down on us as mere "enthusiasts".[9] This academic group carefully analysed the relative costs of "autonomous" and "reticulated" (i.e. public) servicing and generally found

---

9   This tension between academic experts and activists is hard to avoid. These days, the boot is on the other foot, with a new generation of academics coming up with all manner of good-sounding ideas, only to be met with scornful criticism from previous generations who had "been there, done that" and been painfully disillusioned.

that public provision was much cheaper, used less stuff and was generally better all round. Subsequent analysis at the Centre for Alternative Technology (somewhat with gritted teeth) confirmed this.

"Rolling your own" can be very expensive. Robert and Brenda Vale were part of the Cambridge group and carried out a three-year joint PhD programme exploring self-sufficiency at a smallholding level. Subsequently asked whether self-sufficiency was actually possible, Robert replied, "Well, yes, almost – but you need to have a bloody good job to be able to afford all the equipment" (personal communication).

- Inflatables

These were not part of the original plan but turned up anyway in response to our call for "alternative structures". They were mainly play objects (as many have become in subsequent years) and visitors were invited to step inside zippered inflatables and "walk on water" just a few metres from the exhibition door (Figure 6).

Figure 6: Giant inflatable at the Exhibition of People's Technology. Photographer unknown.

POWER

- Wind power
- Basic principles of wind energy
- Fixed windmills

I have grouped these together because they were intended to introduce the general idea to exhibition visitors. Of course, everyone was aware that windmills were used in the past, but it was assumed wind was an old and rather feeble, erratic source of energy and not suitable for a modern economy.

Figure 7: A Gedser wind turbine.

As so often, we got the scales wrong. We really loved the old-style windmills and thought they could be repurposed to produce electricity. Of course they can, but at a ridiculous cost and to little effect, but we hated the idea of large commercially run industrial-scale turbines. However, at the exhibition we had a lovely foot-high model of the Danish Gedser-type wind turbine, that eventually led to the modern Danish (and thence, world) wind industry (see Figure 7). We thought this model was pretty cool, but we didn't sit down and work out the implications if wind were to be a serious contributor to grid electricity supply.

Now we understand. They cannot look traditional. They've got to be aerodynamically designed. They've got to be big. And there have to be thousands and thousands of them. But it is happening.

- Unorthodox wind-powered devices
  - Tree pump
  - Flying windmill

These illustrate very well the kind of approach we preferred and show how they might work, or not as the case may be. They were developed by the wind enthusiast David Stabb at the Architecture Association (Figure 8).

Figure 8: Wind device, designed by David Stabb. This was later redrawn by Derek Taylor and reprinted as "Natural, Endless, Free" in Radical Technology. *Photograph: Björn Gustafsson.*

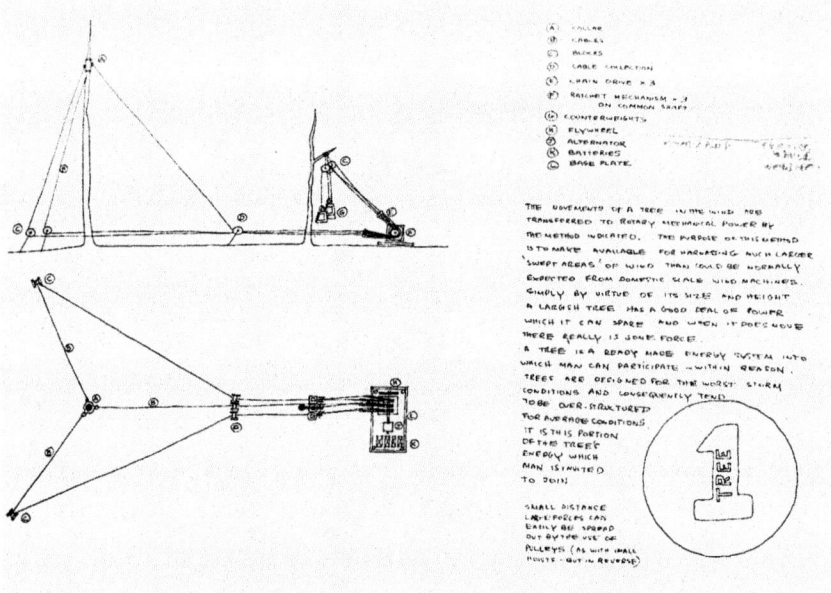

The tree pump is based on the idea that a tree has a large surface area and can sway substantially in a gusty wind. You just tie ropes to pulleys and run them to some kind of pumping mechanism that can fill a header tank or small reservoir when the wind blows. It could all be pretty low-tech and made by the local blacksmith.

I don't know anybody who's tried this seriously, but it could work. We did test it on trees outside the exhibition, using a 10-kg spring balance to measure the effect, and this impressed visitors on windy days. We too were impressed when we turned up one morning to find the spring balance ripped to pieces after a storm!

The Flying Windmill is based on the idea of kites, which clearly do fly and demonstrate that the wind is stronger the higher you go. This is quite impractical on a small scale, but has been seriously proposed for multi-megawatt machines a kilometre up, tethered by giant cables. It might yet happen.

- Direct sun power

The rationale for sun power was the same as wind. Carbon emissions were not an issue then, but we believed fossil fuels were limited and would run out, hence the fondness for renewables, which were in principle "free", and therefore (we thought) cheap. We did not grasp the extreme difference in energy density between sun/wind and fossil fuels and hence the need for very large machines to harvest renewable flows on an industrial scale.

We delighted in the simple thermosiphon solar collector. No moving parts. It could be made from readily available materials in an afternoon, set out in the sun, and behold! Hot water! Well, warm water. It always did *something*.

We thought the same principle – passive harvesting of high-energy radiation – could be used to operate an Electrolux-style vapour-absorption heat pump in order to harvest low-temperature heat. And so it can, in principle, but experience shows that the efficiency is low, and although there are no "moving parts" it is still a highly sophisticated assemblage of industrial components. It cannot be made by the village blacksmith. Might as well have a compressor and all the best kit. Today? Heat pumps can perform the alchemy of turning low-carbon electricity efficiently into heat and are destined for mass take-up.

Perhaps a better idea would have been "external combustion" heat engines such as the Stirling Engine, operating on solar heat. This does have moving parts, but can operate on just heat rather than a concentrated chemical fuel. Somebody brought along a model Stirling engine for the exhibition, and it was regarded as a kind of pet. It operated in complete silence. We thought it was bound be the Engine of the Future, but we are still waiting.

Such passive solar heat engines were a lemon. But of course solar water heating became much more sophisticated, industrialised, relatively cheap, and ubiquitous in sunny places. Even more important were solar photovoltaics, still ridiculously expensive in 1972 and somewhat off our radar. But nearly 50 years later, they are now cheaper than coal, deployed on a colossal scale, still improving, and competing with wind to power the world.

- Small-scale water-power

This has not changed as much as most other things. The rationale is still the same, and enthusiasts are finding all sorts of little local sources that could power a community. Still, they are marginal in the wider picture.

We thought you could have direct mechanical functions as well as electricity, as water mills did, but although agreeably low-tech, that turns out to be much less efficient. Better to generate electricity and use that flexibly for all other functions. Electricity is bound to be the energy lingua franca for the next hundred years.

- Methane from animal wastes

Well, we tried it at the exhibition. We had no idea what to do, but we had the notion that AT had to be simple, so we just got on with it. We'd seen the reports from India and China with quite small digestors, using animal dung, so we filled a cylindrical tank with cow manure and waited to see what would happen. Nothing. Well, a small increase in pressure that could be released as a smelly gas.

Nowadays, much more is known about how to digest animal and plant wastes efficiently, and the gas is mainly used to generate electricity for the grid. It is a sophisticated mainstream technology and part of the suite of systems for backing up the electricity system if supplies from the variable renewables are low. Once again, it's got to be big to be worthwhile.

- Storage of energy

As just remarked, electricity from sun and wind is variable and needs storable back-up. Biomass like animal manure and plant wastes can make methane or can be thermally converted like fossil fuels. Almost certainly it will be supplemented by hydrogen, which can be generated in times of electricity surplus – which you often get with wind. The exhibition plan mentions this, but I cannot remember that we actually demonstrated electrolysis of water, or that we mentioned anything more about energy storage.

- Flower power

I think this was just a joke.

TRANSPORT

- Methane-powered bus

Naturally we were against private cars and envisaged a world dominated by public transport. We knew that you could run vehicles on "CNG" or compressed natural gas, which is pure methane, but of course that was a fossil fuel, and we wanted to use biogenic methane.

It never happened in the exhibition, but sustainable transport has moved on and there are now electric-, hydrogen-, methanol- and bio-propanol-powered vehicles. We probably hate cars less but favour shared systems like car clubs, which we didn't think of at the time.

- Canals

Here we found the sheer retro-chic irresistible. Canals had been displaced by railways, then roads, and had not moved on. They were beautifully stuck in the early 19th century and operated with pre-industrial technology. They were consistent with the slower, steady-state world we envisaged. We thought they could be redeveloped to take much more tonnage of freight, and this is probably true, but could never compete with the vast tonnages currently charging around the planet on roads.

A nice try.

- Airships and balloons

Perhaps these are the aerial equivalent of canals. They recall a bygone age of the slow and steady. Steerable lighter-than-air craft emerge fairly regularly as useful adjuncts to the aviation industry, but never seem to, as it were, take off.

My sense of the process is that they await certain technical developments and a much higher fuel price, perhaps as a result of carbon taxes. If (as seems likely) it will no longer be possible to live on a rapid turnover, "just in time" basis, then they will greatly suit a slower pace of life. They will be back.

MEDICINE

- Malaria control

This might seem an odd item for an exhibition such as this. It is partly based on the understanding that pesticides could be terminally harmful. In one of the preparatory meetings, we had met the Iranian environmentalist M. Taghi Farvar,[10] who had worked with Barry Commoner on DDT in mother's milk in Guatemala (dichlorodiphenyltrichloroethane, an insecticide). He had produced a massive tome of cautionary tales entitled *The Careless Technology* (Farvar/Milton 1972), which convinced us that Nature was easily disturbed by artificial chemicals and other interventions. Which it is. But of course, we were searching for technologies that were *not* careless.

We were also seeing the beginnings of a "systems approach" to sustainability, understanding that there could be no simple "silver bullet" solutions, but much

---

10 Peter Harper subsequently worked with Taghi Farvar in Iran, continuing the spirit of the exhibition in the Faculty of Ecodevelopment of Avicenna University. The research and teaching programmes were summarily terminated after the Iranian revolution of 1979.

more subtle measures based on analysis of the relations between components. You cannot simply change one thing and imagine the rest of the system will not also change, often in unpredictable ways – as Commoner himself insisted.

The topic also draws on the obsession with China, where it was thought that, free from the shackles of capitalism and consumerism, they were more able to think, and act, outside the box. We were much taken with the idea of "barefoot doctors" dealing with a wide range of common medical problems, leaving highly trained specialists to take difficult cases. There seemed to be something romantic about it, like Médicins Sans Frontières. But of course this is simple market forces at work: we now have exactly the equivalent in the form of "paramedics".

- Acupuncture

This also relates to China, and we were confident that the Chinese would not embrace anything that was simply a superstition. It seemed an excellent system because it involved whole-body understanding, without drugs, persuading the body to heal itself by redressing imbalances. Another attraction was that, because the so-called acupuncture meridians could not be found anatomically, it suggested a radical incompleteness in received western medicine, and indeed western science altogether. It hinted at the possibility of a subtle "other world" beyond materiality that could possibly be the basis of radically alternative way of proceeding.[11]

TEXTILES AND CLOTHING

- Handloom

This was a straightforward ancient technology, entirely transparent in terms of its structure and operation, and we had one on display. For native English speakers, the Swedish name *vävstol* ("weaving-chair") was charmingly literal. Of course you can produce real cloth on such a device, and you can make up clothes and wear them, but the time taken is far more than most people would tolerate and it is not surprising that we now rely on mechanised looms that produce cloth at a hundred times the rate.

This of course is true throughout the economy, and productivity is perhaps the principal difference between traditional and modern societies. It was a critical misunderstanding of ours, that we tended to think mechanised industrial production was only *somewhat* more productive than the "old ways", perhaps 50 percent better, perhaps even 100 percent, but not enough to justify all the downsides. The reality of course is that it is 1000 percent, even 10,000 percent more productive: that makes a big difference and allows us the leisure to play with hand looms if we wish.

It is striking that the celebrated Arts and Crafts movement promoted by William Morris and others praised the production and use of handmade useful

---

11   See, for example, "Inner Technologies" in *Radical Technology* (Boyle/Harper 1976).

objects, in contrast to the tawdry industrial products of their day. In the exhibition, we applauded too, without realising that only the wealthy could afford this kind of thing. Today perhaps we have come to appreciate the contribution of the Bauhaus and even IKEA in providing well-functioning, stylish products at reasonable cost.

WASTE DISPOSAL

- Clivus Multrum composting toilet

This is famous in Sweden as a common item in country houses without sewerage connections, invented by the engineer Rikard Lindström. It is very large and an impressive item in the exhibition (but was not in actual use!). Its attraction for us was that it does not require or pollute water, but turns a potentially pathogenic waste into valuable fertiliser. It has no moving parts and operates passively by gravity and small differences in temperature. This was just the kind of self-acting non-industrial alchemy we were looking for.

Composting toilets seemed such a simple no-brainer that we assumed they would soon take over everywhere (Harper/Halestrap 1999). This was not be, and they remain on the fringes, although a significant presence in remote fishing clubs, allotments and country parks. People everywhere seem to prefer the "porcelain standard" and are prepared to pay for the network of sewers and treatment plants then required. (See also Figure 9.)

Rikard Lindström's son Carl came to visit during the course of the exhibition. As his father had become a bit of a hero, we were very pleased to meet him.

Figure 9: An exhibit about the accumulation of non-degradable waste around the world. This continued to be a problem and is now considered a very serious concern. Photograph: Björn Gustafsson.

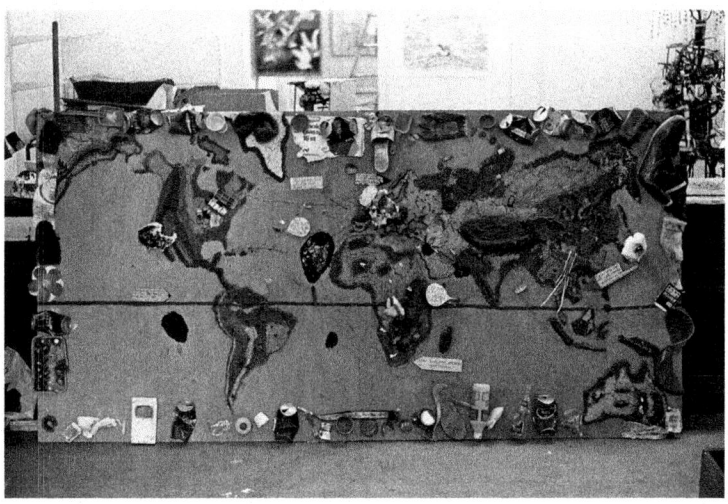

COMMUNITIES

- Biotechnic housing estate

This was not much more than a student exercise, but it was based on all the latest AT lore and had lovely illustrations. It was more or less a large greenhouse with livestock, hydroponics, solar heating and water-power. It was entirely fantastical but pressed all our buttons and looked gorgeous. Sadly, the drawings are lost, except for a much-reduced sample in *Radical Technology* (Figure 10).

- Chinese village technology

We knew nothing about China but we were suckers for the propaganda and the travellers' tales. They seemed to have all the right ideas, relying on local resources in a spirit of mutual self-help. They also had inspiring slogans, many of which we adopted, such as "The Taming Power of the Small".

It is my impression that the founders of the Chinese Communist Party, and particularly Mao Zhedong himself, shared many of our pro-rural, anti-consumerist, anti-technological tastes, and that is perhaps why we were so drawn to the stories that emerged. Later of course, China embraced the opposite of all this, and it was quite clear which path the people preferred.

Perhaps the most striking visual commentary on Chinese self-reliance was provided by Varis Bokalders, a Swedish architect and planner who contributed a great deal to the exhibition. In the early 2000s, he was invited to submit plans for a Chinese town, which would provide enough land to provide its own food and process its own waste. Having done the calculations, the allocation of areas was roughly as follows:

Living areas, circulation, transport	15%
Food production areas	35%
Waste treatment areas	40%

The waste treatment areas (mostly wetlands) can also contribute hugely to biodiversity and ecosystem services, but the proportions still come as a surprise.

- Alternative technology research community

This was supposed to combine the full, all-singing, all-dancing alternative dream: communal living, rural life, self-sufficiency, renewable energy, closed-loop recycling, zero waste and novel uses of traditional materials. It was supposed to record its results and make them known for others to follow – or avoid. An illustration for some of the proposals is shown below. It is worth comparing the implied areas with the results of Varis Bokalders' study above: this is the difference between naïve theory and practical experience.

Figure 10: Clifford Harper, Alternative technology research community. This drawing was displayed in the exhibition and subsequently reproduced in Radical Technology.

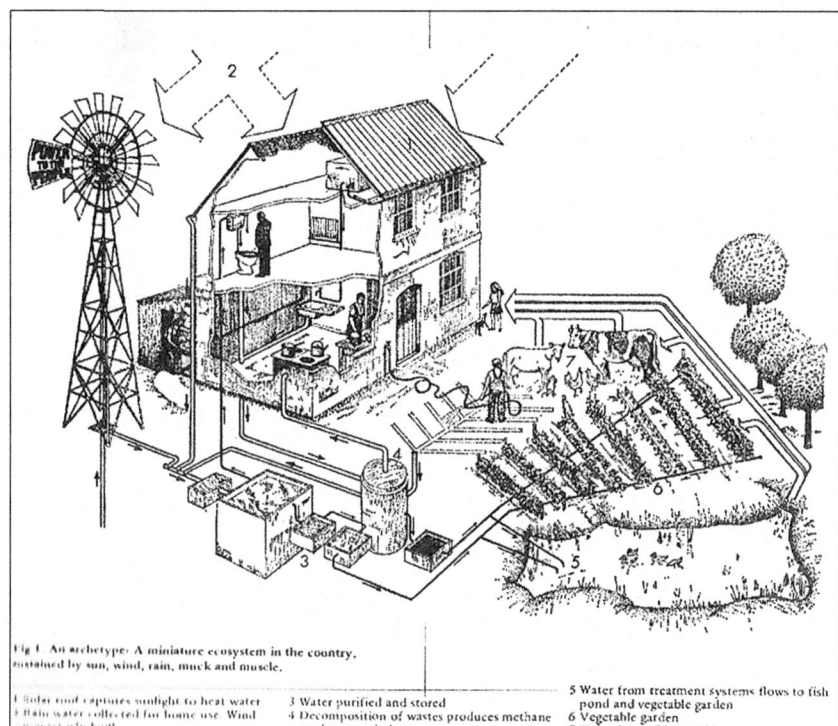

This project did not in the end materialise, but another did: the Centre for Alternative Technology in Wales, founded in 1974 under the influence of the same ideas, which continues to exist 45 years later.

A Conversation Between Peter Harper and Simon Sadler about The Exhibition of People's Technology

SS: The talisman of the current "Maker" might be somebody in Silicon Valley prototyping some new gizmo, which they would take to a TED talk, and then get angel investors, and the idea is that while making a profit, that gizmo will lead to a greater future, led out by somebody with a degree from MIT. And what I think this special issue of the journal *Digital Culture & Society* is trying to do is to go back into history and ask: does that really exemplify what making is about, or was about? And is there a possibility of re-writing history, in a way that makes us think more laterally about what the so-called Maker Movement is about? And I think that is where they landed on you. Because appropriate technology, Alternative Technology, radical technology, is and was about making, and it was a type of grassroots activity. It would have led to a different sort of future, in which we would think about the relationship between technology and society differently.

PH: Sometimes an idea I have now is actually the same as one I had long ago, but have forgotten. Sometimes I look back at my old notebooks – I've got notebooks going right back to that period – and it's astonishing, I'd forgotten I even thought that! But one of the big things that we were interested in was whether you would use technological developments to *maintain* existing functionality, but *reduce* the impact on the environment, or other externalities of various kinds. It's the opposite of what actually tends to happen: "let's take an acceptable level of damage and use the advancement of technology to increase the functionality, making it faster or better or bigger". You've always got that choice, what are you going to do with your new technology, your innovation? On the whole, what's happened is that everyone has run off with the extra functionality, while the environment can just look after itself. Indeed, to some extent it can, but we've pressed it too far and now we are in a serious crisis. And so, our answer all the time would be, keep an adequate level of functionality, reduce your impact. But what we thought adequate by historical standards tended to generate the response: "sorry, that's just not good enough, we want more than that".

SS: What would you have been displaying at Stockholm that had a low level of functionality?

PH: Well, for example, the Clivus Multrum, the big composting toilet. In a way, it is an amazing thing, everyone and every house should have one. You are turning some potentially noxious and pathogenic waste into something rather valuable. And you are not using any water, you are not contaminating water, so you don't have to clean it. But most people would say "Sorry, I'm not having one of those smelly, fly-ridden things. I want a proper toilet that I can flush. And send this stuff away to someone else to sort out!". What we thought was a reasonable level of functionality, for most people it wasn't good enough. The same thing with small-scale energy systems, it just wasn't good enough for many people. They want loads of energy, just like that. Just at the flick of a switch. Anything less than that is the Dark Ages.

SS: It reminds me of how the Bill and Melinda Gates Foundation is again studying the toilet and sanitation.

PH: Absolutely, yes! This composting toilet is one of the inspirations for Alternative Technology, and for Schumacher's idea about intermediate technology. What he meant by that was that it was better than what people had, but it wasn't a great leap to super modernity. Instead of just having a hole in the ground, or a pile behind a bush, you would have a proper toilet, with sanitation and a ventilation stack. But it wasn't a *flush* toilet. And I think that Bill Gates has stumbled on the same thing Schumacher did, basically getting people from the really lowest level to the intermediate level, which, arguably, is where we need to get. It was something of a novelty to suggest that, just as the people in developing countries are at the lower level and then bringing it up, maybe we have reached too high a level and need to get ourselves down a bit. Maybe there is some way you can meet in the middle, where you can find some kind of reasonable, global, level of functionality.

SS: So you would have imagined the technology that you were showing at Stockholm to be the sort of universal technology that would equalise the Global South and the Global North, around one toilet, with an equivalent level of functionality North and South?

PH: Yes! That's right, I think that's what we were aiming at. I'm not saying that there is something existentially wonderfully about that standard, but we were looking for something that was sustainable. Here is the standard, can you meet it with the technology that you have and ensure sustainability? Then we are not sawing off the branch on which we're sitting. That was the main question. So once you got some sort of a stable situation, you could say, right, now where do we go from here? Now we can increase functionality, as long as we don't create further damage. We weren't against high functionality, with lots of possibilities. Having said this, I must admit there was a puritanical streak that considered "high standards of living" to be in some sense "unconvivial",[12] but paradoxically perhaps, we also embraced countercultural hedonism: we liked to have a bit of fun.

SS: I would like to get back to that, because one of the things that I love about *Radical Technology* is that in the book there is a delightful wit and good humour. But I am going to see if I can stick for a moment with the toilet – it sounds like I might have a bit of a toilet fixation, but you could think of that as a great place to start asking about issues of design and politics and the human. One quick historical question, did you ever come across Sim Van der Ryn's book on *The Toilet Papers*.[13] It is a little bit later I think, but he was proposing almost something almost identical.

PH: Yes. We tried a lot of those ideas at the Centre for Alternative Technology. In fact we had a kind of zoo of alternative toilet systems, many of which were fully operational. We had the Clivus of course, and several other Swedish and Norwegian variants; we had the Sim Van der Ryn model; we had the Twin Vaults

---

12 The term "conviviality" was introduced by the influential theorist Ivan Illich in such works as *Tools for Conviviality* (Illich 1973). Illich considered much of modern life to be illogically damaging to a general sense of well-being that he termed "conviviality".
13 Van der Ryn 1978.

from Vietnam, all sorts of things. Eventually I wrote a book called *Lifting the Lid*, cataloguing our experiences with dry toilets and showing how to make them using very basic materials.[14] You're not the only one with a toilet fixation!

Our designs were widely used in the UK, and I should mention Japan, where dry toilets have been a core part of rural culture for centuries. I was especially charmed when, after a lecture in Japan, a person approached me and asked me to sign a copy of, blow me down, *Lifting the Lid*, which he had translated into Japanese and published himself. I still treasure the copy he gave me.

SS: So many great puns.

PH: Yes, mostly untranslatable British humour.[15] Jokes and puns are almost unavoidable if you are writing about toilets.

I went all over the world looking at toilet systems, not all of the dry/composting type; some might be described as "semi-wet" but were not connected to the sewerage system. They didn't always work. Lots of things work okay in California or Australia, just five degrees hotter, but they don't work in the UK: there are no completely universal technologies. They fit certain climates and certain places and perhaps certain cultural habits. You can't easily generalise.

SS: That would be something that I'd like to ask about. When I try to explain to students the principles leading to modernism and universalism, I'm describing an alien culture. They are brought up to understand difference, but to talk about sameness, to talk about the universal, for them is a mode of Eurocentric colonial arrogance. I try to explain the historical assumption that as a globalising, industrialising society, we would eventually alight upon a universal aesthetic and technology that would unify humanity. I contextualise this as the outcome of three or four centuries of thought going back to the Renaissance founded on capitalism, scientific revolution, enlightenment, empire, and in that framework, it would seem to make a radical sort of sense; and however problematic it looks in retrospect, it nonetheless is the undergirding of IKEA and IKEA's systems.

PH: Yes. We were very keen in 1972 on the Arts and Crafts ideal of hand production. But we failed to realise you had to be pretty rich to afford all of that Arts and Crafts stuff. And of course by historical standards we *were* rich. Even the 19th century movement was wealthy on the back of miners, mill-workers and the British Empire, but they were no doubt unaware of it. Ruskin, Morris and Co. were opposed to rubbishy mass production, but the Bauhaus said, look, we can have really cool designs that are functional and cheap and can be mass produced – brilliant! And IKEA has run with that, as far as I am concerned. It

---

14 Harper/Halestrap 1999.
15 As it happens, both interviewer and interviewee are British.

is excellent design, it works very well, it is thought up with people in mind, and it is cheap.

SS: You seem to have concluded that at a small scale, let's say at the household scale, stuff was not going to work, and you needed to find a way to scale up. Is that right, or is that wrong?

PH: Well, let's take hydroponics as an example. I've known people who have done it, and I've done a bit myself; you can grow vegetables and things in a greenhouse, without soil. And you can get good yields. What you don't get is your staples. You would hear people say, "look at me, growing my own food", but actually they are growing flavour molecules, not calories, or protein, or oil, or anything substantial. We get these things from farmers very cheaply, because farmers do it very well. I grow loads of veggies and all that sort of stuff, that's fine, but I know I am still dependent on farmers, God bless them. But look, hydroponics has now been ramped up to huge factories covering hundreds of hectares, producing salads in greenhouses heated by cogeneration from local power stations. Is that the future of food? No, but the future of *part* of our food, which keeps the costs down so we can all engage in craft-scale activities, even most of the time.

And it is the same with the maker movement, you are making one-off things. We are so rich now. We have a lot of free time because of the high productivity of society as a whole that we can then do craft stuff again. In principle, in the course of a life, you could probably make all of your own cups. You could make all of your own shoes, you could make all of your own clothes. It's interesting that you can do these things as a result of the high productivity of the industrial system that provides all the bases that we essentially need, all the warmth and the shelter and the transport. Back in the 1970s, we were thinking … it should be *all* craft stuff. But we were wrong there: it only worked because of the incredible productivity of the industrial system just keeping us all afloat, without our noticing it really. I think what's happened now is that we are coming to accept that, okay, not only modernity, the Bauhaus, the factories, everything, it has got to be there to keep us all going, because we can't survive without it. We are all dependent on it, but now we need to humanise it in some way. We need to find some way to stop it screwing up the planet.

SS: In 1972, at the UN conference, you were cutting against the grain of the universalist, governmental, top-down pro-development and pro-planning approach to environmentalism. It was almost like Karl Marx's vision of the future, where because the basic necessities are taken care of, you can go fishing…

PH: You seem to be alluding to the industrial vision of socialism, exemplified in Edward Bellamy's *Looking Backward*, that – interestingly enough – provoked

William Morris's *News from Nowhere* as a kind of rebuttal.[16] The maker movement should go back and look at these two books again, because they paint two different conceptions of how to deliver the Good Life for all. Back in 1972, we were quite clearly Morris-ists, but as you can tell, over the years we have become Bellamytes as it were. Morrisism offers Maker creativity to an elite few; Bellamism potentially offers it to all.

Bellamy's vision does presage a wealthy welfare society, but only a few today take full advantage of it. The big "winners", it seems to me, are those we might call Bohemians, who, while maintaining an easy-going middle-class discipline, have reduced their aspirations below the average productivity of the system, leaving them time to think, innovate, relax, and – yes – Make. It seems to me that in a post-modern society, everybody could live like this if they wished. They could live out old Marx's dream. Could I be wrong about this? A terrifying thought.

SS: In the 1970s, the emphasis was on small scale; now, we're carefully, critically accepting of the advantages of scale, of production. Nonetheless, it still leaves the question of distribution, justice and sustainability following relentless economic growth. In terms of what the maker movement might be doing now, is it some sort of recombination of handicraft and mass production? What should makers be making?

PH: We were fascinated by household, local and regional self-sufficiency, meeting our own needs from the materials at hand. But this quickly proved impossible in practice. You could "make" a simple thermosiphon solar water-heater, and we did. But you had to get the copper tubing, and the joints, and the solder, and the black paint, and the wood for the box, and the glass, and so on. Although that is not very high tech, it is still industrial. And that does presuppose that there are copper mines somewhere, and there are people making tubes. Could we have made our own tubes, panes of glass? Surely not.

We did occasionally dream of a general-purpose, local-scale manufacturing process that could fabricate almost anything from given raw materials. We thought this would be the ultimate "liberatory technology". Today we have 3D-printing which comes quite close in spirit, but you would still need the appropriate raw materials. Having said this, we would have given our eye-teeth for a 3D printer!

SS: But then, can you make a 3D printer? This is some sort of infinite regression. It is funny, it reminds me of how young designers and engineers, now, doing maker-thons and hack-a-thons and whatever, it is a little bit like you with the copper pipe in the 1970s. Sure they are reconfiguring technology, but they can't make the chip, the Raspberry Pi. They can get the chips to do good things.

---

16   Bellamy 1888; Morris 1890.

PH: Yes, I see, but most of these "good things" do not need to be customised. They might as well be mass-produced in the cheapest possible way. Customisation tends to come at a higher level when you buy standard items from (say) IKEA and combine them in unique ways at home.

Some things are in our favour. Moore's law means that tiny things with marvellous capacities can be reproduced endlessly. On the other hand, miniaturisation and acceleration does not apply to meals, houses, roads, clothes, landscapes and furniture. We could "make" lots of these, but probably most people wouldn't.

There is a worry about specialised skills and supply chains: key people, industries or locations withholding supplies. I find myself unworried by this. I am more worried by the brittleness of the system, forced to rack up greater efficiency at the expense of resilience.

If you want to be more resilient, to simplify, where do you start? That is your infinite regression. This was the question often asked within the circles of people we might call "collapsists", who held the apocalyptic view that a total collapse of modern societies was likely, perhaps inevitable. ...To some extent we were all collapsists then! You've got to remember, that was the time of the bomb and the Cold War: there was a possibility of a nuclear exchange at almost any time. And then you would have the definite collapse of central authority, and that was always at the back of our mind. But then we also thought that the industrial society might have the seeds of its own destruction, and it might just implode and fall apart, in which case, we had to ask the question, "who is going to rebuild afterwards?". In that situation, you cannot take anything for granted, so you might absolutely have to make everything from scratch.

This was one of the notions for the New Alchemists and the CAT in Wales. We were the modern arks, and we would come out and help everyone rebuild civilisation. But you had no idea what would be left.[17] The presumption was that you should try to keep it as simple as possible, because you couldn't just walk down to the hardware shop and get yourself a metre of 19 mill copper pipe.

SS: And then adding to that potentially end times quality of the era, a year after Stockholm, you had the Energy Crisis.

PH: Yeah.

SS: And increasing industrial unrest, all through the 1970s, and at least in France, the UK and the US, increasing racial tension. And recession; and we've said about the Cold War. By 1972 as well the neo-Malthusian tenor of the Club of Rome.

---

17   This question has been given a modern treatment by Lewis Dartnell in *The Knowledge: How to Rebuild Our World after an Apocalypse* (2015).

PH: Of course we knew about that as well. We'd read all of their stuff. We'd met them in fact, the Club of Rome people. They were in Stockholm then, too.[18]

SS: And Ehrlich's *The Population Bomb*.[19]

PH: Yeah.

SS: And Carson's *Silent Spring*.[20]

PH: And others of the same era, such as Barry Commoner's *Closing Circle*.[21] Carson and Commoner both stressed the significance of applying technology in an ethically driven rather than commercially driven manner, and this had a strong bearing on the notion of alternative technologies, of having the technology but with alternative values.

SS: Politically, historically, socially, how did you and your friends find each other and come together? There seems to have been a thrilling intersection of Red and Green – a sort of socialist anarchism meets deep ecology. Not Arne Ness deep, but deep-ish. And why is that interesting again now? (It clearly is, because we are doing this interview; the journal guest editors want to know about it, and my students are curious about it.) How did you get to Red and Green?

PH: Hmm. I guess I haven't been thinking about that recently. The Green bit for me just came from the evidence. I was just paying attention to all of that Malthusian stuff throughout the 1960s, starting with the population data, because you could see the exponential pattern. If there is an exponential going on somewhere, it just can't continue, so you knew that was "unsustainable", although we didn't have that word then. And then on top of that, we started to understand more about pollution. Remember that in the immediate post-war period, there was tremendous technological optimism that the bad could be transformed into good: "swords into ploughshares". For example, chemical warfare technology went into pesticides, while munitions technology went into fertilisers. It's all the same chemistry. And the tanks turned into tractors. Of course, commercial interests promoted these things and they came to seem like technological silver bullets. DDT was the classic silver bullet. You've got all these pests, you just zap them and they go away: what's not to like? And that can keep going for about a decade before the side effects start building up. It takes a while for this to happen, and that of course was Rachel Carlson's contribution. She was showing how things were

---

18 The exhibition was visited by Aurelio Peccei, then head of the Club of Rome.
19 Ehrlich 1968.
20 Carson 1962.
21 Commoner 1971.

happening that we simply did not expect. We didn't expect the DDT to dissolve in body fat and work its way up the food chain and then result in raptors having no chicks because the eggs were too thin.

And one by one, we kept seeing these unexpected things. Another one that struck me was the increase of noise in the ocean. Meaning that ocean creatures like whales that depended on long distance communication with sounds couldn't manage. It was so noisy in there, they could only communicate a few hundred yards. Nobody thought of that, "ships, whales, noise". Of course you didn't. All of these things are unexpected effects. I had pages of these things and I thought, god, this is awful, everything is falling to pieces, and nobody realises because they are so intent on using their own magic bullets. An important paper, Garrett Hardin's "The Tragedy of the Commons", came out in 1968, that explained a lot of this process, with malign collective effects emerging that nobody really wanted.[22] I did not necessarily buy into the author's other agendas, but the basic pattern is surely a universal one, on a par with, say, natural selection. Our answer to the 'tragedy' was essentially the kind of relocalisation that had governed local collective resources for centuries. People would say, "well alright you're a critic. Do you have an answer?" And then we said "Yeah, we do have an answer, it is a bit weird, but here it is. We think it is an answer." And that was our decentralised, low-tech concept of Alternative Technology.

Then gradually as the 1980s rolled on, the key thing that happened to me is that I realised that the different nasty technologies don't necessarily add up to a joint disaster. You can pick them off one at a time, impose regulations at a national level and get results. So you might be able to find a way to have the benefits without the nasty downsides, if we are very clever and pay attention. Not that we did always pay attention, but I began to see that you *could* have high-tech without irreversible damage, and that it is hard to run a modern society without high-tech. So then I began to switch towards what a lot of people call "eco-modernisation": a dirty word in some circles, emphasising technical innovation rather than lifestyle change, to achieve a sustainable modern society.

But my confidence that pollution impacts did not synergise, and could be successfully tackled one at a time, was ruined by the arrival of the greenhouse gases, which behave exactly like the "limits to growth" pollution curve, much criticised for lumping them all together. Damn! I had gone through a rather optimistic phase in the 1990s, and now I had to accommodate a much more pessimistic view, which roughly parallels the great doomsday clock on the cover of the *Bulletin of the Atomic Scientists*.

SS: When you mention Garrett Hardin earlier, you said, you weren't sure about the rest of the agenda. What do you mean by the rest of the agenda?

---

22   Hardin 1968.

PH: Well, he's infamous for being in favour of eugenics and advocating privatisation as a solution to the Tragedy. A lot of people won't use the term "the tragedy of the commons" because it is associated with him. But you need to have some kind of terminology to talk about these malign collective action patterns, and nobody has come up with a better term that is universally recognised as referring to the same processes. I'm taking the essential "political economy" of it, without the rest of the luggage. It is striking that many subsequent "solutions" to Hardin's tragedy share many of the limitations of our own alternative response: they are too local; they solve the problem at one level but leave it unaddressed at the greater, global level.

SS: I think the pessimism you're referring to is one reason that we are going back into history, into the archive, to look at the 1970s and the sorts of interventions that you made, and it could be that the journal is doing this revisiting again, because if the maker movement began during one of those optimistic phases when we believed that we could innovate our way out of crisis.... I think that pessimistic swing of the pendulum is one of the things impelling the journal to say, "well okay, let's then think about a pessimistic making". But I still want to back up. Because a phrase that you used earlier was "alternative values". There is right now, Peter, a hunger for alternative values. I think that an appeal of Alternative Technology is that it seems to posit an alternative set of values. One of the things that you seemed to be doing was that you seemed to be trying to pre-figure (as anarchists would say) what happens next, whether that was in those exquisite illustrations by Cliff Harper, or whether it was by trying to fabricate things, or make things, to see if it works, or whether it was through speculative texts, where in *Radical Technology* you see what socialism would be like. If the United Nations was overall in favour of what would become known by the 1980s as sustainability – that basically you can have your cake and eat it, you can have responsible economic growth that takes care of the environment – it would seem that on the fringe of Stockholm you were "hacking the sustainability" before it is going to be sustainability, and saying "well you know, we might not get there. Things could fall apart before then, we may have to think in a much more grassroots way". And in that, there was also something that we would today call a "hacking", "speculation", "decolonisation" – you were showing that there is an industrial and technological system out there that is a form of colonisation that has made us all dance to the beat of one drum, which is that of "relentless growth" and relentless production, a globalised clock. That it can be kind of hacked, and we can speculate on what comes next. We are yet again back to ruminating on what happens as capitalism stumbles, seems to become more unequal, seems to become more violent, and seems congenitally unable to deal with racial inequality, global inequality; I think one reason we are back in the archive of the 1970s is because analogously, and sometimes literally, it was asking the same questions. Can we do something exciting with crisis? That's a big preliminary to my final question: what happened to bring socialism into the mix of thought in the early 1970s, and what happened to it?

PH: Okay, I've given you the Green, and I think that came from the evidence. The Red I don't think came from the evidence. That was just sort of in the water, I think. I wasn't particularly critical about it. It was the hip thing. Everybody around me seemed to be some kind of libertarian socialist. There were lots of radical tendencies of course at the time, and I used to meet Trotskyists a lot, and members of the Communist Party, old Stalinists, and all sorts of Marxists. It's worth remembering that at that time you could not say that the Soviet Experiment had definitely failed. I should also remark that anarchism was a greater influence on alternative technology than Marxism, and indeed proper Marxists tended to look down on us "mere environmentalists". History has been kinder to us than to them.

SS: Was Maoism circulating?

PH: Yes, Maoism was important too, and you can see the fetishism of China in *Radical Technology*.

PH: In a sense, there was this ... shopping mall of different ideological styles, and you could go in there, and say, "Oh I think I'm rather one of those". It was like choosing a dress! And *these* people are cooler than *those*. Anyway, there were some things which were unquestionable, and one of these was "The Revolution". The Revolution was a universal solvent: almost everybody seemed to agree it was both necessary and inevitable. I am astonished today looking back on it, it was assumed that from this incredible chaos would emerge a beautiful new butterfly. It would be ordered, equitable, everybody would know what to do, and everything would be good – as orderly as iron filings around a magnet.

Now we are sadder and wiser, and today I think just the opposite. The more chaos there is, the more you end up with thugs, guns, Mad Max and political opportunists. We still need a fairly rapid transformation, but it must be orderly and retain the basic civilities. To deploy a metaphor, we mustn't curdle the milk.

In the 1980s and 1990s, as I've already said, I became more sanguine about the physical prospects, but that was also the era when neoliberalism, which is intrinsically anti-ethical, was taking over the planet like a virus. We desperately needed an ideological framework to counter it, but (however unfairly) Marxism was buried in the rubble of the Soviet Union. Gradually, the old humanism exerted itself and finally Thomas Piketty and others have revived the old Marxist spirit. Good for them, we need it.

But I must still say that, in my professional life, I'm at pains to try to persuade my colleagues that if you've got to solve a physical problem – because climate change, etc. are physical problems – you have got to come up with physical solutions, which have got to be technological. And then you have to build your politics and your economics around *that*. It is very important to do it this way and not the other way round. It's very tempting and easy to say, "well let's get all the politics sorted out, and we'll just hope that the physics and the technology will play nicely". It won't. You've got to get that physical side of it sorted out first. Only some patterns are possible.

But it seems to me that the two bits of jigsaw that fit together nicely are again Red and Green, in the sense that if you have a rational environmental perspective, it fits in with a kind of rational evidence-based, careful, social democracy I suppose. It fits together because on both the environmental and political sides everyone is trying to think things out in a reasonable and honourable way. I hope I am not sounding too naïve here. I wouldn't call it Red though; it's more pink, boring social democracy. Boring is good! And the Green is not so deep green – you referred before to "deep ecology". The texts about deep ecology, I am sorry to say, are a kind of populist fantasy, projecting human values and human wishes onto nature. It assumes nature is a bit like us, and that you could actually have dealings with nature as if it were a person. No, Nature is its own thing, and it is not like us. You mustn't project your own values onto it. It has its rules that you have got to obey…. So in that sense, the political context is light green and pink. It is not deep Green and blood Red, as it used to be. Shame really, but there it is.

SS: Would that be a difference between now and where you were in 1972, 1976?

PH: Definitely. Definitely. In those days, I was more Green in the sense that I believed in a neo-primitive, back to nature, fundamental restriction on economic progress. On the other hand, I was Red enough to believe in The Revolution and that capitalists all wore top hats and smoked cigars! But I must admit, it was a laugh.

References

Allen, J. P./Nelson, M./Alling, A. (2003): "The legacy of biosphere 2 for the study of biospherics and closed ecological systems." Advances in Space Research 31(7), pp. 1629–1639.
Bellamy, E. (1888): Looking Backward, 2000–1887. Boston: Ticknor and Co.
Block, M./Bokalders, V. (2010): The Whole Building Handbook. London: Routledge.
Bocco Guarneri, A. (2020): Vegetarian Architecture: Case Studies on Building and Nature. Berlin: Jovis.
Boyle, G./Harper, P. (Eds.) (1976): Radical Technology. London: Wildwood House.
Carson, R. (1962): Silent Spring. Boston: Houghton Mifflin.
Commoner, B. (1971): The Closing Circle: Nature, Man, and Technology. New York: Knopf.
Dartnell, L. (2015): The Knowledge: How to Rebuild Our World after an Apocalypse. London: Vintage.
Ehrensvärd, G. (1972): Före – Efter: En Diagnos. Stockholm: Aldus.

Ehrlich, P. R. (1968): The Population Bomb. New York: Ballantine Books.
Farvar, M.T./Milton, J.P. (eds.) (1972): The Careless Technology: Ecology and International Development. Garden City, NY: Natural History Press.
For a Technology in the Service of the People [För en Teknik i Folkets Tjänst!] (exhibition) (June 1972): Moderna Museet Filialen, Stockholm, Sweden.
Gericke, W. F. (1937): "Hydroponics: Crop Production in Liquid Culture Media." Science 85(2198), pp. 177–178.
Gilman, R. (1991): "The Eco-village Challenge." In Context, Summer, p. 10.
Hardin, G. (1968): "The Tragedy of the Commons." Science 162(3859), 1243.
Harper, P./Halestrap, L. (1999): Lifting the Lid. Powys, UK: Centre for Alternative Technology.
Hart, R. (1996): Forest Gardening: Cultivating an Edible Landscape. Bideford: Green Books.
Illich, I. (1973): Tools for Conviviality. New York, NY: Harper and Row.
Mollison, B.C./Holmgren, D. (1978): Permaculture 1: A perennial Agricultural System for Human Settlements. London: Corgi.
Morris, W. (1890): News from Nowhere; or, An Epoch of Rest, Being Some Chapters from a Utopian Romance. Reprinted in: The Collected Works of William Morris, Vol. XVI, Longmans Green and Company. London: Cambridge University Press, pp. 373–395.
Rappaport, R. A. (2000 [1967]): Pigs for the Ancestors: Ritual in the Ecology of a New Guinea People. Long Grove, IL: Waveland Press.
Scott, F. D. (2016): Outlaw Territories: Environments of Insecurity/Architectures of Counterinsurgency. New York, NY: Zone.
Van der Ryn, S. (1978): The Toilet Papers: Recycling Waste and Conserving Water. Sausalito, CA: Ecological Design Press.

Moments
in Alternative (Hi)stories

The Craft of Small Wind Turbine Making
The Windmills of Scoraig and the Alternative Technology Movement in the UK

Kostas Latoufis and Aristotle Tympas

On the isolated Scottish peninsula of Scoraig, Hugh Piggott and his neighbours have been building "windmills" over the last 40 years by reusing materials sourced at the local scrapyard. Picking up a technological thread from American farmers, who built "windchargers" during the years of the Great Depression by reusing automotive parts of the Model T, the crofters of Scoraig have mastered, over time, the craft[1] of small wind turbine making.

With a fresh critique of industrial society, based on the emerging themes of environmental degradation, resource depletion, nuclear threat and the limits to capitalist growth, the Alternative Technology movement of the 1970s in the UK cross-pollinated the counterculture with ideas on ecology and low impact lifestyles, along with participatory politics based on the anarcho-utopian tradition. In 1972, the term "alternative technology" was first used by Peter Harper in one of the early issues of *Undercurrents*, a magazine for alternative science and technology published at the heart of the UK counterculture scene in London. A year later in 1973, Gerard Morgan-Grenville and many young environmentalists initiated the Centre for Alternative Technology (CAT), on the lands of an old slate quarry in Wales, inspired by organic agriculture, renewable energy and cooperative principles. In light of the 1973–1974 oil crisis, the emerging environmental and antinuclear movement organised the first Community Technology (COMTEK) festival, which took place in the town of Bath in 1974, exhibiting windmills, solar energy converters, methane digesters and simple dwelling constructions, all put together by young Do-It-Yourself (DIY) enthusiasts, showcasing a bottom-up process of technological innovation in alternative technologies (see Figure 1). In 1976, these efforts accumulated in the book *Radical Technology: Food, Shelter, Tools, Materials, Energy, Communication, Autonomy, Community* (Boyle/Harper 1976) which was published in the UK as a hands-on practical guide for the creation of an alternative lifestyle, and would soon find its way into the toolboxes of young pioneers moving back-to-the-land, along with similar publications from the US such as the *Whole Earth Catalog* and *Mother Earth News*.

---

1   Our understanding of craft is in conversation with an emerging literature on the importance of technology maintenance and re-use (see Vinsel/Russel 2020).

Such young pioneers were Hugh Piggott and his neighbours, who settled in the rural community of Scoraig, on the west coast of the Scottish Highlands, in 1974. Most of the newcomers on the peninsula were part of the 1970s counterculture and were actively mixing environmentalism with the traditional crofting lifestyle. With a limited income, the new settlers had to use their ingenuity, locally available natural resources and whatever they could reuse from the scrapyard, to build and furnish their homes, repair their boats, vans and agricultural machines and cultivate their gardens. Electricity was almost non-existent for most of them, and lighting needs were met with oil lamps and candles, as they could not afford a diesel generator like some of the older and more established crofting families on the peninsula, who used electricity for washing machines, shearing sheep and workshop tools. Some of the newcomers did have tape recorders though for listening to music, but that was about it. Hugh had a tape recorder too, which he powered from an old car battery he had recycled. Sometimes, when his battery had run out of energy, he used to carry it over to one of his neighbours, who had a second-hand Lucas Freelite wind turbine from the 1940s mounted on an old wooden telegraph pole. Hugh gradually developed an interest in the old wind turbine, and in the realities of producing electricity from the wind, as did several of his friends and neighbours. The old Lucas Freelite was slowly sparking a wind rush in the community of Scoraig.

It was in 1978, four years after he had first settled on the peninsula, that Hugh started to experiment with building small wind turbines. One of his neighbours had managed to successfully imitate the design of the Lucas Freelite, proving that it was possible to make one from scratch. But word was also coming from other places of people sharing the same enthusiasm and being on the same learning curves. The "Low Impact Design (LID) Windgenerator" was an experimental small wind turbine, developed by the *Undercurrents* magazine team in London, which was documented in issues 11 and 12 published in 1975. The team described the successes and failures of the project, but without managing to reach an operational design. The *Mother Earth News Handbook of Homemade Power* was published in 1974 in the US (see Figure 2), which included an inspiring interview with Marcellus Jacobs, a 1930s farmer and pioneer of wind energy, who managed to successfully commercialise his designs in the US under the name of Jacobs Wind Electric (Mother Earth News 1974). In addition, the handbook included the design and manufacturing instructions of a wooden two-blade rotor, as a republication from the 1940s LeJay manual, a popular handbook among US farmers of the time with design plans for common DIY farm applications.

Hugh went through seven prototype machines in the first year using a limited number of tools and materials he could source in the scrapyard. A car dynamo was the obvious part to use, as it was designed to charge a car battery from a rotating shaft, on which a two-blade wooden rotor could be directly coupled, carved out of a single piece of wood using the LeJay manual's 1940s blade designs. Car dynamos were designed to operate at high speeds though, so Hugh managed to get his hands on a low-speed bus dynamo from the local scrap yard, to which he mounted a three-blade rotor so as to build a system that could produce 700 watts of electrical power in strong winds, enough to provide sufficient electricity for his croft. It was erected on a 10-metre high tower, made from a telegraph pole, supported with steel fence wire rope, which was used for animal fences and connected to wooden fence posts in the ground. By the end of 1978, Hugh had a fully operational wind turbine, the design of which he could trust, that would charge his car batteries during most winds. Gradually, many of his neighbours wanted to be part of this new innovation and Hugh was more than willing to provide this new service to them.

A nearby neighbour, who was also experimenting with windmills, was now using a rewound Champ Jeep dynamo for his wind turbine and that seemed to match well the speed of the two-blade wooden rotor while producing about 300 watts of power, which was sufficient for most Scoraig crofts. Hugh soon found a scrap merchant in London who was selling used Champ Jeep dynamos in bulk and decide to place an order and drove down to London with his van to buy 50 of them. By the end of 1981, Hugh had installed more than ten systems for his neighbours on Scoraig. All wind turbines were based on the original design which he had learned to trust, but at the same time, all windmills were unique in some way, as they had new ideas built into them, some introduced by the owners and others introduced by Hugh, based on his growing experience on producing electricity from the wind. By the end of the 1980s, more than 40 wind turbines could be seen on the skyline of the peninsula, which in combination with reused telephone exchange batteries provided a viable electricity source for most of the newcomers' crofts (see Figure 3).

Since the 1990s, Hugh Piggott has been teaching wind power courses at the CAT in Wales and has been publishing manuals on how to build small wind turbines based on new materials such as permanent magnets, used for manufacturing low-speed alternators. The hands-on construction courses which he has delivered in several parts of the world have led to the creation of a global network of wind turbine builders, called the Wind Empowerment association. Since its initiation in 2011, the association has grown to include more than 50 organisations based on all continents, who have installed more than 1000 locally manufactured small wind turbines in various parts of the world, using the windmill designs developed in Scoraig[2].

---

2   The material on the Scoraig community has been based on interviews conducted by Kostas Latoufis with Hugh Piggott on Scoraig, during the months of April 2015 and May 2017.

Figure 1: Cover of the 1974 Community Technology (COMTEK) festival brochure, with notes and photos of the event. Image credit: COMTEK festival.

Figure 2: Cover of the Mother Earth News Handbook of Homemade Power published in 1974. Image credit: Mother Earth News.

Figure 3: Hugh Piggott standing on a small H frame clamped onto the tower while performing maintenance on an early Scoraig windmill, with a 5-litre bottle clipped to his safety belt used for holding tools. Image credit: Hugh Piggott.

References

Boyle, G./Harper, P. (Eds.) (1976): Radical Technology. London: Wildwood House.
Mother Earth News (1974): Mother Earth News Handbook of Homemade Power. New York, NY: Bantam Books.
Vinsel, L./Russell, A. (2020): The Innovation Delusion: How Our Obsession with the New Disrupted the Work That Matters Most. New York, NY: Currency.

Made in the Russian North

Narratives of Inventiveness from the Geographic Periphery

Svetlana Usenyuk-Kravchuk

The project[1] described here explores the inventive potential of the Russian northern periphery – the rural areas, distant from administrative centres, large industries, and infrastructures, where people pursue a literally de-modernised way of living. In such settings, we sought local inventions – particularly transport vehicles – that people made for themselves. We looked for practical solutions to problems of daily mobility that involved minimum effort and material. The objects we found provided a new understanding of the "beauty and utility" formula, which appeared to be unique for each locality and personality of a maker.

Our data set consists of historical data that were drawn from museums, archives and other public domains such as magazines and newspapers on the Soviet phenomenon of Do-It-Yourself (DIY) enthusiasts grounded in a broader historical and social context of a so-called "repair society" (Gerasimova/Chuikina 2009), as well as first-hand observations of contemporary realities of the Russian northern periphery obtained through in-depth field studies on local technologies and practices in three areas: Arkhangelsk Oblast, Perm Krai and the Sakha Republic. By combining theoretical insights from historical sociological approaches to the study of technology, such as the social construction of technology and geographical construction of technology, we deepen the concept of "proximal design" (Usenyuk/Hyysalo/Whalen 2016) that puts forward not only users' ability to adjust, repair and redesign their machines, but the very ability to create entirely new kinds of technology and, eventually, to come up with enduring design principles without the participation of design professionals.

As we discovered, the common basis for developing local transport solutions consists of the following:

- Parts and materials in close proximity (e.g., reused parts and industrial scrap from local landfills, yards, sheds, garages, and homes);
- Embedded practical knowledge of tools and machinery (in our cases, this knowledge resulted from the Soviet system of mass secondary/professional

---

1 This study is a part of larger ongoing project "Arctic Design: Methods of Technical Aesthetics in Development and Appropriation of the Russian North" funded by Russian Science Foundation grant no. 17-78-20047.

education that enhanced technological literacy and promoted rich handcrafting experience); and
- Practical knowledge of the local geographical conditions and climatic factors in their interdependence and complexity.

While the first point summarised as *hardware* is provided by the environment and therefore differs from place to place, the latter two have always depended on making as *soft* proactive strategies of surviving and comfortable living in a particular environment. Those sets of practical knowledge – tacit, non-verbalised but embodied in technological artefacts – constituted the matter of our design inquiry.

Cosmic Conversion

One of the innovative local solutions in our database is "Cosmic conversion" in Moseevo, a remote village in Arkhangelsk Oblast with limited transport accessibility to the "outer world". The primary transport vehicle is a traditional wooden boat called "zyrianka", which is used throughout the region of the Mezen River basin. But in this particular village, since the 1990s, these boats have been made of metal: not of conventional steel or aluminium, but a high-quality rust-proof alloy.

Figure 1: (a) Rocket parts found in the vicinity of Moseevo (left). Courtesy of Igor Gmyrin (personal archive, early 2000s). (b) A typical boat made of "space metal" (centre). Courtesy of Alexandra Raeva, 2018. (c) A handmade tool for cutting four-millimetre thick metal converted from a mass-produced chainsaw (right). Courtesy of Alexandra Raeva, 2018.

Where do the locals get the material? The answer is clearly in line with the proximal design concept (Usenyuk/Hyysalo/Whalen 2016): the village is situated on the course of space rockets launched from Plesetsk Cosmodrome (200 km south of Arkhangelsk). When rockets accelerate, their exhausted stages fall to the ground. The villagers search for them, collect fallen fragments (Figure 1a) and reuse them in a new, practical way by making boats (Figure 1b). The locals call their small manufacture – partly as a joke – "cosmic conversion". To deal with the high-tech material, they have invented and locally produced specific low-tech tools (Figure 1c).

The space vessels are longer than the original traditional wooden boats – up to 2–2.5 m – and their lifting capacity is up to 2.5 tonnes. The space boats also bypass mass-produced factory models made of duralumin alloys in terms of performance data and lifting capacity. It takes about two to three weeks to make such a boat; the duration of use without repair is practically unlimited (while a wooden boat lasts about two years). Today, when the spaceport is far from being in full use, and the metal is not widely available, people have adjusted to new realities: they have begun using drones to search for remote crash sites.

Pozhva Jeeps

The second example is "Pozhva Jeeps": lightweight all-terrain vehicles (ATVs) in the village of Pozhva, a factory settlement in Perm Krai (Figure 2).

Figure 2: Vladimir Germanovich on a "jeep" made by himself. Courtesy of Ilya Abramov, 2018.

Pozhva is a factory settlement that belongs to the Pozhva Machine-building Factory in Permskiy Krai, in the European North of Russia. In the early 2000s, it became famous among ATV makers and users because of its unique community-centred manufacture of lightweight ATVs on low-pressure tires, called "jeeps". The first jeep was made more than 30 years ago, and, to date, there are about 200 vehicles in the village.

Each jeep is an exclusively produced, manual assembly of uniquely sourced components, combined with unique and individual engineering and design solutions. A small share of the parts (e.g., drive sprockets and frames) were made in the factory workshops – those that required turning, milling and welding operations – while general assembling, tuning and alteration were conducted in personal home garages. In terms of hardware, the primary source of spare parts and materials was also *not* the factory, but backyards, metal stores and landfills of the local kolkhoz (collective farm) with broken tractors and other machines, as well as a network of friends, workmates and acquaintances. The set of components – always limited and non-repeating – forces makers to modify or modernise the original scheme each time, and it is still not optimal. For example, today, the apparent shortage of Izhevsk engines requires the adaptation of Chinese engines, which are of poor quality, in general, and do not go well with Soviet motor parts.

Among the 200 machines, there are no two jeeps alike, although there is an easily recognisable "Pozhva frame". Pozhva jeeps are famous because of their ergonomics and reliability: the unique design resulted from numerous experiments in field conditions. Local makers tried different schemes – from front skis and three-wheels to all-wheel drive and other modifications. They finally came to the "golden standard" of all-weather use, easy-to-handle and light machine that entails four wheels, a motorcycle engine, an automobile chassis, a luggage box at the rear and a cargo platform in front. Today, jeeps are unique handicraft production, which is not associated with any commercial enterprise or collective.

These DIY vehicles provide insights into the Soviet development of mass secondary and professional education, which enhanced the rates of technological literacy, promoted rich manual experience and contributed to the formation of a community of peasants who can independently dismantle almost any machine and – from this pile of details – assemble a "self-propelled wagon". Everyday life in extreme, remote, peripheral areas is, and to an even greater extent will continue to be, marked by the need for a more environmentally conscious and sensible use of resources. The phenomenon of inventiveness we discovered stems from precisely such sense – through local knowledge, oral history, through makers' own craft and economising. It is not about re-shaping the environment but allowing it to shape choices. These examples of low-tech creativity provide new insights into the concepts of recycling and improvisation; they are about bricolage as well as about shifting the control (and responsibility) over the object and the situation to the user.

References

Gerasimova, E./Chuikina, S. (2009): "The Repair Society." Russian Studies in History 48(1), pp. 58–74.
Usenyuk, S./Hyysalo, S./Whalen, J. (2016): "Proximal Design: Users as Designers of Mobility in the Russian North." Technology and Culture 57(4), pp. 866–908.

Czech DIY
A Historically Contingent Landscape

Petr Gibas and Blanka Nyklová

Even though the Do-It-Yourself (DIY) movement is starting to garner more and more scholarly attention, this is less so in the case of Czech DIY. This omission is surprising, as DIY is widespread in the Czech Republic with a distinct history and vibrant presence. Our colleagues and we have been researching Czech DIY (*kutilství* in Czech) since 2018, thus trying to at least partially fill in the gap in our understanding of DIY, its uses and meanings, in a project titled "Do-It-Yourself Culture and Its Importance for Czech National and Cultural Identity" funded by the Czech Ministry of Culture.[1] The project aims to provide a peek into the multifaceted and diverse activities which today's DIYers devote themselves to, how these have changed over time and what DIY means (not only) to the people who engage in it.

DIY has a long and culturally significant tradition in the Czech Republic. Paradoxically, and just as in some other countries (in Europe and beyond), Czechs and Czech media perceive *kutilství* as a national trait, which refers to the specific historical experience and memory of the nation and propagates the view of Czechs as a nation of DIYers *(národ kutilů)*. While DIY historically emerged at the beginning of the 20th century in what was the Czech Lands at the time, it is – in the general awareness – mainly linked to state socialism, the four decades between 1948 and 1989 when then Czechoslovakia was part of the Eastern Bloc of countries governed by Communist parties and under direct geopolitical influence of the Soviet Union. Specifically, DIY is mostly associated with the normalisation period which started in 1968 with the invasion of Warsaw Pact armies to suppress the liberalising movement of the Prague Spring and ended with the Velvet Revolution in 1989.

While the 1950s are associated mainly with Stalinist-style purges, the 1960s with some relaxation of the regime climaxing with the efforts of transforming the socialist state into a sort of democratic socialism, the 1970s and 1980s, following the violent crushing of hopes pinned on the 1968 reforms, are perceived as a timeless period. A boom in DIY is associated particularly with this period because of the perceived loss of credibility of the state socialist system exacerbated by its inability to deliver on the promise of a sustained and substantial growth of state-backed and state-planned production for (leisurely) consumption similar to capitalist countries. This failure led to shortages of some goods and problems with the general consistency of supply and quality. This, together with the rise of free time – the five-day workweek was

---

1   For more details, see http://kutilstvi.soc.cas.cz/en.

established in 1968 – and limited possibilities to spend it as well as a growing lack in available goods and services led to a rise in moonlighting (i.e. work by those skilled enough to substitute the failing formal economy) on one hand. On the other, this resulted in an increase in DIY practices especially in relation to weekend houses, the care for which became and continues to be a massively popular pastime activity. Weekend houses would comprise both newly erected small constructions close to cities *(chata)* and adapted rural houses newly in use only over the weekend *(chalupa)*. This activity – *chataření and chalupaření* – was taken up by broad swaths of mostly urban population with little differences regarding their social-economic status.

In normalisation-era DIY, the materials at hand were often repurposed, giving birth to now-iconic "products", such as – perhaps most notably – a lawnmower built around a discarded washing machine engine. A special venue, which made the iconic status of some products as well as of the whole set of activities popular across the nation, came about with the emergence of the weekly TV show *Receptář nejen na neděli* ("Recipe Book not just for Sunday") in 1987. It was hosted by its founder – a "king of DIY" – Přemek Podlaha, a well-known TV personality until his death in 2014. In the show, various activities, improvements, DIY hacks and artefacts would be regularly presented together with a wide range of associations: fishing, various breeders of small farm animals and pets and fanciers, growers and so on. The show was broadcast on Sundays and quickly became extremely popular, at least partly also because of the contemporary interest in mostly self-led projects of weekend houses.

What makes the association of this type of historically, economically and sociopolitically conditioned and locally contextual DIY with socialism is paradoxically the fact that its media image, created by *Receptář* and promulgated by numerous other similar TV programmes and magazines, emerged at the turn of socialism to capitalism and thus reflects both socialist and post-socialist realities. This is visible in how swiftly the show and its host turned to promote entrepreneurs, an endeavour de facto started at the very beginning of the show in 1987 with the promotion of "crowdfunding" of prototypes not readily supported but also not opposed by the socialist regime. Such an approach and change after 1989 was contingent on the lack of open political subversion and indeed of an explicit political dimension of the extant DIY. This sets *kutilství* apart from other DIY activities that have been emerging since 1989 and especially in recent years including environmentally and politically conscious forms as well as more business-oriented ventures based predominantly on home-made design and being exchanged, but also sold at various design markets and on online platforms. The most recent trend in big cities, namely in Prague, as a response to the Right to Repair, is a growth of community workshops where anyone can come and use the tools freely available. These emerging DIY activities intertwine with *kutilství* in both practice and their media and popular image. The landscape of contemporary Czech DIY is thus diverse and growing, organically fusing the long-existing historically conditioned forms with new ones. In terms of studying both material and digital culture, this is an exciting field both empirically and theoretically.

Halasuru Traverses
Alternative Local Histories

Anupama Gowda

Workbench Projects embarked on its journey as a public laboratory in Halasuru, in the heart of Bangalore's Central Business District, in 2015. Halasuru is a neighbourhood that had lost part of its identity with the coming of the Bangalore metro, and with this in mind, we decided to set up Workbench Projects, a fab lab and co-working space, as an inclusive space, as well as a place for the community to write its own history.

When Workbench Projects was initially set up, people in the neighbourhood came, thinking they were about to visit a concept restaurant and a few hoped for employment. Little did they imagine that the space within the metro station would be a place to tinker. Once they were taken on a tour of the space, local parents and children were reassured that there was something in it for them too. They started frequenting the place and making it their own, hoping to discover something extraordinary each time, as members were constantly working on compelling projects, from creating vertical hydroponics garden to building everyday furniture, to experimenting on a unicycle.

With the children in the neighbourhood becoming regulars, we took the opportunity to speak with a neighbourhood school that had been around since 1873, providing affordable education to the local Tamil population. Over the years, the school had lost patronage to private schools, and to this day, it continues to battle for its existence. The school's quest was to enable young children to look at life more positively and educate them as useful members of society, relieving the distress of being poor and downtrodden. It was timely to initiate a more committed conversation with the school, as the children were curious and eager to explore the things that they had seen at Workbench Projects. We thus embarked on a ten-month arts education project, which ultimately had several phases and involved multiple methods, such as writing histories, puppet making with paper and CAD (computer aided design) technologies, and a public showcase.

Our journey began as a more freewheeling exploration, as the children invited us to take us on neighbourhood walks, opening their doors to us with geniality. During our first walk, it became apparent that these little children were introducing us to their own troubled lives, as they wove local stories that yearned to be documented and retold in their own ways. It was then that the structure of the project became defined in my head. For me personally, having worked with teacher educators and community facilitators for more than a decade, it was heartening to see the children waiting every Sunday morning to take us for a walk and share their everyday lived experiences without reservation. Despite the heart-wrenching stories of their single parents, their homes being vandalised, siblings under threat and abuse, all these children mindful of their circumstances were seeing every day as another hopeful day.

At Workbench Projects, I decided that we structure the experience for the children with the support of local historians to introduce them to the rich history of the place to which they belonged, to inspire them to write a story as they imagined their neighbourhood. A series of walks helped them retrace the history, documenting the neighbourhood, accompanied by an experienced photographer. I emphasised that the group, about 30–40 pupils, continue sketching in their spare time and look at elemental details that they otherwise would not observe. Once I saw that their sketches had started to capture the nuances of their lived realities, we started on an intensive storytelling and writing workshop. Three months of active engagement had led them to write regularly, and now the time had come to piece it together for a production.

Taking cues and elements from the history walk, I encouraged them to develop a narrative based on a plot they wished to present to their community. The result entailed a popular Tamil film icon as the protagonist, who visits Halasuru to inaugurate the Murphy Town Library. The children happen to strike a conversation with the film star about the history of the neighbourhood, which could serve as a plot for his next blockbuster movie. With this storyboard, we sought the support of a veteran leather puppeteer to give children first-hand instruction in the material, form and construction of puppet making. The children were encouraged to explore leather as practised in traditional puppet making in the region. Given the unforgiving nature of leather as material for first-time learners, we also provided art paper and cardboard to develop the characters. Once children were confident with the characters and the material understanding of leather, they were encouraged to use it.

The children also expressed interest to try working with a CAD tool. As a natural progression from pen and paper to computer-aided design, the children were introduced to SketchUp. They spent hours using the basic version and becoming familiar with the functions. Some of the pupils were able to prepare the architectural elements of the sites in Halasuru ready for laser cutting and, awestruck by the precision of the first results, they continued to detail their design files. Now, equipped with storyboard, design, machine operation and the final output in their hands to colour, the children felt more connected to their puppets (Figures 1 and 2). It was time for rehearsals.

The Halasuru Traverses project finally came to an end, celebrating the ten-month long process by staging a community event in a public park with the blessings of the local officials. Pupils, teachers and all fellow collaborators kept their fingers crossed for good weather. Before the performance, there was an exhibition of puppets, a robotics workshop and a visual artist continually gathering

Figure 1: Making theatre sets at Workbench Projects, Bangalore, India. Photograph: Workbench Projects.

Figure 2: Hands-on making, at Workbench Projects. Photograph: Workbench Projects.

stories of Halasuru and drawing it on rolls of paper that kept the crowd engaged. At the entrance of the park, a visual documentation of the project process was projected on a screen to set the context for the visitors. Teachers on the microphone invited the public and presented the work of their students with pride in their local language (Tamil). Surprise ceremonious visits from local politicians attracted even more people. The performance began and held the audience gripped to their seats. Parents and family members cheered for their children; it was a moment that will remain deeply etched in memory for all invested in this journey.[1]

When I look back, I recall quoting that day on the fundamental truth about education, "Regardless of what backgrounds children or teachers come from, if

---

1   See the video at: https://www.youtube.com/watch?v=c94xN7xx9Kw

one can create conditions for alternate and humane experiences, the choices that they make for their own future is well-informed and responsible". Projects such as this often remind me of Mao's saying, "Let a hundred flowers bloom and a hundred schools of thought contend", to promote the flourishing of the arts and the progress of science and technology. We, at Workbench Projects, as a public laboratory will stay committed to processes such as Halasuru Traverses that make us human and embrace the nuances of each and every community that we will work with, to strengthen them.

The Trade Educators' Syndicate
Making 10 Retirement Lathes in the Twilight of Australian Manufacturing

Jesse Adams Stein

Melbourne, Australia, 1978

Peter Williams, 16 years old, has just commenced an apprenticeship in the manufacturing trade of engineering patternmaking. He will train in this trade until 1981. As part of his education, he attends the George Thompson School of Foundry Technology, a department of the Royal Melbourne Institute of Technology.

When interviewed in 2017, Williams reflected on his time at the George Thompson School:

It was a *fascinating* place, I *loved* it [...] It was the only purpose-built foundry and patternmaking training facility in the Southern Hemisphere. There was nothing else like it in the Southern Hemisphere. To find a better place for patternmakers and foundrymen to do their technical schooling, you'd have to go to London, or maybe Philadelphia or somewhere like that. [...] Because the school was well staffed you didn't have to wait for help. [...] They would roam the room [...] They would stop and demonstrate, it was all very practical and hands-on. (2017)

In the mid-1990s, Williams became a patternmaking teacher at this very school. We will revisit his story further on.

Melbourne, Australia, 1985

A group of trade educators are gathered at a meeting at the George Thompson School. These teachers train apprentices in patternmaking, foundry moulding, metallurgy, woodwork, machining and welding. The mood is grim. Australian manufacturing is just beginning its palpable decline. Like other wealthy capitalist economies in this period, Australian politicians are increasingly embracing globalised free trade, privatisation and cuts to public services and education. It is not a good time to be a manufacturing worker. And it is certainly not a good time to be employed as a public educator of manufacturing apprentices. These teachers gather for a lunchtime talk on the lowering of the retirement age for state government employees. They learn that if they take early retirement at age 55, they could retire on half-pay through their superannuation. It is not a lot, but it is a little better than the aged-pension.

John Looker, a patternmaking teacher, is 50. While he is passionate about teaching the craft of patternmaking, the institution in which he works has changed in recent years. There are pressures to rationalise the content: to teach more in less time. Everything now has to be configured into a "module", whatever that means (Looker 2011). Faced with rising paperwork and time constraints, his colleagues grumble that they have become more like "clerks" and less like tradespeople (Walker 2018). Looker knows that the likelihood of finding a patternmaking job in a rapidly deindustrialising Melbourne will become increasingly difficult in the coming years. Retirement seems an increasingly attractive option.

These tradespeople are highly skilled woodworkers. They are forever making something or other, usually to solve a problem: jigs, patterns, furniture and bespoke hand tools. The school's workshops get a great deal of use, and not just for student training. Looker imagines what his retirement might involve:

One of my first thoughts was the realisation that I would no longer have use of a fully equipped workshop [...] My immediate concern was to have a lathe [...] The thought of retiring and not having a lathe was not acceptable. (2011: 245)

A lathe was an expensive piece of equipment, and given his future would be more financially restricted, Looker was reluctant to buy one.

After some thought I came to the realisation that I was working in the very place where I could produce one. I could make the patterns. The foundry downstairs could produce the castings in iron, and the small machine shop attached to our department was just the place to machine and fit all the components together. (2011: 245)

Looker's lathe project requires the assistance of others: he needs the foundry staff on board, and the machine shop staff. Word swiftly spreads of Looker's plans.

The Head of the Patternmaking Department, Jim Walker, is also considering retirement. He too is tired of the rising bureaucracy and is beset by stress.

We had too many teachers for the student numbers, and they were at me to sack some of them. [...] But, you know, I didn't want to sack them. (Walker 2018)

Walker needed a "Staff Development" project to keep his staff busy, and Looker's lathe idea fitted the bill. In this way, Looker's project began "on the sly" – as an unauthorised project – but it emerged with tacit institutional approval from one of the bosses (Smith 2009). Retirement was also on Walker's mind; he, too, needed a lathe. Looker was asked to "collect money from each syndicate member on a fortnightly basis" (Looker 2011: 246).

Ultimately, nine trade educators joined the Syndicate. They decided to make ten lathes, so as to defray the materials costs by selling the tenth machine. As Walker explains, the project involved the full production of bespoke lathes, from start to finish:

We made the drawings, the patterns, the castings, machined them, and we made the lathes over a period of about eighteen months. (2018)

Looker worked throughout lunchtimes and school holidays to get the lathes finished in time for Christmas. The Syndicate was not without its tensions or difficulties. Looker explained that

When it became obvious that all members would get a lathe as long as people kept up their payments, the majority of the work was done by John Noke, our machine-room supervisor, and myself [...] The tenth lathe was taken by a member of the Syndicate who said he might have a buyer for it. We could have reasonably expected $1500 for it, but we never saw it again, or any money. (2011: 246)

In the end, Walker was disappointed with his lathe, believing he got the "lemon", with a fault in the transmission. "You had to hold your hands just right to get it to work properly." Looker's lathe was akin to a "Rolls Royce" and worked beautifully (Walker 2018).

This story is shared not so much as a story of ingenuity or skill in Do-It-Yourself, but as an example of the ways in which manufacturing tradespeople have strategised and collectivised, in unpredictable ways, when faced with impending change. These educators did everything they could in order to continue *as makers*, which was more important to them than staying in a job.

Melbourne, Australia, 1996

Around 10 years after the Syndicate completed their lathes, Peter Williams became a patternmaking educator at the George Thompson School. This time, he was one of only two patternmaking teachers. The department had downsized considerably since Walker's and Looker's time.

One day when we were all summoned to a lecture theatre [...] And this fella stood there on the stage [...] and basically said [...] this faculty is overstaffed to the tune of 32 people [...] I suggest you consider your options elsewhere. [...]
I actually became quite depressed about it because it was now clearly evident to me that everything I'd loved previously about my trade, and what I'd learned, the skills I'd developed, the kids that I'd taught, the facility that I was now working in as a teacher [...] I could see that it was all doomed [...] It was all going to go. (Williams 2017)

Unlike the patternmaking educators in the mid-1980s, Williams was too young to retire. A "retirement lathe" would have been welcome, but what he really needed was secure employment. His only option, then, was to retrain. Without the support of a collective of workers experiencing the same thing, Williams was more or less on his own, having to carve an individual pathway amid systems not designed to support worker transition.

Author's Note, 2020

These are scraps of experiences that I am still in the process of piecing together, from oral history interviews with twelve Australians who trained as engineering patternmakers. Despite the diverse demographic profile – I interviewed men and women aged between 33 and 90 – there are consistent overlaps in their stories. While the interviews form an incomplete patchwork of experiences, they all attest to a deeply felt commitment to manual skill and creative making. They also speak of a fear of what is to come, in a social and political landscape that does not value industrial makers.

References

Looker, J. (2011): I Want to be a Patternmaker: A Memoir. Melbourne: Memoirs Foundation.
Smith, S. (2009): "Foreigners: 'The Forbidden Artefact'". In: J. Harris (ed.), Foreigners: Secret Artefacts of Industrialism. Perth: Black Swan Press, pp. 14–25.
Walker, J. (2018): Interview by Jesse Adams Stein, Reshaping Australian Manufacturing Oral History Project, 7 December, audio recording and timed summary, National Library of Australia, Canberra, BibID: 7889849, https://nla.gov.au/nla.cat-vn7889849.
Williams, P. (2017): Interviewed by Jesse Adams Stein, Reshaping Australian Manufacturing Oral History Project, 26 November, audio recording and timed summary, National Library of Australia, Canberra, BibID: 7540153, https://nla.gov.au/nla.obj-584861891.

Politics of Patents

Researching, Making and Wearing Alternative Histories of Clothing Inventions

Kat Jungnickel

On 6 December 1895, Alice Louisa Bygrave registered an English patent for "Improvements in Ladies' Cycling Skirts". The patent tells us she was a dressmaker living in South London, at No. 13 Canterbury Road, Brixton. She explains the objective of the invention is "to provide a skirt proper to wear when either on or off the machine". While the design makes use of "an ordinary skirt" and "ordinary knickerbockers", the novelty lies in the infrastructure of the garments. Inside the seams, waistband and hems is a unique *pulley system* (see Figure 1). Through a careful combination of "cords", "suitable guides" and "weights", Bygrave's innovation operates by "raising the skirt before and behind to a sufficient height".

Figure 1: Alice Bygrave's 1895 patent for "Improvements in Ladies' Cycling Skirts" (image used with permission of the European Patent Office [www.epo.org]).

Bygrave's convertible cycling skirt is remarkable. Her carefully concealed design gathers the material at the front and rear of the skirt, up and out of the way of moving machinery – bicycle pedals, chain and wheels – to enable the wearer to

secretly switch from walking skirt to safe and comfortable cycling costume when needed. Sewn into the seams of the skirt, this convertible system also deliberately hides her cycling intentions from parts of society who might otherwise hurl abuse or stones at "the hapless women who dared to reveal the secret that she had two legs" (Marshall 1899: 40). Bygrave's invention, and others like it, carved out means and space for women to not only imagine, but also furnish themselves as independent, mobile citizens in new social, political and economic worlds.

This is one of the many fascinating invention stories from research conducted in the European Patent Office digital archives. I have been exploring what historic clothing inventions and inventors can tell us about the changing nature of citizenship over time in two projects: "Bikes and Bloomers: Victorian Inventors and Their Extraordinary Cyclewear" and "Politics of Patents (POP): Re-imagining Citizenship via Clothing Inventions 1820–2020". This research takes a gender/queer, decolonial and science and technology studies (STS)/feminist technoscience approach to the study of clothing inventions, embodied knowledges and the history of clothing as wearable technology.

My research team and I approach the patent archive to ask: *How are citizens made and re-imagined through clothing inventions?* From an STS lens, this means viewing clothing as a sociopolitical device that enables, constrains and organises bodies in different ways. We explore clothing inventions as "acts of citizenship" (Isin/Neilson 2008), which opens up possibilities of studying how people socially, spatially, materially, performatively and economically "do" and "make" citizenship in terms of claiming space, interrupting order or otherwise engaging in or attempting to shape social and political worlds on a more daily basis. In the POPLab, we are investigating how inventors create new forms of clothing that resist, subvert or disrupt social and political norms and beliefs and in the process bring new expressions of citizenship into being.

Historic patents provide a valuable record and rich source of alternative sociotechnical data. Patents are problem-making and problem-solving devices. Inventors explain what concerned them and how to fix it, materially and technically. In the process, they reveal glimpses into the sociocultural context of the time, the politics of clothing, historic maker communities and feminist cultures of invention.

Patents get us closer to the experience of a range of inventors far beyond that of popular discourse. We learn of smaller and lesser-known inventions and get beyond the usual focus on "heroes, big men, important organisations, or major projects" (Law 1990: 12) and take into account more diverse and often radical contributions of women and other marginalised people more commonly silenced or systematically erased from the histories of technology. Zorina Khan writes: "Patent records present a valuable perspective on female inventive activity and market participation in an era when marriage meant the virtual 'invisibility' of married women in terms of objective data" (2000: 163).

Patent archives are critically important sites of data because they provide evidence of women, and other marginalised groups, actively driving change. They

Figure 2: Reconstruction of Alice Louisa Bygrave's 1895 patent for "Improvements in Ladies' Cycling Skirts" (image used with permission of Charlotte Barnes www.charlottebarnes.co.uk).

were not passively waiting for the situation to be resolved. They were not simply buffeted by social waves of change. Rather, many were actively attempting to drive it. By making and declaring their designs in public, they became important actors in socio-technical change – legitimising women's cycle wear as valid inventions, their bodies as rightful actors in mobile public space and claiming a place for women in politics and business.

Like many inventions, Bygrave's convertible skirt is fascinating on paper. It is even more remarkable when transformed (back) into wearable technology (see Figure 2). An integral part of our methodological approach involves analysing patents via text and image and also materially and physically. We follow inventors' instructions step-by-step and stitch-by-stitch to reconstruct their inventions. In previous work, I have argued that this approach enables us to interrogate clothing patents as three-dimensional dynamic knowledge objects. In the process, we participate in choreographies of ideas, materials and practice; party to the productive mess, mistakes and mishaps of making. There is an intimacy in sewing and wearing the clothes of others, especially when the owners of these garments lived over a century ago. Distance in time and space is diminished as we get up close and into the research in new ways (Jungnickel 2018, 2020). This is especially important with dynamic wearable technologies like these, designed to switch from one modality to another and to be worn on lively moving bodies.

There are many striking features of Bygrave's convertible skirt, not least the fact that its inventiveness was hidden in plain sight. Her design deliberately concealed the wearer's cycling intentions, enabling her to cycle safely when desired, while also offering some protection from the daily threat of harassment. These were very real experiences for early Victorian women cyclists. Convertible cycle wear inventors reveal to us not only how individuals managed to continue to participate in a much-loved activity, but also how collectively their radically dressed bodies played a small but nevertheless critical role in intervening in social norms and legal systems around mobility and public space, helping to legitimise new mobile forms of gendered citizenship in public place.

Acknowledgements

Politics of Patents (POP) is a 5-year research project (2019–2024) funded by a European Research Council consolidator grant #819458 (www.politicsofpatents.org).

The article also references images and research undertaken in *Bikes and Bloomers*, part of the Transmissions and Entanglements: Making, Curating and Representing Knowledge project supported by an Economic and Social Research Council Knowledge Exchange grant and Intel Corporation (ES/K008048/1) (www.bikesandbloomers.com).

References

Isin, E./Neilson, G. (eds.) (2008): Acts of Citizenship. London & New York: Zed Books.

Jungnickel, K. (2018): Bikes and Bloomers: Victorian Women Inventors and Their Extraordinary Cycle Wear. London: Goldsmiths Press.

Jungnickel, K. (ed.) (2020): "Making and Wearing." In: Transmissions: Critical Tactics for Making and Communicating Research. Cambridge, MA: MIT Press, pp. 66–88.

Khan, B. Z. (2000): "'Not for Ornament': Patenting Activity by Nineteenth-Century Women Inventors." Journal of Interdisciplinary History 31(2), pp. 159–195.

Law, J. (1990): "Introduction: Monsters, Machines and Sociotechnical Relations." The Sociological Review 38(S1), pp. 1–23.

Marshall, I. (1899): "Correspondence." The Rational Dress Gazette: Organ of the Rational Dress League, No. 10. Accessed at the University of Hull, UK.

Biographical Notes

Yana Boeva is a postdoctoral researcher at the University of Stuttgart studying the socio-technical transformation of design and architecture through automation.

David Cuartielles Ruiz is a teacher and researcher of interaction design at Malmö University, Sweden, exploring the co-creation of socio-technical platforms.

Ellen K. Foster is a postdoctoral researcher in the School of Engineering Education at Purdue University and research affiliate at Drexel University.

Kerstin Franzl manages research projects at the nexus Institute in Berlin with a focus on stakeholder involvement and co-creation.

César García Sáez is an independent researcher specialised in maker culture and digital fabrication, and publisher/producer of the La Hora Maker podcast.

Petr Gibas is a researcher at the Institute of Sociology of the Czech Academy of Sciences.

Anupama Gowda is an educator and co-founder of Workbench Projects, a fab lab, public laboratory and co-working space for tinkering and responsible innovation.

Peter Harper teaches Sustainability at the University of Bath. He was formerly head of research at the Centre for Alternative Technology in Wales.

Felix Holm is co-founding director of Cape Town's Maker Station makerspace, founder of Maker School and co-founder of Flat Rock Studio.

Kat Jungnickel is a Senior Lecturer in the Sociology Department at Goldsmiths, University of London.

Cindy Kohtala is a postdoctoral researcher at Aalto University examining how fab labs address socio-environmental sustainability in their visions and practices.

Kostas Latoufis is a researcher and PhD candidate on small scale renewable energy sources at the National Technical University of Athens.

Blanka Nyklová is a researcher at the Institute of Sociology of the Czech Academy of Sciences.

Isaac Robles is a Fab Lab UTEC Coordinator, Academany Global Reviewer and advisor of innovation projects.

Daniel Rodríguez is a Salvadoran painter with a degree in Fine Arts from the University of El Salvador.

Simon Sadler is Professor of Design at the University of California, Davis, researching the history and theory of design and architecture.

Kate Samson is a PhD student in Psychology at the University of Chicago.

Samantha Shorey is an Assistant Professor of Communication at the University of Texas at Austin. She is an ethnographer of technology design communities.

Regina Sipos is a Research Associate at the Technical University of Berlin researching critical making, grassroots innovation and open source movements.

Suné Stassen is the founder, executive director and custodian of Open Design Afrika, committed to grow Afrikan pride and develop change-makers.

Jesse Adams Stein is a Senior Lecturer and Chancellor's Postdoctoral Research Fellow at the School of Design, University of Technology Sydney.

Peter Troxler is a Research Professor at Rotterdam University of Applied Sciences studying the impact of the digital manufacturing of makers on various industries.

Aristotle Tympas is professor of the history of technology at the National and Kapodistrian University of Athens.

Svetlana Usenyuk-Kravchuk is head of the Arctic Design School, Ural State University of Architecture and Art / Tomsk State University.

Emilio Velis is the Executive Director of the Appropedia Foundation and Adjunct Lecturer at the Heller School, Brandeis University.